ISBN 978-0-282-92612-0
PIBN 10873611

English
Français
Deutsche
Italiano
Español
Português

www.forgottenbooks.com

Mythology Photography **Fiction**
Fishing Christianity **Art** Cooking
Essays Buddhism Freemasonry
Medicine **Biology** Music **Ancient**
Egypt Evolution Carpentry Physics
Dance Geology **Mathematics** Fitness
Shakespeare **Folklore** Yoga Marketing
Confidence Immortality Biographies
Poetry **Psychology** Witchcraft
Electronics Chemistry History **Law**
Accounting **Philosophy** Anthropology
Alchemy Drama Quantum Mechanics
Atheism Sexual Health **Ancient History**
Entrepreneurship Languages Sport
Paleontology Needlework Islam
Metaphysics Investment Archaeology
Parenting Statistics Criminology
Motivational

CONTENTS OF VOLUME III.

XIX.

Delaware Doctors,   *By Dr. Thos. C. Stellwagen.*

XX.

Old Delaware Clockmakers.   *By Henry C. Conrad.*

XXI.

Memoir of Judge Leonard E. Wales.   *By S. Rodmond Smith.*

XXII.

Jacob Alricks and his nephew Peter Alricks.   *By Edwin A. Price.*

XXIII.

Memoir of Nathaniel B. Smithers.   *By William T. Smithers.*

XXIV.

—— William Penn and his Province.   *By Manlove Hayes.*

XXV.

Dedication Exercises at Unveiling of Crane Hook Monument.

XXVI.

Gunning Bedford, Junior.   *By Henry C. Conrad.*

XXVII.

John Fisher.   *By Henry C. Conrad.*

XXVIII.

Memoirs of Deceased Members of Society.   *By Pennock Pusey.*

XXIX.

Life and character of Richard Bassett.   *By Robert E. Pattison.*

XXX.

John Dickinson,   *By Robert H. Richards.*

XXXI.

Letters of James Asheton Bayard.

XXXII.

Sketches of Prominent Delawareans.   *By Samuel W. Thomas.*

XXXIII.

The Bombardment of Lewes.   *By William M. Marine.*

PAPERS OF THE HISTORICAL SOCIETY OF DELAWARE.

XIX.

DELAWARE DOCTORS.

BY

THOS. C. STELLWAGEN, M.A., M.D., D.D.S.,

PROFESSOR OF PHYSIOLOGY, PHILADELPHIA DENTAL COLLEGE.

Read before the Historical Society of Delaware, February, 1896.

THE HISTORICAL SOCIETY OF DELAWARE,

WILMINGTON.

1897.

DELAWARE DOCTORS.

As a nursery and training-school for great men, it is evident to even a casual observer that the climate, the food, the surroundings of Delaware, must be particularly well adapted by nature for producing the highest intellectual and moral attainments. Singularly enough, the shape of your State on the map bears such a resemblance to the old-fashioned cradle that to one who is not attracted as much by glitter as by human grit, it is no small matter of surprise that it has not been called the "cradle" rather than the "diamond" State. The political, industrial, and moral influence of your men and women has been beyond all proportion to the size of your State.

It seems useless to remind this learned body that insular and peninsular people have, in the past, played a mighty part in the government of the world. Ancient Babylon, Assyria, Egypt, and Palestine were countries traversed by mighty rivers and pierced by gulfs or seas. To these doubtless they were greatly indebted for the commerce which broadened their views and made their kingdoms and empires the residence, and their rulers the protectors of the more intelligent and enlightened of mankind. Grecian, Roman, Mohammedan, Spanish, Portuguese, French, Dutch, and English, people largely peninsular, have, each

in their turn, swayed the sceptre of greatest power at some
time during their existence.

Delaware may be compared with Greece as to the climate
and general conditions of the peninsula of which she forms
a part. Surrounded on three sides by great political neighbors, with the fourth open to the sea and bay, she, like
Greece, has maintained a position always independent, and
often controlling; like Greece, when compared with her
neighbors, she is famous; like Greece, she is fertile, agri-
culturally and mentally. Many are the names of her sons
and daughters that are written in brilliant tints upon the
roll of fame.

Fortunately, it fell to my lot to look up that portion of
her history which relates to the medical profession of your
State. The richness of what, at first, appeared to be a field
of limited possibilities, soon made the work a delight. The
noble deeds, the scientific attainments, and the intelligent
pursuit by her devotees in the healing art were unfolded
before my eyes. The pleasure of rendering homage to
Delaware's most modest worthies repaid, many fold, the
labor and the time demanded by the research.

Soon perturbation disturbed the serenity of the work,
from fear that my weak efforts would not be sufficient for
the occasion. Then came a consciousness that made it
seem to be a duty to the silent dead whose very delicate
humility during life had much concealed their true merits.
Finally, the hope arose that by the sounding of the call
some slumbering giant might be awakened to fittingly
recount the grand lessons of scientific charity and humanitarian love that your State's history unfolded.

The intelligence of a community and the accomplishments and culture of its professional men may be fairly
estimated by the differentiation of the occupations of the
individuals that compose it. Although great wealth does
not, *per se*, always indicate the grade of mental enlighten-
ment of the body politic, still thrift, capability, responsibility, prosperity, and financial solidity are invariable attri-
butes of a State wherein the community of the learned
professions is supported with sufficient liberality of emolu-
ment to encourage men of notable ability to cast their lot
there and become citizens.

The Colony of Delaware was very early the home of
distinguished disciples of Æsculapius. Her record shows
that in 1654 she had Dr. Tyman Stidham as a settler, one
hundred and twenty-two years before his adopted country
issued the Declaration of Independence.

For twenty years this good man labored in his chosen
field with marked success, for the annals of the Colonial
government show that at his death he was possessed of
considerable estate. His family, together with their descendants, whose names grace the archives of the Settlements, were people of note and of great respectability.
Many of the latter are still found within the vicinity of New-
castle and Wilmington.

To J. Thomas Scharf, A.M., the compiler, and Dr. Lewis
P. Bush, the author of the work devoted to the history of
the medical fraternity of Delaware, it is a pleasure to acknowledge obligation. The accuracy of the biographical
sketches has been verified in many cases by the testimony
of Delawareans, by correspondence with George M. Stern-

berg, Surgeon-General of the United States Army, and by
others in positions that entitle them to be authority of
greatest merit.

Dr. Henry Fisher, who came from Ireland in 1725, was a
well-educated physician. He was the father of several
children, among whom a son, Henry, became noted for his
patriotic devotion to the cause of the Revolution. His
efforts materially supported his struggling country, and the
success of the war, in your section, was in no small degree
assisted by and due to his personal service in supplying for
the patriot army vessels for river defence and pilotage. He
was the progenitor of an influential family of your State,
which, by fortitude and patriotic example, combined with
personal thrift, trustworthiness, and satisfactory discharge
of responsible duties, together with charity to their fellow-
men, have won respect and success.

Frequently has Delaware honored herself by selecting
her most trusted statesmen from this body of her specially
educated men. Of the numerous examples that may be
quoted as evidence of the appreciation by your country of
this profession's eminent scholars, we cannot omit the names
of the first President of the State, Dr. John McKinley; Dr.
Joshua Clayton, its last President, and Governor for two
terms, who closed his earthly career so full of honors while
serving as a United States Senator. In its Legislature, Dr.
Henry Latimer likewise attained distinction that gained for
him the envied position of a seat in the United States
Senate, where Dr. James Sykes also served our country for
fifteen years, and was finally elected Governor. Dr. W. T.
Burton, Governor; Dr. Saulsbury, Speaker of the United

States Senate, and Governor; and in the State and United States Senate, Dr. Arnold Naudain was another whose entrance into public life was originally through the doors of a medical college. In your own city there have been chosen as chief magistrates men renowned for their skill, as Drs. James H. Hayward, J. P. Wales, Evan G. Shortlidge, and Charles R. Jeffries.

The history of your State shows that it was the third to recognize the importance of and to establish a State Medical Society. This was inaugurated by twenty-eight physicians as early as 1789. Later acts of the legislature empowered this Society to form a Board of Medical Examiners, with authority to regulate the practice of their profession, and without whose endorsement parties practising medicine were liable to penalties and fines. Now we find in the various States laws based upon those entrusted to this initial society. The first President was Dr. James Tilton, of whom we shall have occasion to speak as one of the most important factors in the war of the Revolution.

The study of the diseases peculiar to your locality was very materially advanced by the labors of the members of this Society, notably Drs. Snow, Barratt, Capelle, Tilton, Wilson, David Bush, and Edward Miller. The last contributed largely to the treatment and successful combating of intermittent and yellow fever by means of the then novel remedy, Peruvian bark, the alkaloid of which, quinine, is to-day one of the most universal and generally trusted remedies of the Pharmacopœia. His correspondence abroad was presumably in his day the most volumi-

nous, and his reputation the most world wide of any one of his profession in this country, except, probably, Professor Benjamin Rush, a distinguished Philadelphian and signer of the Declaration of Independence, who paid the greatest tribute to Dr. Miller, saying that he was "second to no physician in the United States." The first medical journal of this country was founded by Dr. Miller, in New York, where he was appointed to the important position of Port Physician, Professor of Practice of Physic in the University of that city, and attending physician to its Hospital. As a member of the Philosophical Society of Philadelphia he was well known. He was among the first to advise the drinking of water in fevers, which probably has alleviated the sufferings of mankind in this direction more than any other one remedy. He likewise was an ardent advocate of vaccination, together with Dr. Samuel Henry Black, of your State, Dr. J. Redman Coxe, of Philadelphia, and Professor William Handy, of Baltimore. The last two were so enthusiastic in their advocacy of this practice, that they each exposed a son to the dreaded disease to convince their contemporaries of the almost absolute immunity gained by the use of this virus. Dr. John Vaughan, a son of a physician, and a member of a number of famous scientific bodies, lectured upon chemistry and natural philosophy in your city as early as 1790.

In literature, as might be expected from such a body, eminence was early attained by your physicians. Several of these, among whom might be mentioned Dr. Robert R. Porter and Dr. Samuel H. Black, possessed private libraries which were proudly pointed to by their fellows as examples

of choice selections, and also among the largest private book collections in your State.

Dr. P. Brynberg Porter, who was born here, was formerly the editor of *Gaillard's Medical Journal*, and now is the New York correspondent of the *Medical News*, of Philadelphia, the *Journal of the American Medical Association*, and the *Boston Medical and Surgical Journal*, etc., etc. Dr. Robert Montgomery Bird, born in Newcastle, in 1805, was an associate editor and publisher of *The North American and United States Gazette*, of Philadelphia. He was likewise Professor of Materia Medica in the Pennsylvania Medical College from 1841 to 1843. As the author of "Nick of the Woods," and many novels, and the dramatizer of the "Gladiator," "Metamora," and other plays, he is well known throughout this country. Dr. Lewis Potter Bush, of Wilmington, was likewise a prolific author, and his papers upon the history of medicine in your State have made him a name throughout the profession in this country. In recognition of his labors, in 1886 he was elected President of the American Academy of Medicine.

Of the famous medical men of your State, many living to-day, I dare not attempt mention, except of those who in my own city are so widely known that it seems a work of supererogation to speak, and yet it would be an injustice and a positive neglect of my duty if I failed to mention Dr. James P. Lofland, associate of Dr. Franklin Bache, Professor of Chemistry in the Jefferson Medical College; Theophilus Parvin, M.D., the honored and world-wide known Professor of Obstetrics, author of numerous treatises, who to-day is loved and admired by all who know him. Professor W.

James Hearn, M.D., who stands second to none in our great cities for his ability, honesty, and absolute trustworthiness, fills the chair of Clinical Surgery in the same college. Dr. E. O. Shakespeare, the histologist and bacteriologist, Dr. Louis Starr, the author of works on the diseases of children, and the late Professor T. L. Buckingham, M.D., D.D.S., one of the founders of two dental colleges in Philadelphia. Martin W. Barr, M.D., the head of that noble and intellectual charity, the Pennsylvania Training-School for Feeble-Minded Children, which has been a blessing to those afflicted with that most sad of all ailments, imbecility.

Dr. W. G. A. Bonwill, born in your State, holds the credit of the practical adaptation of electrical force to automatic mallets, which probably were the forerunner of the modern wonders of electrical trip-hammers and machines for rock drilling and tunnelling, to which the modern railroad owes an imperishable debt. Like Dr. Physick, who invented the surgical needle, with its eye at the point, without which sewing-machines would probably have been long delayed in their arrival at their present state of perfection, this man was the progenitor of many modern inventions. H. C. Register, M.D., was also the inventor and improver of many delicate appliances for dental and surgical engines.

The late Professor James E. Garretson was born in your city in 1828, where he passed his boyhood. Moving to Philadelphia, he pursued a course in dentistry, and graduated when twenty-nine. Two years later he passed successfully the examination for the degree of Doctor of Medicine in the University of Pennsylvania. From early life he had been an earnest student, with a strong inclination

towards surgery, in which he became deeply interested, and in 1861 his association with Dr. D. Hayes Agnew in the Philadelphia School of Anatomy ripened his attainments, so that he gradually created the new specialty known as oral surgery. In this department he was the accepted authority in this country and throughout the English speaking world. His operations were of the most bold and terrible character, and yet singularly free from fatal endings. As the inventor of procedures for the removal of bone and tumors about the head and face, without leaving deforming scars, he was eminently successful. He filled, at various times, chairs in the Philadelphia Dental College and Philadelphia School of Anatomy, of which former institution he had been dean for many years. In the school of the philosophers he had excited considerable comment by a series of lectures for several winters in succession. Young men and women, mostly students of the colleges with which he was connected, flocked to his Tuesday night discourses, wherein his avowed object was the seeking for the deeper truths of life. He was prominent as one of the practical founders of the Medico-Chirurgical Hospital and the Medico-Chirurgical College, in both of which institutions he served as the president. Their success under his administration soon became phenomenal.

Ceaseless as was his activity, he also gained fame as a literary man. His philosophical writings, designed to teach self-control and restraint as means to the highest end, were published in a series of volumes under the *nom de plume* of John Darby. In addition to this herculean task, he wrote the "System of Oral Surgery," which is

considered the crowning work of his life, the present being
the seventh edition. Through its agency, as I have been
informed by a gentleman lately returned from abroad, he
is probably as well known in Edinburgh as in Baltimore.
As a humanitarian and philosopher he was probably less
widely known than as a surgeon. His love for humanity
and his desire to aid it were such that he realized within
himself the ideal of human brotherhood. None were so
poor or so sinful that they might fear to claim from him a
brother's loving sympathy and help. Few but those who
enjoyed his charity have any conception of its breadth.
Firm in his belief in a divinity, he endeavored to implant
high conception of the wonders of the All-knowing God,
and yet, inasmuch as there were those who could not
encompass his broad outlook, they questioned what his
belief really was. Probably but few modern thinkers have
so completely harmonized the various tenets and creeds of
the Christian church as did he. His social life was the
embodiment of virtue and earthly satisfaction. No words
can adequately express the refinement and depth of his
devotion to duty, love, and purity. Frugality, caution, and
far-seeing preparation for the rainy day made him independent of that world which he never failed to assist, and
it may be said of him, in his pursuit of pleasure as a philosopher, he rarely allowed it to divert his attention from
earthly work to the disadvantage of provision for his
family. When the temptation to give up the world in the
physical sense for the metaphysical is considered, his life is
an exhibition of the most remarkable and refined unselfish-
ness. I quote the following opinion from a religious jour-

nal : "The finer side, the real man was little known, even to many who were in daily contact with him. While Dr. Garretson was prominent as a surgeon, a teacher, a writer, and a deep thinker, and a truly religious man, with qualities of mind and heart, the crowning one was his abounding love for humanity.

"To know the inner man was to have seen him at the bedside of the sick, the poor, the sorrowful, and the sinning. There he seemed God-inspired to try and save, and his tenderness and sympathy were Christ-like.

"Through forty years of arduous professional work he was never too busy to respond to appeals for help, and they were multitudinous."

Distinctions as to charity and self-denial are so numerous and so patent throughout the medical profession that we have come to look upon them as natural and necessary qualifications of the physician. Your State's history is covered with glory in this direction. Dr. Nicholas Way, in 1793, welcomed to his private house in your city those who fled in terror from Philadelphia, and were dreaded by your townspeople lest they should bring with them that awful disease, the yellow fever, which was hurrying hundreds to their last resting-places. His example of unbounded hospitality and fearless love caused his fellow-citizens to soon throw open their houses as refuges for the fugitives. How strange is fate! In the great epidemic of 1797, Dr. Way died in Philadelphia, a shining mark, whose death was undoubtedly caused by his personal and unflinching, steadfast devotion to those to whom he ministered. In 1802, Dr. John Vaughan was the only physician in Wilmington to

fight this fever. Dr. William Draper Brinckle, likewise, in the cholera epidemic of 1832, distinguished himself so markedly at the Buttonwood Street Hospital, Philadelphia, that some of his many admirers had the Commissioner of Spring Garden present him with a magnificent silver vase.

Patriotism, by no means confined to any class or profession in our great country, has, however, flourished and been nurtured in hearts and families of doctors throughout the world.

Probably few, if any, have more truly deserved public recognition of their great works than Dr. James Tilton, before referred to as the first President of the State Medical Society of Delaware, who graduated in 1771, at Philadelphia. His eminence as a physician was, if possible, excelled by his devotion as a patriot. Entering the Revolutionary War as a lieutenant, he served with distinction, as also in his professional capacity as an army surgeon with Washington at Long Island, White Plains, and the retreat to the Delaware. At Princeton he found the army in a sad plight. Its efficiency was almost paralyzed by the enormous number of men sick in the hospital, and the cause of American freedom was languishing and seemingly about to be completely extinguished by the prevalence of typhus fever. To Surgeon Tilton fell the task of preparing for these sick ones, who, by reason of their poor food, confined quarters, and the general depression of spirits, were being carried off more rapidly by disease than by bullets of the enemy. As surgeon in charge he quickly remodelled the entire hospital service, breaking up the large

hospitals, and dividing the sick into parties of six in a hut; each hut thoroughly ventilated and purified by the nascent creosote from the fires which were placed in the middle of the clay floors.

Probably without this device at that time Washington would have been defeated; and we know only too well to what great straits the country had been reduced, and believe that there would have been no hope of success if this scourge had not been arrested. It is but fair to claim that American independence would very likely have suffered either total extinction or a long delay, had it not been for this son of Delaware. At the close of the war, when the number of army medical officers was being reduced, Washington personally advised the retention of Surgeon Tilton. After the final surrender of the British at Yorktown, in 1782, he returned to practice in his State, from which he was sent to Congress, and after holding several positions of public trust he was appointed the first Surgeon-General of the United States Army, doubtless in recognition of his incalculable service at Princeton. Although a great sufferer, he energetically inaugurated and carried out many reforms in the Army Medical Corps. After an amputation of the thigh when nearly seventy years old, he lived some seven years more, to enjoy the honors and love of his fellow countrymen, who delighted to pay him respect. His colleagues of the Delaware State Medical Society erected a monument over his remains, as an humble tribute to his works and his eminent services, both to the profession and to his country. It seems probable that his success was very early provided for by his study on the subject of

respiration, which he wrote upon in his examination for the degree of B. M.

Delaware inscribed on her roll of honor the names of many who were heroes of the wars of the Revolution and of 1812. Dr. Jacob Jones, known to every school-boy as Commodore Jones, commanded the U. S. S. "Wasp" in that ever-memorable battle which terminated within forty-three minutes in the capture of H. B. M. S. "Frolic." When the hearts of the soldiers of our struggling little republic were sickened and saddened by repeated defeats, this, with a series of other glorious naval victories, revived the hopes and renewed and redoubled the efforts of our patriots, both afloat and ashore. To this may be added, at a second fortunate juncture, such a victory by our fleets that it may be said to have virtually closed the war of 1812. From the very jaws of defeat and death the battle of Lake Champlain may be said to have snatched the oriflamme of victory, and thus led the way to the final overthrow of all attempts and long-cherished hopes of the Mother Country to regain by force of arms her sovereignty in our land.

Commodore Thomas Macdonough was the son of a physician who, in his youth, was one of the stanch Revolutionary patriots who served his country in the army as a volunteer. Like many others of his day, it appears that he left but little for his son save an honorable name and that love of his country which made him the winner of that country's most profound admiration, which was publicly attested by well-deserved votes of thanks of State Legislatures and the United States Congress.

This gallant officer, as you well know, has never been duly appreciated by the majority of those who have written the histories of our country. As Delawareans, I trust you will pardon me for dwelling for a few moments upon the importance of this victory against a combined invading English army and fleet near Plattsburgh, and off Cumberland Head on Lake Champlain. All who have read United. States history know that he met twelve thousand men of the English army, under Sir George Provost, and seventeen vessels carrying ninety-five guns and about one thousand men under Commodore Downie, of the English navy. Our hero conquered with a force of only eight hundred and twenty men, with eighty-six guns and fourteen vessels, some of the latter having been constructed and launched within forty days of the felling of the timber of which they were built.

To Macdonough, his officers and men, was due the successful building and equipment of this fleet. To them belongs the glory of having completely defeated a well-disciplined and carefully organized force in what was pronounced by all judges to be the only scientific battle between a fleet of the United States and of Great Britain. To the energy, courage, and training that accomplished the manœuvres that decided the victory, our whole country is everlastingly indebted. It was an almost providential repulse and total overthrow of an enemy and capture of a fleet of invasion which were designed to seize and hold a line of military posts extending along the chain of Lakes and the Hudson River. Had the British succeeded in this project, they would have severed from the United States the eastern sec-

tion of this country. Probably they would have destroyed
our independence, or at least effected the subjugation or
alienation of New England. In parts of the Eastern States,
at least, it is a question as to whether the war was not
already sufficiently unpopular for this blow, if completed, to
have compelled the patriots of this section to succumb to
dark fate,—a condition which would at the very best have so
seriously crippled our infant Republic as to have made a
mighty change, the result of which, happily, we are saved
from even speculating upon. This, therefore, was one of
the greatest and most momentous turning-points in the
world's history, and its success was due to the victorious
leadership of a son of a Delaware doctor.

The hour grows late, and yet the task before me is far
from finished; many are the names omitted of those richly
deserving, whose lives have merited immortal blessings.
Such, however, in the calm enjoyment of their heavenly
recompenses, have passed beyond the border where the
tongue of earthly praise can afford them a moment's thought.
Lifted to the highest moral, intellectual, and heavenly joys,
associated with the spirits of the good of all ages, their lives
are fully occupied in pressing forward with that innumerable
host of angels whose joys can never cease, grow dim, sleep,
flag, or waver.

As you see, my task was confined to members of one
profession of your State. Imagine, if we can, what it would
be if one had the time and the ability to justly portray the
merits, virtues, and deeds of the rest of this truly great
people. Surely no one born or living in Delaware can lack
for examples upon which to model his life for the accom-

plishment of greatness. Three times have you seen in this very limited field the destiny of the whole nation balanced upon the scalpel and the swords of three of Delaware's born and reared sons,—once in the Camp Hospitals, once upon the high seas, and once upon the historic lake. How pleasant it would be, did time permit, to spend a portion in reminiscence of another whose character was as true and pure as his valor was unquestioned.

But I must stop myself, for the subject is as fascinating as my powers are mediocre, and I fear that while the theme could never weary you, the narrator has.

PAPERS OF THE HISTORICAL SOCIETY OF DELAWARE.

XX.

OLD DELAWARE CLOCK-MAKERS.

BY

HENRY C. CONRAD,

LIBRARIAN OF THE SOCIETY.

Read before the Historical Society of Delaware, December 3, 1897.

THE HISTORICAL SOCIETY OF DELAWARE,

WILMINGTON.

1898.

PAPERS OF THE HISTORICAL SOCIETY OF DELAWARE.

XX.

OLD DELAWARE CLOCK-MAKERS.

BY

HENRY C. CONRAD,

LIBRARIAN OF THE SOCIETY.

Read before the Historical Society of Delaware, December 3, 1897.

THE HISTORICAL SOCIETY OF DELAWARE,

WILMINGTON.

1898.

THE FRIENDS' MEETING-HOUSE,

WILMINGTON, DELAWARE.

OLD DELAWARE CLOCK-MAKERS.

INTRODUCTION.

THERE is something about the old-fashioned high clock that commands respect. Whether it is the primness of the tall case, or the imperative tone of the resounding gong as it suddenly strikes the ear, may not readily be determined. We, somehow, cannot get rid of the idea that the generation of a century ago, who not only respected, but venerated this ancient style of time-piece, had a sense of quiet dignity that is most sadly lacking in the bustling activity of these later times. The grandfather's clock is about the last link connecting our homes with the colonial days and the Revolutionary period that followed. We look up into the faces of these faithful sentinels of the olden times, and our minds revert to homespun and the spinning-wheel; we hear the muffled swing of the old pendulum, and are reminded of "The days of birth and the days of death" which the old clock has seen, and of the many lives that have flashed and gone out in all the years that the faithful hands have been making their monotonous revolutions around the dial. There is a character to a high clock that is peculiarly its own,—the plain, old-fashioned high clock, that stood in the chimney corner, or on the landing of the stairs, in the mansion, and in the substantial farm-house of

two or three generations ago. Are they not the truest and fittest representatives we have left of that sturdy race of men who braved the rigors of a perilous ocean to plant in the new world the banner of religious freedom, and worked out for us the most glorious heritage that man has known? True representatives indeed are these old and faithful chroniclers of time of the steady, plodding, faithful men who sowed and reaped, who dug and toiled, who planted and gathered in days of hardship, of sacrifice and privation; building better than they knew, laying, in truth, the foundation-stones of the greatest nation of the earth.

THE FIRST DELAWARE CLOCK.

An item clipped from the *Every Evening* of January 10, 1880, says that "Edward B. Humphries, a gentleman quite celebrated as an antiquarian, has just arrived in New York from Holland. Whilst there he came across an old Dutch clock made by John Moll, who was an old and well known Delaware magistrate, and who held power here anterior to the arrival of William Penn both under the English and Dutch dynasties. He lived and resided upon a large tract of land near Wilmington. The clock was sent to Holland to have the movements put in. Upon it is the 'armorial bearings' of the Moll family. It was made as a matter of amusement by Magistrate Moll, and derives its celebrity not only from being made more than two hundred years ago by a Delaware ruler who was an amateur mechanic, but because it was more probably the first clock ever constructed in Delaware." This item I presume was furnished by Francis Vincent, to whom a description of the clock had

been sent, and the owner promised to send a photograph of the clock; but the photograph I assume never came, and I have been unable to ascertain anything further about this clock.

Assuming that John Moll was the first Delaware clock-maker, I have ascertained that John Moll was a prominent man in New Castle and Delaware in the seventeenth century. He was one of the justices of the court at New Castle during the entire period of the Duke of York's government from 1676 to 1682, and was for some years its presiding justice. He purchased a large tract of land in Mill Creek Hundred from Charles Rumsey in 1669, and on this plantation he lived, except when engaged in his court duties. In the same year a tract of one thousand acres in Red Lion Hundred was patented to him, including the handsome farms which afterwards came into the possession of the Clarks and Reybolds. He was named a commissioner with Ephraim Herman in a deed of feoffment from the Duke of York to William Penn to give possession and seisin of the town of New Castle and a circle of land of twelve miles around it. His account of the ceremony is curious. He says that "on the first arrival of Penn at New Castle from England in October, 1682, the commissioners considered for twenty-four hours the deeds which Penn showed them from the Duke of York, and then, by virtue of the powers given us by the said letters of attorney, we did give and surrender in the Duke's name to Mr. Penn actual and peaceable possession of the fort at New Castle, by giving him the key thereof to lock upon himself alone the door, which being opened by him again, we did deliver to him

also one turf, with a twig upon it, a porringer with river water, and salt, in part of all that was specified in said indenture, and according to the true intent and meaning thereof."

It is recorded that complaint was made that Judge Moll was not fit to sit as judge, but after a full hearing of the matter the judge was vindicated, and resumed his duties on the bench.

John Moll was identified with the colony of Labadists that settled on Bohemia Manor in 1684. He was one of the leaders in the movement, and in company with Ephraim Herman and Arnoldus De Lagrange, early settlers in this county, removed to Maryland and became a member of that peculiar religious sect, where he figured for some years; after which time but little is known of him. In 1698 there is mention made of John Moll, Jr., among the Labadists, very likely a son of the judge.

GEORGE CROW.

Among the earliest clock-makers in Wilmington was George Crow. The first mention I find of him is in 1746, when he was elected high constable of the borough of Wilmington. He served one year. In 1755 he was elected one of the burgesses of Wilmington, and re-elected in 1756 and 1758. The records of Old Swedes show the marriage of George Crow to Mary Laudonet in August, 1746.

I have seen several high clocks bearing his name, but none of them bore any date. He was evidently in the watch and clock business prior to 1754, and continued in business until his death, which occurred in 1771 or 1772. I know of a surveyor's compass, now owned by Jacob H. Emerson, of Middletown, which bears the date 1754 and the name "George Crow." The name of R. Bryan is also scratched on it, and the present owner tells me that Bryan was one of the early surveyors who laid out much land in the vicinity of Middletown and the Bohemia Manor. I find a deed of record from Gabriel Springer, one of the earliest hatters in Wilmington, to George Crow, dated March 26, 1761, for a house and lot on the west side of Walnut Street just above Spring Alley. It is reasonable to believe that Crow lived in this house and carried on his business there, and I am of opinion that the identical house in which he lived is still standing. In addition to this property he owned at the time of his death, in 1771 or 1772, a property at Third and King Streets, where the market-house now stands (southwest corner), and a large lot at the northwest corner of Tenth and Market Streets, having a frontage on Market Street of about seventy feet and running back on Tenth Street to the westerly side of the Friendship Engine House. All of his property, after his death, was divided among his widow and four children, who survived him, by a deed of partition dated March 22, 1773, made by John McKinly, William Poole, and Bancroft Woodcock, all of whom were leading and influential citizens of Wilmington at that time. John McKinly, it will be recalled, was the first President of Delaware under the

constitution of 1776. William Poole was one of the early and successful millers on the Brandywine, and the father of a numerous family, of whom J. Morton Poole was one. Bancroft Woodcock was a noted silversmith here more than a century ago, and owned the old house on Broome Street, which for the past forty years has been the How-land homestead. He was a great walker and skater, and was so spare and thin in flesh that old people used to say he would evaporate.

George Crow left two sons, Thomas and George, and two daughters, Sarah, who married William Nash, and Mary, who married Samuel Goodman. George Crow, Jr., died prior to 1802. I have not been able to find any living descendants of George Crow; nor could I establish his exact age or place of burial, but there is a reasonable presumption that he was buried in the Old Swedes' graveyard.

THOMAS CROW.

Thomas Crow, who seems to have been the oldest son of George, succeeded his father in the clock and watch business, and presumably he learned the trade with his father.

Thomas Crow

Like his father he seemed to be in favor with the public, for I find that he was elected town clerk in 1771, one of the assistant burgesses in 1778, 1779, and 1780, and borough assessor in 1784 and 1785. Notwithstanding his willingness to serve the public in these various modest capacities,

he was a most industrious clock-maker, as is evidenced by the many clocks which bear his name. The number of his clocks now in existence indicate that he carried on a large business. While I know of but half a dozen George Crow clocks, I have knowledge of not less than twenty or twenty-five clocks made by Thomas Crow, and they are scattered from Caroline County on the Eastern Shore to the Manheim Club at Germantown. Thomas Crow owned in 1814 a property on the south side of Second Street, just east of Market, and here I think he plied his trade, although Betsy Montgomery says that "Thomas Crow, a watch-maker, and a worthy man, was on Second Street on the north side of the market-house." At the time of his death he owned a small place on the Philadelphia Turnpike in Brandywine Hundred, near the present residence of William C. Lodge, and this was sold after his death to pay his debts, which seem to have been largely in excess of his assets; as the records recite that he had no personal estate, but that he owed the Bank of Delaware about seven thousand three hundred dollars, and this small farm, which brought only eight hundred dollars when sold by his administrator, seems to have been all the estate which he left. He had two daughters, Elizabeth Ogden and Ann, wife of William Haslett. His death occurred about 1824, and he survived his wife, whose Christian name was Isabella.

His place of burial I have not been able to locate. He seems to have been a member of the First Presbyterian Church, and his mortal remains may be reposing in the graveyard adjoining the venerable building now occupied by the Historical Society.

JOHN CROW.

In a copy of the *Delaware and Eastern Shore Advertiser* of September 7, 1797, a newspaper "printed by Samuel and John Adams at the corner of King and High Streets, on Mondays and Thursdays," I find an advertisement of "John Crow, clock and watch maker," who announces a great variety of jewelled cap'd link wheel and plain watches for sale at wholesale or retail at the corner of Market and Second Streets, Wilmington. It winds up with the announcement that "It is presumed that *Thomas Crow's* shop is so noted that it may be found without further caution."

Who this John Crow was I do not know. I can find no trace of a son of either George or Thomas of that name.

JONAS ALRICHS.

The Alrichs family is one of the oldest in the county. The original settler was Peter Alrichs, to whom land in this county was patented in 1668. Peter had four sons, the oldest being Peter Sigfridus, who married Susanna Stidham, and had twelve children, among whom was Jonas Alrichs, who was born March 22, 1759. Jonas Alrichs was the first clock-maker of the name of Alrichs. He probably learned his trade with Thomas Crow, and succeeded the latter in business in the old Second Street store. I find an announcement of his retirement from business in the following advertisement clipped from the columns of the *Delaware Gazette :*

"Notice.—I take this method of returning my sincere thanks to the public for the encouragement I have received in the Clock and Watch making Business. As I have this

JACOB ALRICHS.

day resigned the same, I request all those who have any demands against me to present them for settlement; and those who are indebted to discharge the same.

"JONAS ALRICHS.

"WILMINGTON, April 6, 1797."

Jonas Alrichs died in 1802, leaving five children, one of whom, Thomas C. Alrichs, was for many years a useful and influential citizen of Wilmington.

JACOB ALRICHS.

Jacob Alrichs, a nephew of Jonas, was the son of Sigfridus Alrichs and Rachel Colesberry. He was born September 8, 1775, presumably in Wilmington. He learned the trade of clock- and watch-making with his uncle Jonas, with whom for a short while he was associated in business under the style of Jonas and Jacob Alrichs; but in 1797, as shown by the following advertisement taken from the *Delaware Gazette*, he started business alone:

"Jacob Alrichs, Clock and Watch maker, North side of the lower market, three doors from Market Street (In the shop formerly occupied by Jonas Alrichs and lately by Jonas and Jacob Alrichs), has received in addition to the stock already on hand, eight-day clocks of the first quality; silver watches from London, Liverpool and Dublin, such as can be warranted, watch main springs, glasses, dials, gilt and steel chains, keys, seals, &c, &c. Those who continue to favor him with their custom, he flatters himself will receive satisfaction. An apprentice wanted to the above business. April 15, 1797."

Presumably he continued in the clock- and watch-making

business for many years, although he did not devote his
entire time to it, as in 1810 he, in company with Samuel
McClary, started the first machine-shop in Delaware at the
northwest corner of Seventh and Shipley Streets in this city,
under the firm-name of Alrichs & McClary, and it is said
that an old horse served to make the power which ran the
machinery. The machine business seems to have been a
success, as Jacob Alrichs bought the property occupied by
the machine-shop three years later from Job Harvey, and
continued to own it until 1837, when it was sold to " The
Delaware Academy of Natural Sciences," an institution
that has long since ceased to exist. Alrichs afterwards had
a machine-shop on the site of the present pumping station
on the Brandywine near the head of French Street, and as
a testimonial of his efficiency as a skilful mechanic it is
only necessary to add that Elijah Hollingsworth learned his
trade with Alrichs, and afterwards, as we of this generation
know, became a leading and influential member of the firm
of Harlan & Hollingsworth, and by the development of
the mechanical ideas that were taught by Jacob Alrichs in
this primitive shop founded and successfully conducted the
large and important industry whose fame is world-wide.

The clock and watch business was removed from the
" upper side of the lower market" to Market Street, between
Third and Fourth Streets, at what is now known as No. 311
(David P. Smyth's recent location); from there to Arcade
Row on the east side of Market Street below Eighth (a row
of one-story stores erected by David C. Wilson on what for
years was known as Wilson's sand-hole); and later on, on
Market Street, west side, the second door above Seventh,

between the dry-goods store of Mary Dixon, on the corner, and Mary Slack's ice-cream saloon above. Both Miss Dixon and Miss Slack have been in business in my day and generation, although several years back.

Jacob Alrichs was evidently a man of strength of character, and of superior intelligence and capacity. He was unusually successful in the two lines of business which he conducted, and accumulated considerable real estate. As early as 1805, when only thirty years of age, he was elected an assistant burgess of the borough of Wilmington, and in 1810 was elected a member of the first City Council of Wilmington, being re-elected year by year until 1823. In 1830 he was elected a member of the State Senate from this city.

I find among the collections of our Historical Society a very exact and carefully prepared survey and level made in 1804 by Jacob Alrichs and Edward Roche of a route from the spring of Cæsar A. Rodney, Esq., to the centre stone at the corner of Chestnut (now Tenth) and Market Streets for the use of the Wilmington Spring Water Company. Evidently the idea had entered the brain of Jacob Alrichs almost a century ago to supply the citizens of Wilmington with water from "Cool Spring," an idea that nearly seventy years afterwards developed into a reality by the construction of the Cool Spring Reservoir, which is now so important a factor in our unsurpassed water-supply.

Jacob Alrichs was a prominent Whig in his day, a great admirer and close friend of John M. Clayton, the Whig leader, and under the administration of President Harrison served as postmaster of Wilmington when the post-office

occupied a small store-room on Third Street between Market and Shipley Streets.

About 1813 Jacob Alrichs built the house No. 1017 Market Street, at that time a large and imposing edifice. In it he lived during the remainder of his life. He died October 29, 1857, in his eighty-second year, and was buried in the Friends' Burying-Ground at Fourth and West Streets. He left four children, two sons and two daughters; his son, Henry S. Alrichs, continued the watch- and clock-making business after his father's death, and the only branch of the family who survive are descendants of Henry S. Among these are William J. Alrichs, a son of Henry S., who, true to the family calling for four generations, is a successful jeweller and watch-maker at Elkton, Maryland, and through his courtesy I was able to present to the Historical Society a few months ago a copy of the only portrait that is in existence of Jacob Alrichs, a copy of the same appearing in this publication.

DUNCAN BEARD.

I recall that several years ago I ran across a high clock having engraved on its face the name "Duncan Beard," "Appoquinimink," and since that time I have seen a half-dozen clocks with the same inscription. There was a feeling born within me to find something about this man, to ascertain, if possible, when and where he lived, who he was, and what he did.

The records disclose that in 1767 Duncan Beard, who is described as a "clockmaker," bought from William Hanson, Jr., one acre of land in Appoquinimink Hundred, in

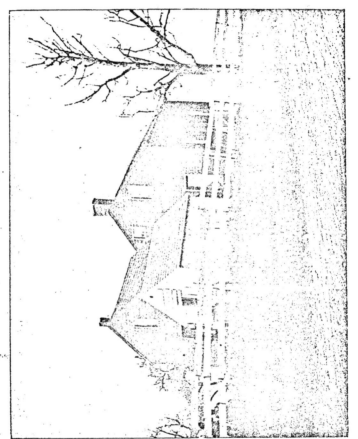

DUNCAN BEARD'S WORK-SHOP.

this county, for which he paid eight pounds English money. The price paid would indicate that he bought only the bare ground, without buildings, so that he seemingly began his active business life with that purchase; and I assume that by dint of his own labor and industry he put up on "the acre" a dwelling and a shop in which to live and carry on his vocation.

"Duncan Beard, Scotchman and skilled worker in metals," is the tradition that has lived in the neighborhood through the hundred years that have gone by since his life ended. Duncan Beard's acre was on the King's Highway, between Cantwell's Bridge and Blackbird, at both of which places the creaking sign of the country tavern sent forth a rather melancholy invitation to all passers-by to come within and find refreshment for both man and beast. Here Duncan Beard built and made his home. A little more than a mile south of Cantwell's Bridge, just across the marsh that skirts the sluggish Appoquinimink, and within a stone's throw of the colonial home of James Moore, of the Delaware line, who entered Colonel John Haslet's regiment as a lieutenant and came out a major, bearing with him an almost mortal wound received at Germantown.

Here he toiled and worked out the delicate and complex mechanism which went to make up the sturdy and truthful timepieces of that day; everything by hand, from the tempered steel spring and the nicely balanced pendulum to the ponderous, clumsy weights hung on catgut strings.

To this day the faithfulness of his clocks as correct time-pieces attest his thorough workmanship and conscientious labors. He was not only diligent in business, but he was

interested in the affairs of his neighborhood. The old
records still preserved of Union Lodge, No. 5, A. F. and
A. M., show that Duncan Beard became a member June
24, 1765, the year that it was instituted. This was the first
lodge of Masons instituted in the State, and it met monthly
at Cantwell's Bridge, Beard being one of the most regular
attendants at its meetings for a term of thirty years. The
minutes record that he was Senior Warden within a year
after his initiation, that he served as Worshipful Master
from December, 1767, to December, 1769, and Treasurer for
one year in 1772 and 1773. The last mention of his name
in the minutes is on November 27, 1794, three years before
his death. Under date of September 25, 1777, a minute is
made that " The lodge did not meet last month on account
of the enemy landing at Elk.". This recalls the stirring
events of the Revolution ; the British landed at the head of
the Elk early in September, the battle of Brandywine having
been fought on September 11. Here was a small country
village, fifteen miles away, so alarmed and excited over the
advent of " the enemy" that a quorum of the lodge could not
be gotten together. It was the custom of the lodge to go
once a year to Parson Read's meeting-house to hear a sermon from old Dr. Thomas Read, the patriotic preacher at old
Drawyers, who, during " the times that tried men's souls,"
ministered in holy things to the whole countryside, and was
beyond question the leading man of that community. Robert Kirkwood, the gallant major of the Delaware Regiment,
joined this same lodge in 1783, after his settlement at Cantwell's Bridge, at the close of the war, where for some time
he was engaged in mercantile pursuits. Union Lodge, a

good many years after its institution, was removed to Middletown, where it is still in successful operation. In the present lodge-room in Middletown is a Duncan Beard clock, presented to it several years ago by Richard T. Lockwood, it having been in the possession of the Lockwood family of St. George's Hundred for several generations. It is a plain old clock, in running order, and seemingly but little the worse for wear, notwithstanding its hundred years and more of life. In addition to the clock the lodge has a trio of candlesticks (wood-gilded) and a chest, that were made by Duncan Beard for the lodge on its express order. The candlesticks represent the three orders of architecture, the Ionic, the Doric, and the Corinthian, and in design and finish show skilful handiwork.

It was in the fitness of things that Duncan Beard should be a Presbyterian in faith and religion; so I am not surprised to find that when Parson Read succeeded in getting his membership enlisted in the building of a new meeting-house to take the place of old Drawyers, that after three-quarters of a century of use was falling into decay, that Duncan Beard was named as one of the building committee; and the substantial, dignified structure which under his direction was built and dedicated to the service of Almighty God in 1773 still stands as a monument and memorial to Duncan Beard, "the skilled worker." Truly, he builded better than he knew.

The will of Duncan Beard was proved before the register of wills of this county on June 29, 1797. The will, the original of which is still preserved, was written by his own hand, and he begins with the words, " [I] , Duncan Beard

Clockmaker of Appoquinimink Hundred." It is neither dated nor signed, but the requirements of the law regarding two witnesses having been complied with, it was duly proved and allowed after his death. Two of his neighbors, Christopher Weaver and Richardson Armstrong, served both as witnesses and executors. The will mentions his wife Rebekah, but no children. There is a small bequest to Duncan Beard, son of John Beard, who presumably was a nephew or other relative. After the death of his wife provision is made that his real estate go to "Drawyers Meeting House," and the will also contains this item: "I give and bequeath unto the congregation of Drawyers Meeting House my silver pint for the use of the sacrament of the Lord's supper and that forever." The records of Drawyers are very incomplete and fragmentary, and whether "the silver pint" reached the congregation I cannot say. I have been unable to find any trace of it.

Thus imperfectly have I gotten together the scraps of information that remain of this plain old man who lived a quiet, sheltered sort of life, hidden away from the turmoil and strife, far removed from the bustle and confusion of the business world.

In his narrow sphere, in the little clearing that was bounded on the north by the Appoquinimink and on the west by the great Blackbird Forest, he lived out the measure of the days that were given him, patiently and faithfully laboring from rise to set of sun, intent only upon doing the duty that lay before him, little dreaming that a century after his life's work had closed any one would be interested in recalling the simplicity and beauty of his life.

Duncan Beard's body has been resting one hundred years in the quiet graveyard beside Drawyers Creek, in the shadow of the church he loved so well. Many of the high clocks which his mind and hand fashioned still remain, mute but impressive reminders of his modest but faithful work.

JOHN CHANDLEE.

In the latter part of the last century I find evidences of an old watch-maker in Wilmington named John Chandlee. As far as I have been able to ascertain he did not make high clocks. He was from the old Chandlee family that settled at Nottingham, in Cecil County, Maryland. The emigrant who planted the family name at Nottingham was Benjamin Chandlee, who in 1710 was married to Sarah, daughter of Able Cottey, "Watchmaker of Philadelphia," with whom Benjamin seems to have learned his trade as watch- and clock-maker. On his marriage he settled at Nottingham, where he established his trade in a small way, doing also iron-work for the neighbors.

In 1741 he removed with his younger children to Wilmington, among whom was John Chandlee, who carried on the business of "watchmaker and limner at his new store nearly opposite the Academy." Another son of Benjamin the emigrant was Benjamin, who remained at Nottingham, where he attained much eminence in the manufacture of scientific, mathematical, and chemical instruments. His clocks are among the best. In 1749 he proceeded in marriage with Mary Follwell, daughter of Goldsmith Edward Follwell, of Wilmington, "according to the good order established among Friends." This Goldsmith Edward

Follwell was for many years clerk of the borough of Wilmington. A clock made by Benjamin Chandlee, of Nottingham, is now in the possession of Josiah Lewden, at Christiana, in the old Lewden house, where it has been for more than one hundred years.

ZIBA FERRIS.

Among the old Delaware families that made an impress upon this community was that of Ziba Ferris, the elder, who served the public in many capacities. Among his children were Benjamin Ferris, the author of " Early Settlements on the Delaware," the most reliable and carefully written history of these parts. The service he rendered this State as a historian in examining, authenticating, and preserving the early records has never been fully recognized and appreciated. It is not generally known that Benjamin Ferris was a clock- and watch-maker by trade, having served his apprenticeship in Philadelphia, where he afterwards plied his trade for some years, and then removed to Wilmington. His younger brother, Ziba, learned the trade of clock- and watch-making with his brother Benjamin at the corner of Second Street and Church Alley, in Philadelphia, and then opened his shop in Wilmington, at the southwest corner of Fourth and Market Streets, where he continued in business for over fifty years.

Ziba Ferris was born January 25, 1786, at the northeast corner of Third and Shipley Streets, and lived there all of his life until his removal in 1851 to a country-seat called "Clifton," which he built near Edgemoor, in Brandywine Hundred, and which of recent years has belonged to the

ZIBA FERRIS.

Sellars family. In 1816 he was married to Eliza Megear, daughter of Michael Megear, one of the early Wilmington hat-makers. He was a birthright member of the Society of Friends, and was always a regular attendant at the West Street meeting. During his long and successful career as a clock- and watch-maker he had several apprentices, among whom were Joseph Haslet, son of the famous Colonel John Haslet who led the Delaware Regiment in the Revolution, and lost his life in the battle of Trenton. Joseph Haslet was afterwards twice elected governor of Delaware, an honor that has never been shown to any other individual. Other apprentices were Charles Canby (whom I mention later at more length), Thomas J. Megear, William F. Rudolph, and his son Ziba Ferris, Jr., the latter being for several years associated with his father in business.

Ziba Ferris was a public-spirited citizen as well as a diligent business man. He served in the Borough Council in 1811 and in 1816, and for two years, from 1841 to 1843, was treasurer of New Castle County.

His long and useful life ended on the fourteenth day of December, 1875, being within a few months of ninety years of age. He was buried in the Friends' Burying-Ground at Fourth and West Streets.

Many are still living who bear witness to the cheerfulness and geniality of his disposition and of his delightful companionship. In many regards he was an unusual man. Two of his children are still living.

CHARLES CANBY.

I have before me the face of a kindly-looking man who sat with John Brooks at the head of Friends' meeting on West Street, thirty-five years ago, when I occasionally went to meeting with my father. This was Charles Canby, another of the old Delaware. clock-makers. He was a descendant of Thomas Canby, who came to America about a year after Penn, from Yorkshire, England, and settled in Bucks County, Pennsylvania. The mother of Charles was Catharine Harlan, a daughter of Caleb Harlan, for many years a leading citizen in Mill Creek Hundred. Charles in his youthful days spent much time with his grandfather near Mill Town, and it is supposed that his fondness for bathing in Mill Creek led to an attack of white swelling which rendered him a cripple for life. It will be remembered that he always walked with two canes in after-life. He began his trade with Ziba Ferris in 1808, being his first apprentice. Born in Philadelphia in 1792, he started in business in Wilmington very soon after arriving at age, and for forty years was in active business. His first store was the first door above the Farmers' Bank at Third and Market Streets, having bought out the store of Jacob Alrichs, and he succeeded so well that in 1827 he bought the property at No. 311 Market Street (lately and for many years occupied by David P. Smyth). The new front which he put in this building was the talk of the town and quite a revelation to the tradespeople of that day. He remained there until about 1852, when he sold out to George Elliott and retired from active business. George Elliott had learned his trade

CHARLES CANBY.

with Canby, and among other apprentices who learned with him were P. Sheward Johnson, who afterwards became a school-teacher, and still later on a lawyer; Jacob F. Robinson, for many years a watch-maker and jeweller near Third and Market Streets; Thomas Conlyn, who is still living at Carlisle, Pennsylvania; John A. Rankin, who within the last year died at Elkton, Maryland; and Thomas S. Dawson, who died a few years ago, and is still remembered.

Charles Canby in his young days was fond of horseback-riding, and on one occasion having had a rather perilous experience while indulging in his favorite pastime, a friend suggested "that he sell his horse and get a wife." He acted on this advice, and on October 11, 1821, was married in the Friends' Meeting-House to Ann Richards.

By this marriage there were three children, one of whom, Catharine Garrett, wife of Henry Garrett, is still living. Although the fact that she celebrated within the past year her golden wedding would indicate that the "threescore and ten" are more than passed, yet she is a living example of those who never grow old, having many of the amiable and pleasing characteristics of the honored father from whom she sprung.

Charles Canby's latter years were spent quietly and peacefully at his home on Quaker Hill, No. 311 West Street. He was a Whig and afterwards a Republican in politics. He took a lively interest in public affairs, although never holding public office. In the anti-slavery movement and in the first steps that were taken looking to the education of the colored race he took a leading part. A man with strong convictions, he made himself felt when he en-

listed in a cause that had been prompted by a sense of duty.

He died January 13, 1883, in his ninety-first year, and his remains lie in the Friends' Burying-Ground at Fourth and West Streets.

SAMUEL McCLARY.

A few clocks still in existence bear the name of Samuel McClary. He was a native of Wilmington, being the child of John and Mary (Wallace) McClary, and was born on the 19th day of June, A.D. 1788. He learned the watch- and clock-making business with Thomas Crow at the latter's shop on Second Street near Market. When twenty-two years of age he formed a copartnership with Jacob Alrichs, and they established the first machine-shop in Delaware, using the firm-name of Alrichs & McClary. After being together only a few years the firm dissolved, as I find in the directory of 1814 Samuel McClary alone as a machine-maker at the corner of High (now Fourth) and French Streets. In 1827 he and Charles Bush went into business together, and it is said that the first steam-engine built in Delaware came from the shop of this firm, at the corner of Eighth and Orange Streets, in 1832. Samuel McClary was evidently a man who possessed mechanical ingenuity, and he was a man of industrious habits. Most of the clocks made by him were made between 1803 and 1816, as after the latter year his time seems to have been fully occupied in the machine business. A large mantel clock bearing his name is still in the possession of the descendants of his son Samuel McClary, Jr.,—at the latter's late residence, No. 404 West Seventh Street in this city. A high clock of his make

SAMUEL McCLARY.

has for years been in the possession of the McCullough family of Northeast,—the family of McCulloughs for whom the iron company is named.

Samuel McClary died August 24, 1859, and is buried in the Wilmington and Brandywine Cemetery. He was a good citizen, a useful and successful man, and, as I have shown, was a pioneer among the men whose originality and mechanical ability tended to make Wilmington the active and important industrial centre that it is to-day. For many years he was a director in the Bank of Wilmington and Brandywine.

The two sons of Samuel McClary, Samuel, Jr., and Thomas, followed in the footsteps of their father, and achieved unusual success in the lines of trade and business which they adopted. Until their deaths, in very recent years, they were active and influential business men in this community, and their fair fame in business circles is now upheld by William J. McClary, a son of Samuel, Jr., and grandson of Samuel the elder, who is the proprietor of one of the largest and most prosperous morocco plants in this city. The name Samuel McClary is perpetuated by Samuel McClary the third, the only son of William J., who is just about reaching his majority.

GEORGE JONES.

Contemporary with Samuel McClary was George Jones, an important figure in the business world of Wilmington in his lifetime. He was six years older than Samuel McClary, but they learned the trade of watch- and clock-making together with Thomas Crow; and for many years after

attaining his majority George Jones followed his trade and
conducted a successful business in that line at No. 29
Market Street, and afterwards at No. 407 Market Street,
the stand so long occupied by Benjamin S. Clark, who
became the successor of Jones in business at that location
about 1850. George Jones was a dentist as well as a
clock-maker; or rather, it might be more exact to say,
that he "pulled teeth;" as it was before the days of pain-
less extracting, and before the art of skilled dentistry had
been developed. There are people still living that can
bear witness to the thoroughness, if not to the skill and
painlessness, of the tooth-pulling of George Jones.

In an advertisement of George Jones in the *Delaware
Gazette* of May 13, 1833, in which he announces his removal from No. 25 to No. 95 Market Street, and sets forth
the merits of his watch- and clock-making business, he adds
an N. B. which says, " The subscriber, as usual, attends to
the various branches of setting, filing, plugging and cleaning
teeth. He also keeps a good assortment of teeth brushes."

I have never seen but one tall clock that bore his name.
It is fifty years old, and is owned by Elwood Garrett.
Another, I learn, is still in the family of his son John M.
Jones, in New York City; and a third, smaller, but bearing
the name of George Jones, is in the possession of his
daughter Elizabeth A. Jones Dod, who is living at an advanced age in Wichita, Kansas. George Jones was identified
with the important business enterprises of his day. He
served as president of the Delaware Fire Insurance Company
for many years. This was then the leading fire insurance
company in this city, and much of its success was due to

GECRGE JONES.

the care and attention given to its affairs by its president. The company was located on Market Street, just below Second, at what is now known as No. 117.

He was among those who organized the Wilmington Savings Fund Society in 1832, and remained a manager from its organization to the time of his death. He was a member of City Council in 1819, 1820, 1821, 1823. For many years he was a director of the Bank of Wilmington and Brandywine, and was one of the founders of the Friendship Fire Engine Company.

He was a leading member, and for fifty years an elder, in Hanover Presbyterian Church. At the celebration of the one hundredth anniversary of that church in 1872, Rev. Carson W. Adams, in an address on the elders of the church, speaks as follows of George Jones:

"George Jones was for most of the years of his life a member of this church, and also an elder. His life was a quiet one, spent in the diligent pursuit of business, in which he was very successful. He was an amiable, genial man, a great favorite with his friends. When this church edifice was erected he had his fortune still to make, but like his contemporaries, he made great sacrifices to secure the completion of the building. He had a love for the walls of this sanctuary; within it many of the happiest hours of his life were spent. He was punctual in the duties of his office as a member of session. He died in the hope of a blessed immortality, after he had passed fourscore years on the earth."

George Jones died August 15, 1867. Funeral services were held in Hanover Church, and his remains were buried

in the Wilmington and Brandywine Cemetery. His residence at the time of his death was at No. 711 French Street.

JOSEPH & ALEXANDER KINKEAD.

In the old Allen homestead at the south end of Christiana Bridge, on the outskirts of the village of Christiana, is a high clock bearing the name of " Joseph & Alex'r Kinkead, Christiana Bridge." A few years ago I saw another Kinkead clock in the town of Newark. I have been unable to gather but little information in regard to them. May we not assume that Joseph Kinkead was the veritable clock-maker who is described so charmingly by "Gath" in his "Ticking Stone." His hero "resided in the little village of Christiana (by the pretentious called Christi-anna, and by the crude, with nearer rectitude, called Christene), where was kept a snug little shop full of all manners and forms of clocks, dials, sand-glasses, hour-burning candles, water-clocks, and night tapers." Over the door of the whitewashed cabin of Gath's clock-maker was the sign of a fat jovial person, bearing some resemblance to himself, in the centre of whose stomach stood a clock inscribed "My time is everybody's." And Gath goes on to explain that "Past this little shop went the entire long caravan and cavalcade by land between the North and South, stage-coaches, mail-riders, highwaymen, chariots, herdsters, and tramps, for Christiana Bridge was on the great tide-water road and at the head of navigation on the Swedish river of the same name, so that here vessels from the Delaware transferred their cargo to wagons, and a portage of only ten miles to the head of Elk gave goods and passengers reshipment

down the Chesapeake. This village declined only when the canal just below it was opened in 1829, and a little railroad in 1833. It was nearly a century and a half old when the clock-maker set his sign there, before General Washington went past to be inaugurated."

Joseph Kinkead, clock-maker, owned a lot in the town of Newark as early as 1781, which he and his wife Martha conveyed to John Ochletree in 1796. Four years later he bought a tract of four acres on the road from Newark to the Welsh Tract; and in 1788, by deed of Benjamin Ogle, became possessed of twenty acres near Christiana Bridge on the road to Newark. In this deed he is described as "Watchmaker of White Clay Creek Hundred." I assume that it was after this that his clocks were made which I have seen. I presume that Alexander was his son. Joseph and Alexander have been sleeping many years in their graves, and I presume that their resting-place is in the little graveyard that surrounds the Presbyterian church that crowns the hill at Christiana, where the Calvinistic faith has been preached for a century and a half.

THE LOWBER CLOCK.

There is an old eight-day high clock in the possession of the descendants of Michael Lober that is worthy of notice, even though not made in Delaware. It is probably the oldest clock in Kent County, and is still keeping good time. It has a walnut case, with brass works and a brass face. It was brought to this country either by Michael or Peter Lober from Amsterdam. Peter owned land in Kent as early as 1684, and it is a tradition in the family that he

brought the clock with him about that time. From Peter the clock descended to his son William, and then to William's only child, Catharine, who married Thomas Cooper, and from Catharine Cooper the clock went to her daughter Letitia, who married John Gruwell. It is now owned by John C. Gruwell. The names of the successive owners are written on the inside of the clock. It bears no date, but its history has been handed down by Catharine Cooper, who learned it from her grandfather, Peter Cooper. The eighth generation from Michael Lober is now living, among whom is Peter Lowber Cooper, Jr., a member of our Historical Society and the respected deputy attorney-general of this State.

ROBERT SHEARMAN.

I have heard of a high clock now in Chester County, bearing the name of "R. Shearman, Wilmington." I find that Robert Shearman, clock-maker of Wilmington, as early as 1768, owned three lots of land in Wilmington: one at the southeast corner of High (Fourth) and Walnut Streets, one at the northeast corner of Queen (Fifth) and Walnut Streets, and the third on the southeast corner of the same streets. These facts which I have ascertained from the records are all that I have been able to find of R. Shearman.

S. EVANS AND WILLIAM FURNISS.

At the sale of the personal effects of Mary Ann Barlow at Milford Cross-Roads, in Mill Creek Hundred, in 1889, a tall clock was sold bearing the name on a brass ball on the face " S. Evans and Wm. Furniss, New Castle County,

Fecit." This clock afterwards came into my possession, and about two years ago became the property of Howard Pyle, the artist, who still owns it.

Of S. Evans I have been unable to learn anything; but my presumption is that he belonged to the same family as Oliver Evans, the famous millwright and inventor, who lived on Red Clay Creek near Faulkland. William Furniss' bought a small lot on the west side of Marshall Street in Newport-Ayre from Samuel Marshall in 1739, and the records disclose that this same William Furniss died about 1748, and in an application made to the Orphans' Court by James Kelly, his administrator, to sell his real estate to pay his debts, he is described as a "clockmaker." This was under date of October 16, 1750, and establishes the fact that the above clock is more than one hundred and fifty years old, and was likely made in the town of Newport.

NICHOLAS LE HURAY.

There are people still living who remember a clock-maker of the above name, who plied his trade in the little brick shop at the cross-roads at Ogletown, on the public road from Christiana to Newark. The only information I have been able to obtain of Le Huray is from his will, which was probated on February 16, 1834, and remains of record in this county. In his will, which is dated January 8, 1834, he describes himself as a watch- and clock-maker, a son of Nicholas, who was a native of the parish of Tortmal in the island of Guernsey. The will mentions his wife, whose name was Elizabeth, and eight children. The executor named was Jonathan Bee, a respected citizen of that local-

ity. He was possessed of the farm on which he lived and died at Ogletown; and a small tract of land on the Frankford Turnpike, three miles above Philadelphia. His personal estate seems to have been considerable, as the executor gave a bond of fifteen thousand dollars. I assume that he was buried at the old Welsh Tract Baptist Burying-Ground. I have never seen a clock bearing his name, but clocks of his make are remembered by people in that vicinity.

JOSEPH H. JACKSON.

I have knowledge of two high clocks bearing the name " J. H. Jackson, Mill Creek Hundred, Delaware." One is owned by Robert C. Justis, at Faulkland, having descended to him from his father, for whom it was made about 1810, and the other owned by James G. Longfellow, of Clayton, he having procured it recently from a party named Morrison.

Joseph H. Jackson lived on part of the Mermaid Tavern farm on the Limestone Road, in Mill Creek Hundred. Under date of April 1, 1817, he bought a tract of fifteen acres from John Hanna, Jr., which is described as on the Limestone Road and adjoining lands of Mary Black (widow), William Bracken, and William Ball.

There is no record in this county of any administration on his estate, so that he may have removed from this county before his decease, and the above is all that I have been able to find concerning him, except that he was an Englishman by birth, and presumably came to this country after reaching his majority. His name is not mentioned in an assessment list for Mill Creek Hundred for 1804, which I have seen.

A RITTENHOUSE CLOCK.

The old clocks that command the highest prices are those that were made by David Rittenhouse. Rittenhouse was the leading scientific man of his day. He resided near Norristown, Pennsylvania, and was a leading man in public affairs in Revolutionary times. A clock of his make is now in the possession of the family of Alfred Gawthrop of this city. It has an interesting history. During the prevalence of the yellow fever in Philadelphia David Rittenhouse, who resided there, sought his own safety by removing temporarily to Darby, and for some time lived with Samuel Stroud at that place. In recognition of the kindness shown him, Rittenhouse presented Samuel Stroud with one of his clocks. It afterwards descended to a son of Samuel Stroud, and then to two of the grandchildren, Mrs. Alfred Gawthrop and Elizabeth Stroud, in whose possession it has been for many years, and by whom it is highly prized.

I have spanned a century with the simple records of these modest lives,—not the fame and renown won in military and naval warfare, but every-day, commonplace lives that were spent over the work-bench and amid plain and unpretentious surroundings.

With the glamour and display, the tinsel and the glitter so prevalent in this age, is it not refreshing to recall the patient industry and sturdy manhood of the generation of a century ago represented in these quiet, unassuming lives, which in a fragmentary and imperfect way I have endeavored to recall? "Time and tide wait for no man." They have

passed from the scenes of their earthly labors. Only the influence of their lives survive. If in their lives they added to the store of human knowledge, if in a little measure, even, they made the world brighter or better, or happier, then were their lives not lived in vain; and, being dead, they yet speak to us in the handiwork which they wrought.

HON. LEONARD EUGENE WALES.

LEONARD EUGENE WALES.

A MEMOIR.

BY

SAMUEL RODMOND SMITH, ESQ.,

CLERK OF THE UNITED STATES COURTS FOR THE DISTRICT OF DELAWARE.

Read before the Historical Society of Delaware, September 20, 1897.

THE HISTORICAL SOCIETY OF DELAWARE,

WILMINGTON.

1898.

LEONARD EUGENE WALES.

Mr. President and Members of the Historical Society of Delaware: In accordance with the request made
by your honorable body, I have prepared a brief memorial
of the life and public services of the late Judge Wales. In
the discharge of this pleasant duty of commemorating his
useful life and distinguished services, I have investigated
with more particularity and care than would be necessary if
the memorial were not intended to include historical data;
and, in accordance with his views often expressed to me, I
have endeavored to avoid indiscriminate praise, and to hold
up as admirable only those traits of character for which he
was particularly distinguished.

Leonard Eugene Wales was the son of John Wales,
who was elected in 1849 to represent this State in the Senate
of the United States, and of Ann, his wife, who was the
only daughter of Major John Patton, of the Revolutionary
Delaware line. He was born in this city on the twenty-
sixth day of November, 1823. His boyhood days, as far as
I am informed, were not remarkable for unusual precocity
or aptitude for learning; but, like the generality of youths,
he possessed a healthy appetite for exercise and amusement,
which resulted in a robust although spare form and a
strong constitution, which preserved his life for more than

the allotted period of threescore years and ten. His college days, too, at Yale, as was also true of his preparatory studies at the Hopkins Grammar School at New Haven, Connecticut, were not, as I am informed, conspicuous for a display of mental powers and achievements beyond the average.

After his graduation at Yale, in 1845, he commenced the study of law under the instruction of his father, and was duly called to the bar of this county on May 8, 1848. He was for a while associated with his father, until the failing health and increased infirmities of the latter threw the burden of office work, and the preparation and trial of causes which were entrusted to their care, almost entirely upon him. His association with his father in this way, although of inestimable advantage to him in after life, doubtless dwarfed him in the popular estimation, as the prominent figure in the trials at court by them was naturally that of his father, whose position, ability, and tact as a lawyer had long been favorably known and recognized. In July of 1853 he was elected city solicitor, and discharged the duties of that office so acceptably that he was re-elected for another term in the following year.

He became clerk of the United States District and Circuit Courts for this district under the appointment of Judge Hall on May 8 and 29 respectively, 1849, and held these offices until September 13, 1864, when he resigned, and was appointed associate judge of the Superior Court of our State under the commission of Governor Cannon. He was sworn in and assumed the duties of this latter office on October 1, 1864, and remained upon the State bench, attending to all the various duties of that office, to the great satis-

faction of the members of the bar and the citizens of our
State, until his appointment by President Arthur as the
United States district judge for this district. He took the
oaths of office pertaining to the latter office on March 24,
1884, and remained on the Federal bench in that position
until his death on February 8, 1897, a period of nearly
thirteen years.

It is difficult, in contrasting the record of Judge Wales
during the nineteen and one-half years he was on the State
bench with his record during the thirteen years he was on
the Federal bench, to avoid comparisons which may seem
to belittle his work as a State judge. It must be remembered, however, that during the whole time he sat as associate justice of the Superior Court of Delaware there
were but two terms of the Superior Court annually in each
of the three counties, and that the population of the State
showed but little increase during this period except in the
city of Wilmington, and here the population had only increased in these twenty years from about twenty-six thousand to about forty-five thousand. As a consequence, the
trials were comparatively few and the amounts in controversy usually small. Wealth was not so generally distributed or aggregated in any considerable amount in isolated
cases; it was rare to find a person worth one hundred
thousand dollars. The State was decidedly provincial, and
the condition of the people in material wealth and education was largely governed by the disabilities which sur-
round a frontier settlement. The Delaware Railroad,
which has opened the avenues of trade and commerce of
our State and brought higher civilization, comforts, and

blessings to our people, was but just finished, and the resultant benefits of this and other internal improvements had only commenced to be felt.

Under these circumstances it is not surprising that during the whole period of nearly twenty years during which Judge Wales sat on the State bench, so far as I can ascertain, he only delivered ten opinions in the Court of Errors and Appeals, four opinions in the Superior Court, and one in the Court of Oyer and Terminer.

Of course, he sat in a relatively large number of cases during this time, and doubtless delivered oral opinions from the bench which have not been reported. It must not be forgotten, either, that he transacted considerable business in the Orphans' Court,—business of a very important character which made no show in the reports; and that he sat with his associates in the Court of Errors and Appeals, in the Court of Oyer and Terminer, and in the Court of General Sessions of the Peace and Jail Delivery. In all this latter class of cases he shared, of course, the responsibility of the decisions, except where he dissented, with the other members of the court.

In all of these years he fulfilled every expectation that could be reasonably demanded of him; and it is not too much to say that he met every call upon him with credit to the State and to himself.

We come now to his work in a very different field,—to a period commencing with his elevation to the Federal bench. Here, on his appointment, he found, with a growing, thrifty population around him, a great deal of work in the District Court, in which no one could sit with him or share his re-

sponsibility,—work covering a vast range of jurisprudence, admiralty, bankruptcy, law, equity, and criminal prosecutions for violations of the United States Statutes; issues involving often questions of international law, treaties, and constitutional rights. He found, also, much work in the Circuit Court, more perhaps than in the District Court; and in this work it was the exception, from the great volume of business in the other Circuit Courts in this circuit, that any other judge found the time to sit with him. He found here matters of large import: controversies where the matters in dispute were of great value and importance; questions involving the appointment of receivers and the settlement of insolvent estates in their charge; the construction of patents, the powers and duties of railroad, private, and municipal corporations; the rights and disabilities of corporate stockholders, construction of contracts, international treaties, trade-marks, neutrality laws, constitutional guarantees, insurance, conflicts of jurisdiction with the State courts, mandamus, national banks, insolvency, common carriers, principal and surety, attorney and client, classification of items subject to custom duties, eminent domain, and many important questions relating especially to the admiralty and bankruptcy jurisdiction of these courts.

It might be supposed that the business of two courts with such a wide range of jurisdiction and with increasing work each year coming to his hands, would be enough of responsibility and strain for one judge, but under the United States Statutes any district judge is liable to assignment to another district in the event of the disability of the judge of that district; and so, in July, 1886, United States District

Judge Nixon, of the New Jersey district, having become disabled, Judge Wales was assigned to the New Jersey district, and thus had, until Judge Nixon's decease, about three years thereafter, the whole of the civil and criminal business of the United States District Court for the New Jersey district to transact, as well as the larger part of the business of the United States Circuit Court for that district, in addition to his own work in the District and Circuit Courts for our own district. This work, although exacting, was entered upon with great willingness and remarkable confidence, and was discharged with signal ability. Every appeal which was taken to the Supreme Court from his decisions in this district was dismissed. His labors under this assignment, while approximating closely in general character and scope to the work devolving upon him in the Federal courts in his own district, were yet of greater importance, owing to the extensive interests frequently involved in the controversies before those courts.

It had seemed to me that after Judge Nixon's successor had been appointed and qualified, the remainder of Judge Wales's life might have been well and usefully spent in attending to the growing business of his own courts, but Congress, on March 3, 1891, passed an act for the relief of the Supreme Court and created a new Federal court,—the United States Circuit Court of Appeals. The component members of that court were the United States Supreme Court justice allotted to the circuit, the two circuit judges, and the several district judges of the circuit who might be assigned to duty. The intention of the circuit judges in this court was, as I understood from Judge Wales, to

assign alternately to duty in that court one of the four district judges whose districts were embraced in the circuit; this would have given Judge Wales eighteen months' relief from the duties of the Appeal Court before a new assignment, but in practice it resulted, that owing to the press of business at their respective courts in Philadelphia, Pittsburgh, or Trenton,—all larger, more populous, and more wealthy districts than our own,—none of the judges of these districts when assigned to any term were fully able to complete their tour of duty: so Judge Wales, being the district judge with the smallest district, was called upon and actually sat during every term of the United States Circuit Court of Appeals for this circuit since its organization.

In the performance of all this arduous duty Judge Wales sat in the United States District Court for the Delaware district and heard argument in one hundred and fifty-one contested cases, and handed down seventeen opinions; he sat and heard argument in the United States Circuit Court for the Delaware district in one hundred and seventy-three contested cases, and handed down thirty-two opinions. He handed down in the United States District Court for the New Jersey district twenty-one opinions, and in the United States Circuit Court for the New Jersey district, twenty-seven opinions; and, without knowing precisely in how many cases he sat in these courts, by analogy to the number of opinions rendered in the two Delaware courts as compared with the number of contested cases in which he sat, I think it safe to say that he must have heard argument in the New Jersey District and Circuit Courts in at least three hundred and twenty-four contested cases. He also

sat and heard argument in the United States Circuit Court
of Appeals for the Third Circuit in one hundred and thirteen
contested cases, and handed down twenty-six opinions.   All
told, he sat and heard argument in seven hundred and sixty
contested cases, and handed down one hundred and twenty-
three opinions.   This is altogether aside from the innumerable hearings on *ex parte* applications, both in his own
courts and in the New Jersey courts, often involving considerable investigation and responsibility in their trial and
disposition.   This is a record, it seems to me, of which
any one might be proud.

It must be remembered that many of these decisions related to very large interests, occasionally running into the
millions, and involved questions of most intricate character
and nice discrimination, as, for instance, the question of in-
fringement of patents for cold storage of meats, etc., electric
light patents, celluloid patents, bicycle tire patents, electric telegraph and burglar-alarm patents, metre patents for
measuring flow of fluids, spindle patents for yarn winding in
cotton mills, car-box lid patents, and patents on soda-water
fountains, and that the parties in interest were often represented by the ablest counsel in America, among whom
may be mentioned Roscoe Conkling, Benjamin F. Butler,
George H. Boutwell, Frederick Coudert, John R. Bennett,
J. C. Carter, Roger Foster, Wayne MacVeagh, John G.
Johnson, Courtland Parker, Richard C. McMurtrie, Samuel
Dickson, Edmund Wetmore, Joseph D. Badee, J. H. Ray-
mond, O. Z. Keasby, Samuel A. Duncan, Henry R. Ed-
munds, Henry Flanders, Morton B. Henry, and by many
other prominent members of the New York, Trenton, Bos-

ton, and Philadelphia bars, as well as by the leaders of our
own bar on many occasions.

In leaving this subject, permit me to express the hope
that Congress will at an early day pass laws authorizing
the appointment of a sufficient number of circuit judges to
constitute the United States Circuit Court of Appeals, and
thus relieve the district judges of the duty and burden of
attending that court, and the circuit judges of the duty
and burden of attending the several Circuit Courts in their
districts. Both, beyond doubt, are very much overburdened,
and I believe from the views I have frequently heard expressed that the bar would regard an independent Circuit
Court of Appeals as a great improvement upon the present
constitution of the courts.

Judge Wales, coming from an old Whig family, was
naturally a Republican. In his younger days he wrote
editorials for the *Delaware State Journal*, a newspaper published here, and I think for the *Blue Hen's Chicken.* He
was stanch in his political belief without being intensely
partisan. He did not follow any man's flag, but believed
in principles; he was always ready as a citizen to further
the cause of the party whose principles he believed in.

As a judge he knew no man nor the political party to
which he belonged, and this has been amply demonstrated
to the disappointment of his ardent party friends in the
numerous force bill cases tried before him. No man in this
respect can dispute his absolute fairness. As a citizen he
was always alert for the good of his community. If any
law were proposed especially detrimental in his judgment
to the welfare of the State, it would invariably encounter

his opposition. He was at all times ready to forward any movement towards the betterment of the city or the State or the condition of our people. He proposed and drafted the law which forbids the granting of divorces to non-residents for causes outside this State, unless the same were grantable for like causes in the State from which the petitioner came, and he has suggested various other remedial laws, among which may be mentioned the proposed United States statute to permit comparisons of handwriting of the accused on a criminal charge with his handwriting proved to the satisfaction of the court to be genuine, and not otherwise in the cause. This proposed law, after, as I am informed, receiving the approval of the Judiciary Committee of the Senate, failed to pass. An act similar to the one above suggested was passed in our State Legislature, and was approved March 2, 1881, and has doubtless prevented miscarriages of justice.

As a patriot Judge Wales was ever solicitous for the maintenance of the Union, and he viewed with concern and alarm the spirit of disloyal sentiment in the South during the years immediately preceding the civil war. Few persons who were not adults at the outbreak of this sanguinary conflict have any conception of the intensity of the feeling engendered by this momentous struggle and the controversies which led up to it. On the one hand, the influential and the thrifty class residing in those States whose laws since the formation of the government sanctioned slavery, felt that they were about to be deprived of their lawful and recognized rights of possession and property in this species of chattels without compensation, and without that due process of law which was guaranteed to them in such case by

the Constitution; and that this legalized robbery was to be perpetrated upon them, solely to satisfy the demands of a class of fanatical reformers, whose piety justified the taking of private property against the consent of the owner without compensation. Added to this, many divines in the different religious bodies in the States referred to, declared that slavery was an institution recognized by the Scriptures and sanctioned by the divine law. On the other hand, the great mass of people in the free States, and nearly all the great ecclesiastical bodies in that section, maintained that slavery was the relic of barbarism, radically and inherently wrong, and indefensible from any point of view; that the holding of one human being in bondage to another for life, could not be justified by any of the tenets of Christianity, which inculcated the doing to others as you would have others do to you; and that such legalized enslavement was brutalizing, degrading, and inhuman;—in short, that slavery was against the enlightened conscience of the nation, and that there was an irrepressible conflict which must be settled one way or the other, for freedom or for slavery.

Amid these religious, political, and social contentions, and the intense feelings aroused by the public discussions in the campaign of 1860, which closed with the election of President Lincoln, families were divided, brothers estranged from each other, life-long friendships broken, and the people of the Union were separated into hostile camps by the sectional line of border States.

At such a time every man had to declare himself for one side or the other.

Judge Wales did not hesitate. He threw the whole

weight of his personality and influence into the scale in favor of freedom. At the outbreak of the civil war he enrolled himself as a volunteer in Company E, First Regiment, Delaware Infantry, and was elected second lieutenant in that organization. The regiment was mustered in for three months' service, and was assigned to duty at the bridges over the Gunpowder and Bush Rivers on the line of the Philadelphia, Wilmington and Baltimore Railroad. This duty was uneventful, although at the time serious apprehensions from threatened forays of the enemy's cavalry were felt for the safety of these important bridges, which were the main avenues for the transportation of troops from the North and East to the capital. These apprehensions were afterwards justified by the attempted burning of one of these bridges by Harry Gilmore, a partisan ranger, in 1863.

After Judge Wales's discharge from the military service he became one of the commissioners of the Board of Enrollment for Delaware under appointment of Governor Cannon in May, 1863; and at the time of his appointment as associate judge of the Superior Court of this State he resigned the former position.

In the discharge of this work as enrollment commissioner it became his duty to prepare drafts for the army, to fill the call made upon the State by the national government, to decide on the claims for exemption from military service, and on the qualifications of substitutes offered for those who had been drafted. It was a trying and unpopular task, but was performed conscientiously and to the satisfaction of the State and national authorities.

Judge Wales was a true philanthropist, and was ever

ready to give his aid and countenance to measures for the relief of the poor and unfortunate. He was one of the charter members of the Ferris Reform School,—an institution near this city for the reformation of incorrigible youth,—and by his frequent presence and advice contributed much to its successful institution and conduct. He was prominent in aiding the West End Reading-Room, which was organized largely through the persistent and public-spirited efforts of his niece, Miss Emily Bissell. By his encouragement and interest on frequent occasions he assisted in placing that worthy institution in the position it has since attained for accomplishing great good. He was president of the Delaware branch of the Society of the Cincinnati and the Delaware branch of the Sons of the Revolution, and also aided largely in organizing the latter and reorganizing the former association, which had been disbanded for very many years. He was also president for many years of your honorable body, and evinced much interest in its deliberations and praiseworthy efforts to preserve from loss the authentic personal recollections and records of the distinguished men whose services in military and civil life have added so much to the renown of our State.

Judge Wales possessed a pleasant, kindly manner, which rendered him easy of approach and endeared him to his friends and to the younger members of the bar. Often have I heard the latter speak in the warmest terms of the ease with which they addressed him while on the bench, and the gratification they had in the feeling that their arguments were fully comprehended by the court. As one of the younger members of the bar expressed it

when paying his tribute,—"Judge Wales never left a sore
spot in the hearts of those who addressed him." He
was not insensible to the dignity of the court over which
he presided, but he rarely had occasion to vindicate it,
as it was equally rare for any one to attempt to take advantage of his complaisance. He was true in his friendships, and no man could say that he had fallen in the judge's
estimation by reason only of the change in his fortunes.
He was devoted to his family, and there seemed to be no
service he was reluctant to give for their advancement and
happiness. I never saw him, during the whole thirteen
years of my intimate association with him, entirely lose his
good temper, and I have occasionally seen him under severe
provocation. He seemed always charitable and philosophical enough to overlook the offence. I never saw or heard
him intentionally wound another's feelings, but have often
heard him qualify censorious remarks made by others.

He was one of the finest gentlemen I have ever had the
pleasure of knowing intimately. He was honorable and
true and just in all his transactions, and his death was
an irreparable loss not only to his family, but to his friends
and the community as well. His example, however, is
with us to stimulate the younger members of the bar to
emulate his good qualities, with the certainty before them
that such a life, often involving self-denial, is richest in results
both here and, as we must believe, hereafter; while to those
of us who are fast approaching the other side, his genial
disposition, unfailing good temper, desire to aid all worthy
efforts, his devotion to honor and truth, are examples we
may all find advantageous to more closely imitate.

PAPERS OF THE HISTORICAL SOCIETY OF DELA

XXII.

JACOB ALRICKS AND NEPHEW PETER ALRIC

BY

EDWARD A. PRICE, ESQ.,

OF MEDIA, PENNA.

Read before the Historical Society of Delaware, January

THE HISTORICAL SOCIETY OF DELAWARE

WILMINGTON.

1898.

JACOB ALRICKS AND HIS NEPHEW
PETER ALRICKS.

THE discovery of the North and South Rivers in 1609 by Hudson, while seeking a northwest passage to China in the service of the Dutch East India Company, created great interest in Holland.

A general edict was passed by the States General, granting special privileges to all persons who had or should thereafter discover any new courses, havens, countries, or places.

The privileges of this edict expired by limitation in 1618, but were renewed for limited periods, and up to 1620 several private adventures were taken to the newly discovered land in America called New Netherland.

On February 12, 1620, "the Directors of the Company trading to New Netherland," whose grant had expired in 1618, represented to the States General that "a certain English preacher, well versed in the Dutch language, was inclined to go there to live, and take some four hundred families from Holland, as well as England, provided he could be suitably protected; also expressing their belief that the English were disposed to colonize the land, which would deprive the States of the benefit of their discovery, and asking that the proposed emigrants be taken under their protection, and that, provisionally, two ships of war

be sent to secure the land to them." The petition was held until April 11, and then rejected.

In July, 1620, some of the associates of the Reverend John Robinson (the English preacher referred to) embarked at Delft Haven in the May Flower for the North River or the region south, but by reason of bad navigation struck the shoals of Cape Cod, and after a vain attempt to proceed southward were forced, on December 11, 1620, to land at Plymouth, where they laid the foundation of that colony.

The Dutch West India Company had been organized and chartered by the States General in 1607 for the purpose, among other things, of extending its commerce into the New World, as the East India Company had been organized and chartered for a like purpose in the Old, but on the signing of the truce between the States General and the Archduke Albert and his wife Isabella, on April 9, 1609, and its subsequent ratification by the King of Spain, which virtually recognized the independence of the Republic, no further action had been taken.

The truce expired in 1621, when the young Republic stood, confronted by its old enemy, on the verge of another war. This, together with the threatened loss of the newly found possessions in America by English colonization, led to the reorganization and charter of the Dutch West India Company upon what appears to have been a military as well as a trading basis, as in the charter, dated June 3, 1621, it is set out that, besides the right to traffic in the countries of America and other places, " the company might in the name and authority of the States make contracts, engagements, and alliances with princes and natives of the coun-

tries mentioned, and also build forts, etc, there; appoint and discharge governors, people for war, officers of justice, and other public officers," "transmitting a report of such contracts and alliances, and the situation of the fortresses taken by them."

Nothing appears to have been done by the West India Company towards carrying out the objects of its charter until about 1623, when it seems to have turned its attention towards planting a colony on the Delaware.

To follow in detail its operations and that of other adventurers on the Delaware would be tedious and out of place in this paper. Suffice it to say, that the Dutch West India Company after a time found itself burdened with debt, and having in its efforts to maintain its authority on the Delaware been compelled to obtain financial aid from the city of Amsterdam, negotiations were entered into for the purpose of transferring a portion of its possessions on the river, consisting of Fort Casimer, located on the present site of the borough of New Castle, and the land from the Christiana to Bombay Hook, and so far landward as the boundaries of the Minquaskill, to that city in payment of the debt, over which the city was to have complete control as a distinct colony.

Immediate steps were taken by the burgomasters of Amsterdam to settle a colony and garrison the fort, for which purpose a company of about fifty soldiers, with their captain, Martin Kryger, and lieutenant, Alexander D'Hiniyossa, and one hundred and sixty persons, principally inhabitants of Gulick, as settlers, with Jacob Alricks as director and commissary general, embarked at the expense of the

city on December 21, 1656, in the ships Prince Maurice,
Bear, Gilded Beaver, and Flower of Gelder, from Amsterdam to Manhattan, to report to Director General Stuyvesant
for instructions.

Alricks embarked on the Prince Maurice with his wife, on
which were one hundred and sixty-eight people, including
colonists, mechanics, soldiers, and attendants, and sixteen
sailors. The Prince Maurice was to lead the fleet and to
act as admiral, but it was soon discovered that the vessel
was greatly clogged, and that neither the skipper, pilot, nor
any superior officer belonging to the ship had ever been in
New Netherland or frequented its coasts.

On the night of December 28, 1656, the fleet was over-
taken by a storm, and the Prince Maurice became separated
from the others and remained so for the rest of the trip.
After a very stormy, discouraging, and dangerous voyage,
land was descried on February 17, 1657, a little south of
Cape Romaine, off the coast of South Carolina, and it was
hoped that the Manhattes would be reached in a few days.
This, however, was not to be, as on the night of March 8,
about eleven o'clock, through the ignorance of the skipper,
pilot, or officer in charge, although repeatedly warned by
Alricks not to spare the lead, the vessel stranded on a
shoal, on which she pounded harder and harder, until it
seemed doubtful whether those on board would survive or
perish.

After a night of great anxiety and fear, they found themselves at daybreak to be a gunshot from the shore, between
the shoals and the strand, but in such a position that it was
unanimously resolved, first to save their lives, and then to

exert every energy to save as much as possible from the ship.

Accordingly, on March 9, in severe, bitter, and freezing weather, amid drifting ice, in a leaky boat partly filled with water, they succeeded in reaching the shore, "which was a broken spit or foreland, on which neither brush nor grass grew, nor was any tree or firewood to be found."

On the third day they saw and spoke to some Indians, who informed them that they had been wrecked on the fore-land of Long Island, about twenty leagues north of Man-hattan.

The ship in the meantime had been getting nearer shore, and from time to time they unloaded as much as they could of what was necessary to their comfort.

An Indian was sent to Director General Stuyvesant, at Manhattan, to report their misfortune, who immediately sent them a small sloop, and the second day thereafter came himself. The work of unloading was continued, but before it was completed the ship went to pieces. The goods that were saved were carried to the side of a river that was discovered, called Sichtauagh, and then loaded into nine small vessels and conveyed to Manhattan.

The remaining vessels of the fleet, having on board some fifty or more persons, reached Manhattan in safety about ten days afterwards.

On April 12, 1657, at Fort Amsterdam, Peter Stuyvesant, on behalf of the States General of the United Netherlands, and the directors of the West India Company, transferred to Jacob Alricks, as director and commissary-general of the Colony of the Burgomasters and Governors of the City

of Amsterdam, on the South River of New Netherland, Fort Casimer and the territory above mentioned, agreeably to the first bill of sale and title-deed of the Indians, dated July 19, 1651.

The Gilded Beaver was re-chartered, and on April 16, 1657, the vessel set sail from the harbor of New Amsterdam for New Amstel (now New Castle), having on board the goods that had been saved from the wreck and about one hundred and twenty-five souls, including Director Alricks and his wife, where they arrived on April 25, and on the same day Director Jaquet, who had been in the service of the States General, delivered to Alricks the keys of the fort and vacated the place.

On May 1, following, thirty-eight soldiers and some freemen, together with the captain and lieutenant before mentioned, who had travelled overland, reached the place.

The government of the colony was vested in a Board of Commissioners who resided in the city of Amsterdam, but at his post Alricks was charged, as officer of the city, with the administration of civil and criminal justice, the superintendence of military affairs, and the jurisdiction of matters connected with the revenue.

He found, on his arrival, the government to consist of the vice-director or commander, sitting over military delinquents with military persons as associates, and over civilians with citizens as associates, those in the latter case being two persons acting as schepens, and one other person selected as secretary.

The conditions offered by the city of Amsterdam to settlers provided for a court consisting of a schout or offi-

cer as the head of justice appointed by the deputies of
Amsterdam, three burgomasters to be appointed by the
common burghers from "the honestest, fittest, and richest,"
and five or seven schepens to be nominated and selected by
the director in a certain manner, being a copy of the manner of administering justice in Amsterdam.

This court had full criminal and a limited civil jurisdiction, with the right of an aggrieved party to appeal to the
director general and commissioners of New Netherland.

The ancient inhabitants objected to the proposed change,
whereupon the director permitted the old civil system to
remain, giving the Schepen Court jurisdiction provisionally
over little civil cases, the military council and the director
disposing of all public affairs and whatever concerned the
military and militia, questions between the servants of the
city, such as civil officers and freemen, and misunderstand-
ings arising among and received from the Schepen Court,
until the arrival of more persons in the ship De Waegg, or
Balance, at a later period, when the court as provided by
the conditions before mentioned was organized.

The inhabitants consisted of a few soldiers and some
twenty families, five or six being Hollanders and the rest
Swedes. In the Prince Maurice were "about thirty-five
colonists as free handicraftsmen, among whom were some
few workmen and some future servant men, but the major
part were tradespeople, who did not learn their trade very
well and ran away from their masters too early in consequence of their own viciousness." "There were also forty-
seven soldiers and ten civil servants, with seventy-six women,
children, and maid-servants," making a total of one hundred

and sixty-eight persons. Others subsequently came, so
that on October 16, 1658, there were about six hundred
souls in the colony, among whom were many rough people
who furnished plenty of work in a certain line, " scarcely an
hour passing without the director having trouble or talk
with one or the other of them." Houses were few, and the
fortifications and all the buildings connected therewith were
in a ruinous condition.

A large store, with a loft for a dwelling, a store-house, and
other necessary conveniences, a barrack one hundred and
ninety feet in length just outside the fort for the married
soldiers with their wives and children, a guard-house inside
the fort, a bath-house in the fort square, a dwelling for the
commissary for the distribution of rations, and a burgher
watch-house were immediately constructed, and repairs to
the director's dwelling and the houses of the clergyman
and smith were also made.

Each colonist and tradesman received the free conveyance
of a lot in the square, thirty by about one hundred and
eighty feet, in fee, and up to August 16, 1659, one hundred
and ten houses had been built, making the settlement
" pretty well looking and convenient."

Those erections were necessarily slow and tiresome. On
May 25, 1657, the colonists, free mechanics, civil servants,
with the freemen who were formerly there, and some few
who came and settled afterwards, amounted altogether to
about sixty men.

All building materials, tools, and implements of every
kind were supplied from the mother country, but the
arrivals were few and far between. Three carpenters came

over among the freemen,—one was frequently sick and ailing, another would not work, and the third, being in a measure imbued with the spirit somewhat prevalent among mechanics in the present age, was constantly on a strike and demanding something better, and, to make matters worse, the brickmaker had died. All available help was utilized, but, to use the words of the director in a letter dated October 10, 1658, as many "who came hither are as poor as worms, and lazy with-al, and will not work unless compelled by necessity," the progress was slow.

The schoolmaster was not forgotten. Everet Pieterson, who came with the colony, wrote under date of August 10, 1657, that he had already begun to keep school and had twenty-five children.

By the conditions offered by the city of Amsterdam, the schoolmaster was to read the Holy Scriptures and set the psalms, and he also acted as " Ziecken-trooster," or comforter of the sick. He does not seem to have satisfied the spiritual appetite of the people, as one of the first appeals of Alricks to the burgomasters was for a clergyman, one of whom (Everardus Welius) was sent over in August, 1657.

Agriculture was not neglected, but was attended to according as circumstances permitted. Those inclined that way were directed to look up land for themselves, their selections being measured and marked, and a written record sent to the home government. It could not, however, have been of a very high grade, as farmers were few and poor in quality. The director writes that after the arrival of the first colonists " some others followed in the ships De Wag, De Sonne, and De Meuler, but of no good repute ; scarcely

three good farmers were to be found among the whole lot."

In the first year a great calamity came to the colony, which contributed largely to the difficulties under which they labored.

In a letter from Alricks to Burgomaster De Graaff, dated August 16, 1659, he writes as follows: "There came a general sickness, attended by burning fevers, etc., which sorely fatigued and oppressed the people and made them groan. In consequence, housebuilding for the commencement of a city, and the tillage of the land for the harvest of grain, went both but poorly, and not so much progress followed as was desirable. The second year was so wet and unseasonable that hardly grain enough for the people and cattle could be saved, added to which a multitude of new cases of sickness broke out, so that nearly a tenth part of all the people lingered, and lived in misery under continual sickness and languors. Fully more than a hundred persons perished in consequence, and a great many cattle were lost. By this means most of the labor was at a stand-still. This gave rise to scarcity and dearth; most of what the people had saved was spent in their poverty, whereupon a severe, hard, and long winter followed."

In a previous letter by Alricks to Director General Stuyvesant, at New Amsterdam, dated October 7, 1658, he speaks of this sickness as being a "burning and violent fever which raged badly, almost all the people there having been sick," including himself, two members of the council, Messrs. Hiniyossa and Rynevelt, the sheriff, and all the schepens. Of the deaths he says, "but few old ones have

died, but rather among young children, who cannot endure
it."

Rynevelt, who was also commissary, died, however, October 26, 1658.

A still heavier blow was to fall on the vice-director. In
a letter to Director Stuyvesant, dated January 24, 1659,
Alricks writes as follows : " Almighty God has been pleased
to visit me with a great loss, and to let an affliction come
over me which distresses me exceedingly ; it is the death
of my beloved and dear wife, who on the sixth instant very
piously went to rest in the Lord; nevertheless, such a parting falls very heavily upon me," and then submissively adds,
" The Lord may be pleased to provide for and assist me
with his grace."

It can well be seen that the position of Alricks as vice-
director was a most trying one. The province was not
producing anything in the way of food for the maintenance of the people. Up to May 14, 1659, some five hundred souls had been sent by the city of Amsterdam to the
colony as additional emigrants without bringing along any
provisions whatever. The appeals of Alricks to Director
Stuyvesant and the home government for provisions, building materials, tools, implements, money, etc., had been
slowly and inadequately answered. Jealousies and dissensions had broken out among those in authority. Secret
complaints and false reports as to Alricks and his administration were sent by officials of the colony to Stuyvesant and
the burgomasters, which were in a measure accepted as true,
as appears by a letter from the burgomasters to Alricks
containing insinuations as to dereliction of duty on his part.

Several colonists deserted and removed to the English colonies of Maryland and Virginia and other places, leaving hardly thirty males remaining.

The government of Maryland laid claim to the lands occupied by the colony. Reports of the approach of a large armed force from that quarter, and of a possible massacre by the savages not far away, were frequent. The original force of soldiers of some fifty men had dwindled to one-half that number, two-thirds of which were at the Horekill, so that at New Amstel there were not more than eight or ten soldiers and very few free people. Harassed, suspected, and decried, unsupported by those upon whom he had a right to rely, whether at home or abroad, it is not a matter of surprise that Alricks succumbed at last to the great mental and physical strain under which he labored. He died on December 30, 1659, doubtless of a broken heart. His remains at some time were buried in the yard of the old Draeyers Church, near Odessa, Delaware, and his grave marked with stones, which up to a recent period were still there, but have now disappeared.

He was a Hollander, and doubtless came from the province of Groningen. He was a business man, well up in business matters, and as such probably well known in the city of Amsterdam.

His correspondence shows that he was a man of education. The tone and style of his letters are in striking contrast with the communications of others of his period, whether official or otherwise.

He was keenly alive to the interests of his employers. His letters are full of wise and practical suggestions

whereby the colony might be benefited, and of measures whereby the city of Amsterdam might reap a rich reward. Had he been properly supported, the history of the colony on the South River might have been differently written.

His government was evidently good. Immediately after his death the schepens, the Town Council, and the city officers were all summoned by D'Hiniyossa, who was named as his successor in his will and assumed the office of director, and asked to attest that Alricks had governed badly, which they refused to do, and although summoned a second, third, and fourth time, they declined to appear, for which they were removed.

Director Stuyvesant, in a letter to the Board of Commissioners in Holland, under date of July 21, 1661, in which he had occasion to refer to the late director, speaks of him as a man of discreet character.

Alricks did not leave children. This we gain from a letter written by him to Director Stuyvesant after the death of his wife, dated May 23, 1659, in which, after suggesting a means for protecting the colony from a threatened hostile demonstration on the part of England, he says, "As regards me, you need not make any difficulty, for I am alone and have not the care of wife, children, or any one else."

Nothing definite is known of his family predecessors. His only known relations were two nephews, Peter Alricks and Cornelius Van Gezel, both of whom resided at New Amstel at the time of his death, and appear to have been in the service and employment of the colony. Peter was the son of a brother, whose name is unknown, but Van Gezel was the own nephew of his wife.

By his will he gave Van Gezel a portion of his estate and made him executor. He must also have mentioned his nephew in that document, as in a letter written by William Beekman, the vice-director at Altona (now Wilmington), to Stuyvesant, dated January 14, 1660, he says, " His Honor's death causes a great alteration in the colony, especially among the council and the heirs," but never in his official correspondence does the name of his own nephew appear.

In his will he expressed the desire that D'Hiniyossa, who had come over in the Prince Maurice as lieutenant of the soldiers, and who subsequently became a captain and was prominent in the colony, should be named as his successor. This seems strange, as D'Hiniyossa was antagonistic to both him and Van Gezel, with the latter of whom he was constantly quarrelling, and endeavored more than any other to undermine Alricks in the confidence of the home government and blacken his memory after death. It may be that the will was made when the parties were friendly, and through oversight was permitted to stand after their relations had become strained.

D'Hiniyossa seems, however, to have been on good terms with the nephew, Peter, as during his administration he frequently called him to the public service.

Peter Alricks came from Nykerk, in the province of Groningen, Holland, as indicated by his marriage record.

There were others of the family. Lucas Alricks, of Maryland, a lineal descendant, has in his possession a manuscript hymn in the Dutch language, found among his ancestor's papers, dated 1663, signed with the names of

Harmanus Alricks and Jacobus Alricks. They were probably brothers or cousins of Peter.

In 1664 one Jacob Abrichs (Alricks), of Groningen
Land, is inscribed as a student on the books of the University of Groningen in Holland. He was probably a nephew
or cousin.

There is nothing to indicate that any of the family other
than Jacob and Peter ever came to this country.

When, how, and why Peter came has been a matter of
conjecture. It has been stated that he came over with
his uncle as commissary for the colony, but that could
not be, as Abraham Van Rynevelt was the commissary
from the time of the arrival of the colony to October 28,
1658, when he died; G. Van Sweringen succeeded him, and
served until November 26, 1659, when he resigned. Cornelius Van Gezel was appointed in his stead, and held the
office until the death of Jacob. Another idea advanced is
that Peter came over in 1657 as the bearer of dispatches
from the burgomasters to his uncle, but for this there is no
authority.

The first official mention of him is found in a statement of
debts due in the colonies, made by D'Hiniyossa, December
12, 1659, and sent by him to the commissioners in Amsterdam under the cover of an insinuating letter. This statement was made in the lifetime of Jacob, and was one of the
means employed by D'Hiniyossa to shake the confidence
which the commissioners had in him. It contains the following item, "Peter Alricks, his nephew, four hundred
guilders."

This entry establishes, first, that Peter was a nephew of

Jacob, and, second, that he was then or had been in the
service of the colony in some capacity or other.

The place and character of that service is uncertain, but
may be inferred from the next official mention, which is
found in a letter written by Beekman, at Fort Altona, to
Stuyvesant, at Fort Amsterdam, dated January 25, 1660, in
which he says: "The Hon^bla Mr. D'Hinoyossa has requested Pieter Alrichs to *re-enter* the service to go again to
the Horekill as Commandant in the Spring."

During the administration of Jacob, D'Hiniyossa had
purchased for the colony from the Indians the land on the
west side of the Delaware, lying between Bombay Hook
and Cape Henlopen, and at the Horekill, where Lewes
now stands, a fort had been erected in 1659, which was garrisoned by a contingent of soldiers sent from Fort Casimer
at New Amstel. It is probable that the former service in-
timated by the extract quoted was as commandant at the
Horekill immediately on the erection of the fort, and that
the debt due was for that service, but from which he had
been relieved.

In the new service he held the rank of ensign, and may
probably have been commissary also. Ferris, in a foot-note
on page 127 in his " Original Settlements on the Delaware,"
says, " We first hear of Peter Alrichs as commissary at the
fort near Cape Henlopen built in 1659."

There is, however, an authority which, if correct, fixes
the date of his coming at an earlier period.

Doctor O'Callaghan, in his " Registry of New Netherland," after mentioning the fact of Alricks having been
commander at the Horekill in 1660, states in a foot-note on

page 51 that he had been commissary at New Amstel in the years 1656 and 1657.

This writer was the person employed by the State of New York to translate such of the Holland documents as referred to the early settlements of the Dutch in this country, and in the course of this work looked into a great many official papers. It is hardly likely that he would have authorized the foot-note mentioned unless he had found the fact so stated in some of the documents examined.

It may therefore be safely assumed that Peter Alricks came to this country as early as 1656, and was at that time in the service of the Dutch West India Company at New Amstel as commissary, thus antedating the coming of his uncle Jacob as director of the Amsterdam colony (the successors of the trading company) by probably a year or more.

From 1660 until 1697 he was almost constantly in the public service, and became one of the most prominent figures in the early settlements on the Delaware.

Two soldiers at New Amstel having deserted and run away to the Minquas country and from thence to Maryland, Peter, with several others, was sent in July, 1660, for the purpose of recovering the men, to Colonel Utie in Maryland, who promised to deliver them up when they should arrive in his jurisdiction. The service was trivial, but well performed.

The relations with the Indians of the back country not being as satisfactory as desired, D'Hiniyossa sent Alricks on September 13, 1661, with two chiefs of the river to the government of Maryland, with whom the Indians were

friendly, to negotiate a peace. The chiefs proved unfaith-
ful and left him on the journey, but he continued on the
trail alone, and met the governor and his council at Colonel
Utie's.

On September 21, 1661, he returned to New Amstel, accompanied by three commissioners from the governor, who
were sent by him for the purpose of attending to the case
of the savages, all of which was satisfactorily arranged.

While at the Horekill he was constantly brought in contact with the Indians of the neighborhood and back country,
who brought in tobacco and skins of various kinds to exchange for such articles as pleased their fancy or might be
useful.

Quick to appreciate the opportunity thus presented, he
conceived the idea of opening a trade in tobacco and furs,
and, securing the favor of D'Hiniyossa, obtained from that
official in 1662 the exclusive privilege of trading on both
sides of the Delaware River " from Bompier Hook to Cape
Hinlopen."

To protect him in this project, D'Hiniyossa, on March
29, 1662, posted a placard on the church door at New Amstel (which seems to have been the official bulletin-board),
forbidding any one from trading with anything on the Delaware between the points named on the pain of losing the
goods that might be found in their possession, which notice
gave great umbrage to the Swedes, particularly those located on the east side of the river. Alricks had built a
small vessel or ketch, which was manned by two men and
which he used on the river in transporting goods to and
from the Horekill and New Amstel.

It is probable that during this period he still retained his position as commander and commissary at the Horekill. We have no direct record of this fact, but we know from official sources that he was there in September, 1662. On the twenty-seventh of that month Commissary Beekman wrote from Fort Altona to Director Stuyvesant at New Amsterdam that some Englishmen went to the Horekill for a man named Turck, who had either run away or been captured by the savages, and having been bought by Alricks was then in his service. Scharf, in his "History of Delaware," says that he was there as commissary at that time.

When Alricks came from the Horekill is not known, but it seems that sometime in the month of June, 1663, both he and D'Hiniyossa made a visit to the mother country. They returned together from Holland in the ship Parmeland Church, arriving at New Amstel towards evening on December 2, 1663, accompanied by about one hundred and fifty souls as colonists, thirty-two being Swedes and Fins, and also by Miss Printz, the daughter of John Printz, a governor of the Swedish colony on the Delaware in 1642, the seat of government of which was on Tinicum Island, about four miles above Chester, Pennsylvania.

Considerable feeling existed between Beekman, the commissary of the West India Company on the Delaware, whose headquarters were at Fort Altona, and D'Hiniyossa, the vice-director of the Amsterdam colony, whose headquarters were at New Amstel, and Beekman took every opportunity to lodge complaints against D'Hiniyossa with Director General Stuyvesant and the home government in Holland, and to criticise his management.

One of the purposes of this visit to Holland was to lay before the burgomasters a new plan of colonization, and probably also that D'Hiniyossa might in person answer the complaints and criticisms referred to, and more properly explain the situation of the colony, as to which he would have the substantiating testimony of Alricks.

Another purpose was to interest the burgomasters of Amsterdam in the tobacco and fur trade on the Delaware, which Alricks had already established. The burgomasters became interested in the trading project, and sent over in the ship named two hundred pieces of frieze or duffels and a large quantity of blankets and other goods that were thought suitable for the Indians, making Alricks the super-cargo, and appointed him superintendent of the trade after his arrival.

The administration of justice in the colony, as established by the early conditions to settlers and modified by Director Jacob Alricks, seems to have undergone some change, largely influenced, no doubt, by the former practice of the Swedes in their settlements on the Delaware. The time of the change is not known, but in December, 1663, Israel Helme, Peter Rambo, Peter Cocks, and Peter Alricks were appointed magistrates or commissioners for the Amsterdam colony. These magistrates were appointed by the director general, and the court sat at New Castle. Just what their jurisdiction was cannot be determined, but it was probably the same as the original Schepen Court.

The business enterprises of Alricks seem to have borne fruit, as by the end of 1663 he had acquired considerable real and personal property.

He had purchased of the Indians a tract of land on the south side of Christiana Creek which extended to the Delaware River. It lay just north of where Crane Hook Church was erected, and the monument now stands. The Lobdell Car-Wheel Works occupy a portion of this property.

He had also become the owner of the land lying on the north side of Christiana Creek and extending to the Delaware, called "Cherry Island Marsh." It extended up the Delaware as far as what was then known as "Verdrietege Hook," now Edgemoor, and back to the fast land on the west, and contained about five hundred acres. At high tide it was covered with water, except one small spot of a few acres on which were many forest trees and was called by the Indians "Manathan."

While in command at the Horekill, Alricks had taken up a tract of land on Pagans' Creek containing one hundred and thirty-two acres. He also became the owner of a marshy piece of ground called Apen Island, lying on the Delaware at the mouth of Red Lion Creek, opposite New Castle Hundred, and had a house and some lots in New Amstel, in which house he probably resided. His holdings of personal property were considerable, among which were a number of negroes held as slaves.

He was on the highway to prosperity, but a cloud was forming from which a deluge came that in a very brief time swept away the savings of years and reduced him to poverty.

England, jealous of the foothold which her ancient enemy, the Dutch, was gaining in this western land, laid

claim to all the possessions of the Dutch on this continent, and, though the nations were at peace, proceeded to enforce her claim by force of arms.

On May 25, 1664, an expedition of four war vessels, the Guinea, a frigate of thirty-six guns, the Elias of forty-two guns, the William and Nicholas of eighteen guns, and a transport of fourteen guns, with three hundred soldiers on board, in addition to the crews, set sail from Portsmouth, England, for the purpose of capturing all the Dutch possessions known as New Netherland.

The expedition was commanded by Colonel Richard Nichols, and with him were Sir Robert Carr and two others, the four being charged as commissioners to hear and provide all things for "settling the peace and security of the country."

They were instructed to first reduce the Dutch in and near Long Island to entire obedience.

On August 25 the frigate Guinea arrived in the outer bay of New Amsterdam.

On July 3 Alricks had reached New Amsterdam from the South River in the sloop Princes, a vessel used by him in trading with New York and the Dutch West India Islands, with a cargo of goods worth about twenty-five or thirty thousand guilders. His object was to sell the goods and with the proceeds purchase cattle and sheep in New England for the use of the Delaware colony. The merchants of New Amsterdam raised considerable objection to his trading in their market, but yielded when informed as to the purpose.

The goods were sold and the cattle and sheep secured.

and brought to Manhattan for shipment to New Amstel.
Twelve soldiers had been furnished from the fort to aid in
the work.

On August 27, while the cattle and sheep were being
loaded, the English frigate captured the vessel and all the
stock, but Alricks and the soldiers escaped.

About the beginning of 1664 the city of Amsterdam had
entered into a partnership with the West India Company
to engage in the slave traffic, and on January 20 of that
year had made a contract with one Lyman Gylde to bring
from Loango, on the coast of Africa, in the ship Gideon,
three hundred slaves, of which number one-fourth were to
be reserved for the use of the colony on the South River.

A few days previous to the capturing of the cattle just
mentioned the Gideon had arrived at New Amsterdam from
Africa with two hundred and ninety slaves of both sexes
on board. The portion of New Amstel were hastily run in
gangs through New Jersey overland to the South River by
Alricks. The English captured the boat in which they
crossed the North River and some of the crew, but none
of the negroes.

The remaining English vessels having reached New
Amsterdam, Colonel Nichols on August 30 demanded the
surrender of the fort and place, which demand was repeated
on September 4, and preparations made for an attack in
case of refusal.

After considerable parleying with the English and consultation by Stuyvesant with the inhabitants, and there
"being no hope of relief nor possibility of making head
against so powerful an enemy," Stuyvesant agreed to treat

for a surrender; and after the terms had been arranged,
ratified, and exchanged, on September 9, 1664, New Amsterdam, its fort, and the whole of Manhattan were formally
surrendered to the English, and the name of New Amsterdam changed to that of New York.

The English then directed their attention to the South
River, and Colonel Nichols and two others of the commissioners directed the other commissioner, Sir Robert Carr,
to proceed to Delaware Bay with the frigates Guinea and
William and Nicholas, with all the soldiers not needed in
the fort, and to reduce the Dutch that might be found there.

The instructions as to the terms to be offered to such of
the Dutch as might surrender were very liberal. Acquies-
cence on their part could work no apparent change except
that of masters. The right of conscience and the ownership
of property were guaranteed. The present magistrates
were to be continued for six months on taking the oath of
allegiance, and the laws were to remain as at present as to
the administration of right and justice.

Carr sailed from New York as directed, and on the last
day of September arrived at New Amstel. He summoned
D'Hiniyossa and the burghers, and demanded the surrender of the town and fort. After three days of negotiation
the burghers and townsmen agreed to give up the town of
New Amstel; but D'Hiniyossa, the sheriff, Van Sweringen,
and Alricks, inspired by a zeal which at this time seems
like something beyond the bounds of heroism, refused to
surrender, and retired into the fort with about fifty soldiers.
On the Sunday following Carr landed his soldiers, and had
the ships run down the river below the fort, but keeping

within musket shot, with directions to fire two broadsides each into the fort, while at the same time his soldiers were to attack on the land side. All this was done, and the fort quickly taken by storm, the Dutch losing three men killed and ten wounded, and the English none.

After the battle the soldiers and seamen vied with each other in sacking the fort, which done they proceeded to plunder the town, the inhabitants of which had just surrendered under articles that solemnly guaranteed them protection in the possession and ownership of property.

They took from the Dutch all the produce of the land for that year and many other things, including one hundred sheep, forty horses, sixty cows and oxen, a brewing-house and still, a saw-mill ready to put up, and from sixty to seventy negroes, being some of those brought by the Gideon and which Alricks had run across New Jersey. All the soldiers and many citizens of New Amstel were sold as slaves to Virginia, where white slavery or forced service existed.

The negroes were divided among the captors, and some of those belonging to D'Hiniyossa were subsequently sold into Maryland for "beef, pork, and salt," and "other small conveniences," as stated by Carr in a letter to Nichols giving an account of the expedition.

The amount of plunder obtained was valued at four thousand pounds.

The officers wearing epaulets were not to be outdone by the soldiers and seamen in obtaining their share of spoils. Sir Robert Carr appropriated to his own use the island of D'Hiniyossa, located on the Delaware near the

present town of Burlington, afterwards called "Mattini-
conck," but now "Burlington Island," and owned by that
municipality.

Captain John Carr, his brother, took possession of the
lands of Sheriff Van Sweringen; and Ensign Stock and
William Tom, who was one of the English party, appropriated the lands of Peter Alricks, Tom taking the "Cherry
Island Marsh," "Apen Island," and the tract on Pagans'
Creek at the Horekill, and the house and lots in New
Amstel, while Stock took the tract lying on Christiana
Creek and the Delaware. Stock also took the negroes
which belonged to Alricks and presumably all the rest
of his personal property. However, between them, they
stripped him of all he had.

Not content with the sacking of New Amstel, the expedition proceeded to the Horekill and plundered the settlement of unoffending Mennonites at that place, leaving the
inhabitants there, as has been stated, "not even a nail."

The interests of their sovereign were entirely ignored by
these pirates acting under the cover of authority.

Colonel Nichols, who had remained at New York as governor, did not approve of the conduct of Sir Robert Carr,
and in his report to the secretary of state spoke disparagingly
of the selfish conduct of Carr in respect to the plundering,
and particularly of his presumption in appropriating "the
prize to himself" and of "disposing of the confiscations
of the houses, farmes and stock to whom he doth think
fitt."

Notwithstanding this, the land so appropriated was, upon
the recommendation of Nichols, subsequently, in 1663 and

later, granted to the captors, as a recompense for their
valuable and meritorious services in the reduction of the
fort, the reason for this action being the continued recusancy of D'Hiniyossa, Van Sweringen, and Alricks
towards the new government, which, however, does not
appear to have been true, as far as Alricks was concerned.

The name of New Amstel was at once changed to the
present name of New Castle.

After the disastrous incident at Fort Casimer, Alricks
proceeded at once to New York.

On the " Catalogue Alphabeticall of yᵉ names of such inhabitants of New York as took the oath to bee true Subjects to the King of Great Britain," dated in October, 1664,
his name appears, and in 1665 it also appears in a directory
of New York, then a place of about fifteen hundred people,
as a resident of Pearl Street.

He did not, however, long remain inactive, and evidently
longed for the associations of his original home.

He had doubtless made a good impression on Governor
Nichols, for that functionary on November 11, 1665, granted
him a pass, in which it was stated that he was an inhabitant
of New York, permitting him to go from there " to Delaware with a servant and six horses," and also " to transmit
himself and servant from thence into Maryland and so to
return about his actions, without any Lett, Hindrance or
Molestacon Wʰsoever," and on the same day, at the request
of Alricks, granted unto him " free leave and liberty to
trade or trafficke, either by himself or his deputies, wᵗʰ the
Indians or any others, in and about Hoarekills, in Delaware
Bay, for Skins, Peltry and what other commodities those

parts shall afford," and requiring all persons "to forbear the
giving him or his deputy any unlawful hindrance or molesta-
tion herein."

His new ventures must have proved successful, as in
1667 he reclaimed from Ensign Stock that portion of his
confiscated land lying along the Delaware and south side
of Christiana Creek, and Stock in a spirit of generosity
"did freely restore and bestow to the number of eleven
negroes upon said Peter Alricks as a guift," being some of
those taken from him at the capture of the fort, which
action was approved by Governor Lovelace, on July 7,
1668.

Governor Nichols, by patent dated February 15, 1667,
granted him two islands in the Delaware on the west side of
the river lying southwest of Mattineconck Island above
mentioned. One of them, known as "Kipp's Island," but
called by the Indians "Koomenakanokonck," was about a
mile in length by half a mile in breadth, and the other, somewhat to the north, was about a half a mile long and a
quarter of a mile in breadth, and also a small creek near by,
running a mile inland, with the liberty of erecting a mill
thereon at the most convenient spot.

Those islands were in a part of the Delaware now embraced within the limits of Bucks County, Pennsylvania.
The small one cannot now be traced, having been connected
with the mainland, and forming a part of the meadows below Bristol, but the larger one can readily be identified, the
northern end being near the steamboat landing at that
place.

Its western side is becoming connected with the fast land

by the filling of the intermediate marsh, and it will soon cease to be known as an island.

On a map of the river made by Jasper Denkers, a Lapidist missionary from Friesland, who traversed the same in company with Peter Sluyter, another missionary, in 1679, it is called Peter Alrick's Island. These missionaries spent the night of December 28, 1679, there, Alricks having given them a letter of recommendation to a man named Barent from Groningen, who lived on the island and worked for him. Davis, in his "History of Bucks County," says that Alricks was the first landowner in that county. He held these islands until November 11, 1682, when he conveyed them to Samuel Bordin.

In May, 1667, Governor Nichols was succeeded by Colonel Francis Lovelace.

By the terms made by Sir Robert Carr with the burghers and townsmen of New Amstel in 1664, the present magistrates were to continue in office for six months on taking the oath of allegiance. As Alricks had resisted the English and went immediately to New York, he was not one of those who continued to act. No record has been found wherein any mention is made of how long the remaining magistrates continued in office.

On April 21, 1668, Governor Lovelace issued a set of directions for the settlement of the government in Delaware, from which it would appear that Captain John Carr had been the chief officer in command since the conquest, so that a civil magistracy of some sort had existed.

In these directions Lovelace provided that "Civill Governm^t in the respective Plantacons be continued until Furth^r

·Ord^r", and "That To p^rvent all Abuses or ·Opposicons in Civill Magistrates so often as Complaint is made the Commission Officer Capⁿ Carre shall call the Scout wth Hans Block, Israel Helme, Peter Rambo, Peter Cocke, Peter Aldricks, or any two of them as Councello^{rs} to advise, heare & determyn, by the ^Maio^r vote what is just, Equitable and necessary in the case or cases in Question," and further "That The same Persons also or any two or more of them shall be called to Advise & direct that is best to be done in all cases of difficulty wch may arise from the Indians & to giue their Councell & ord^{rs} for the arming of the seuerall plantacons & Planters who must obuy & attend their summons vpon such occasion."

In May, 1668, an Indian named Tashiowycans, living in New Jersey near Mattineconck Island, thinking himself aggrieved by the death of a sister, who had died from natural causes, said "Manetto hath killed my sister; I will go and kill the Christians." He and another Indian proceeded to the island, which was held by four Dutchmen, and killed two of them, one being the servant of Peter Alricks, another the servant of William Tomm. This event created quite a commotion in the settlement, a general uprising of the Indians being feared.

It was much deplored, however, by many of the Indians, several of whom offered their assistance in bringing in the murderers.

One sachem proposed to invite the men to a kinticoy (cantico, I presume), and to hire some one to knock them in the head when in the midst of their mirth, which was not, of course, acceptable.

The matter hung for a long time, and at the meeting of the council in New York, held on September 25, 1671, at which Alricks was present, he suggested that the authorities wait until later in the season, when the tribe would separate for the purpose of hunting, and the offending Indians could be more easily captured.

In eleven days after the return of Alricks from New York, however, a conference was asked for by the Indian sachems, at which they promised to bring in the murderers dead or alive. One of the criminals made his escape, while the other allowed himself to be surprised. One of the two Indians in pursuit, being his friend, was unwilling to shoot him, but finding the sachems had said he must die, and that his brothers were of the same opinion, he was shot at his own request.

In the latter part of 1672 the councillors appointed on April 21, 1668, held a meeting at the house of Peter Cocke, one of the members, for the purpose of considering what was best to be done with the Indian people, at which Alricks was present, and he and Israel Helme, another member, were sent to the governor in New York to report the result of the conference.

Among the records of the Upland court, held in the town of Upland (now Chester) on Tuesday, November 25, 1679, the following appears: " Jonas Nielsen makeing apeare to ye Court that there was due unto him for Expensis, about the burriells of Peter Veltscheerder & Christiaen Samuels, whoe were by the Indians murthered att Tinnagcong Island, in ye servis of m^r Peter alrichs in ye Jeare 1672, the sume of 106 gilders, and s^d Jonas desiering sattisfaction ;

The Court are of opinion that Either m^r alrichs whoese servants they were, must pay ye same, or Else ye s^d Jonas must be paid out of the Estates of the deceased, if any bee or can bee found." It is not known what the result was.

As before stated, Sir Robert Carr at the time of the capture of New Amstel had appropriated to himself Mattinneconck Island, which either belonged to or was in the possession of D'Hiniyossa. No grant to Carr appears, however, to have been made, but the island and personal property thereon seem to have been placed by the governor in the care of Captain John Carr, the brother of Robert.

Governor Lovelace appears to have made some arrangement with Alricks as to the island and goods, and on December 15, 1668, made the following order: "Whereas I have made an agreem^t wth Peter Alricks concerning the Island of Matinicom als Carr's Island in Delaware ryver & all the Stock Goods and other materials that there upon heretofore in your Care and Custody: These are to require you imediately to make a Surrender of the said Island to the said Peter Alricks or his Assigns and also that you do Deliver up unto him all the Stock and Goods thereupon & belonging thereunto or whatsoever else was delivered to you there by Sr Robt Carr."

This island must have been merely rented, as on November 18, 1678, Governor Andros sent an order to Captain Cantwell to put Robert Stacey in possession, as he had leased it to him for several years.

Alricks appears to have spent a great deal of his time in New York, and to have grown rapidly in the esteem of

Governor Lovelace. Indeed, the relation seems to have been one almost of confidence.

On October 22, 1670, he gave Alricks permission to take a pair of mill-stones lying on the land at the Horekill fit for a horse mill, and dispose of them at his pleasure.

On November 16, 1670, in a letter to Captain Carr urging economy of expenditure, he says: "I hope all Affairs stand now in a peaceable posture since I have not lately heard from you. I have so amply instructed Mᵣ· Alrick that this time I know nothing to be added." Alricks and the governor had evidently been in conference, and Alricks asked to keep an eye on affairs at New Castle.

In a letter to William Tomm, dated September 26, 1671, relating to the murder of the Dutchmen before mentioned, the governor says: "I shall be this Conveyance Transmitt but little to you in regard I know not how and when it may arrive you, but I reserve my more ample Instructions, wᶜʰ I will send by Peter Alrick, who To-morrow will Imbarque in Tom the Irishman."

The danger of an Indian war being still feared, on October 5, 1671, the governor's council at New York made Alricks and Henry Cousturier commissioners to Delaware, and ordered "that Thomas Lewis now bound for New Castle in his sloop, be delayed three or four days, that Peter Alricks and Henry Cousturier may go with him. That general instructions be drawn up for them suitable to the present state of affairs."

In a letter to Captain Carr, dated November 10, 1871, Governor Lovelace with considerable warmth reproached Carr for neglect of duty in permitting the inhabitants of

New Jersey to get ahead of him in organizing a force for the pursuit of the Indian murderers, and charged him with several other serious derelictions of duty, in which letter appears the following sentence: "What hàth now been concluded on, will be brought to you by Peter Aldrick to wch expect a punctual complyance at y^r perill."

At a council held at Fort James in New York, May 17, 1672, it was urged, "That for ye better Governm^t of ye Towne of New Castle for the future, the said Towne shall be erected into a Corporacon by the name of a Balywick, That is to say, it shall be Governed by a Bailey & six Assistants, to bee at first nominated by the Governor." "The Baily to be Precedent and have a double vote, a Constable to be chosen by the Bench" and "to try causes as far as ten pounds without apeal."

The name of Alricks and another having been returned to the governor from which to make a choice as to bailiff of the corporation, he appointed Alricks, and issued a commission in which he says: "Having conceived a good Upinion of the Fittness & Capacity of the said Peter Alricks to Officiate in that imployment, I have therefore nominated & appointed & by these presents do hereby Nominate & appoint him the said Peter Alricks to be Bayliff and Principal Civill Magistrate at New Castle afores^{id} for the year ensuing of the wch all persons concerned are to take Conizance & to give him ye respect & obedience as is due to his Office and Charge."

This did not interfere with his appointment as one of the councillors of the colony, and therefore he held both positions.

In a letter from Governor Lovelace to Captain Edward Cantwell, dated August 24, 1672, he directed that in order to stop the frequent passing through Delaware of runaway servants, in coming and going to Maryland and Virginia, Alricks, as bailiff of New Castle, in conjunction with the high sheriff, should examine all tickets and passes, and give tickets to such as had occasion to use them.

He further directed that the bailiff, the commander, high sheriff, and two others, or any three of them, should inquire into the arrears of the quit-rents, the fines about the Long Finn, and also the taxes and rates for the keeping of the high and low courts in New Castle and Delaware River, and all other public rates and taxes, in order to see how and when they have been disposed of or in whose hands they were, and when any persons were found to be in arrears, to levy the same by distress, of all of which they were to render a speedy and exact account, so that all abuses in the foregoing matters might be regulated.

In another letter from the governor to Captain Carr, dated October 7, 1672, in relation to a threatened attack on the Horekill by Marylanders, after giving minute instructions as to the defence, he says: "In All Matters of Conserne you are to take the Advice of the chiefe officers there. This will come to you by y^r Bailiff, Mr Peter Alricks, who is hastening overland to secure his affayres there in this portending invasion, and to give his best help for y^e Safe-guard of the place & his royall Highness' interest."

In a letter from Captain Cantwell to the governor about the affairs at the Horekill, dated December 10, 1672, he

says : " Y^r Hono^r writt Mr Aldriches of my not writing to y^r
H$_{ono}$^{r}. I had writt^n to Capt. Nicolls att Large of what I
heard and saw in Maryland."

As Alricks was frequently passing from the colony to
New York on business, and was capable and trustworthy,
he was no doubt sought by the governor for information
and consultation as to affairs at home. His readiness and
earnestness in advocating and carrying out measures for
the regulation of the colony certainly repel the charge of
recusancy to the new government before mentioned, and
make manifest that the English were harsh in their treatment of him in 1664.

Alricks was present in New York in the month of October, 1672, at a trial in the Court of Assize, wherein Armi-
grant Printz, alias Mrs. Pappegoya, was plaintiff, and Captain
Carr attorney for Andrew Carr, defendant, for the recovery
of Tinicum Island, in Delaware River, which had been
appealed from the "High Court on the Delaware." The
jury found for the plaintiff; and on March 2, 1673, Governor Lovelace appointed Alricks as one of the commissioners to appraise and set a value upon the island.

War having commenced between the Dutch and English,
a few Dutch ships appeared at New York on July 30, 1673,
and the fort surrendered without a shot being fired on either
side. The larger part of the magistrates swore allegiance
to the States General and the Prince of Orange. Deputies
were sent to New York from the people on the Delaware,
who, in the name of their principals, made a declaration of
submission, and Delaware again returned to the control of
the Dutch.

On August 12, 1673, Nathan Colve, a captain of Netherland infantry, was appointed governor.

On September 19, 1673, Colve appointed Peter Alricks to be schout or sheriff, and vice-director or commander on South River, beginning at Cape Henlopen and covering the same territory as was possessed during the former Dutch government, the governor in his commission stating that Alricks was appointed "on the good report given of him as ensign and commissary in the former times."

He took the oath of allegiance to the United Netherlands, and was required to administer the oath to all the inhabitants of the river from Cape Henlopen unto the head of the same, both on the east and west banks, and was authorized to enlist ten or twelve soldiers at the expense of the government.

It was the general belief, no doubt, that in the recapture Holland had come to stay, and as the authority of that nation had been fully established, it was fitting and right that the inhabitants, particularly those of Dutch nativity, should renew their allegiance.

It seems to have been the habit of Alricks to acknowledge the ruling powers, thus carrying out the injunction given by the Apostle Paul to the Romans, to "be subject unto the higher powers," as "the powers that be are ordained of God."

The Dutch deputies to New York from the South River having asked for certain privileges, all residents of the river were permitted to keep such houses, lands, and personal property as belonged to them lawfully, in which were included the inhabitants of English nationality, provided they took the oath of allegiance.

A general confiscation act had been passed of all the houses, lands, goods, and effects, without exception, in the country belonging to the Kings of England and France and their subjects, and also of the Duke of York, his late governor and auditor-general, and all other military officers in the country, but from the above it would seem that those residing on the South River were excepted.

Captain John Carr, the late English commander, fled to other parts, and Commander Alricks was directed to request him to return, and, in case he did not do so and submit himself and reside within the government, his property was to be taken and confiscated.

It would appear from this that the Dutch did not intend to disturb in their possessions those of the English who had confiscated the property of D'Hiniyossa, Van Sweringen, and Alricks in 1664, but it seems like retributive justice that Alricks had been given so early an opportunity of laying an iron hand on Carr.

Three courts of justice were established, with eight persons for each court, one at New Amstel, or New Castle, with jurisdiction from Christina Kill to Bompjas Hook; one at Upland, with jurisdiction from Christina to head of river; and one at the Horekill, with jurisdiction from Cape Henlopen to Bompjas Hook.

Magistrates were appointed and a few official acts performed, one being the order by direction of the governor that two millstones which had been lying at the Horekill and not used be given to Commander Alricks, as they were wanted by the garrison at New Amstel.

Some Englishmen in Maryland having driven out a

number of subjects of the government and burned their
dwelling-houses, Governor Colve on January 14, 1674, sent
a placard to Alricks which he directed to be published,
stating that all such exiles, Dutch as well as English, who
came to New Amstel with certificates from Commander
Alricks, showing that they were among the sufferers, would
be provided with means of support.

The Dutch government was of short duration. A treaty
of peace having been signed between England and the States
General, on February 19, 1674, all the Dutch possessions
at New York and on the Delaware passed by its terms into
the possession of the English.

Major Edward Andros was appointed governor, who received the government from the Dutch. By an order dated
November 4, 1674, he directed the commissaries who were
in office at New Castle, Upland, and the Horekill at the time
of the Dutch conquest in July, 1673, to resume their places.
Alricks, who was bailiff at New Castle at that time, was
excepted out of this order, the reason for the discrimination
against him being that he was too eager and ardent in his
attachment to the Dutch interests. The record of the
Sussex County court concerning the reappointment of
these magistrates reads in part as follows: "Except Peter
Alricks, Bayliffe, he having preferred himself to ye Dutch
at their first coming of his own motion, and acted v^{e}ry
violently (as their chief officer) ever since."

Captain John Carr had doubtless returned to New Amstel,
as requested by Commander Alricks, and seems to have
gotten into financial trouble. At the last change in the
government, judicial proceedings as to his property seem to

have been pending, which Governor Andros in a letter to Captain Cantwell, at New Castle, confirmed, and in a letter to the same functionary, dated February 23, 1674, he informed Cantwell that he was "not to suffer Capt. Carr or any from him to dispose of, or make way his estate, upon which (if you judge it necessary) you may lay an attachment in his Maties behalf."

In a letter from Governor Andros to Captain Cantwell, dated November 12, 1674, inquiring as to the whereabouts of the King's colors, which before the conquest by the Dutch in 1673 had been in the custody of Carr, he states that Carr had gone out of the government. His land at New Castle appears to have come into the possession of the authorities, a part of which was low or marsh land. The government was desirous that the town should take this land for a commons, on paying what it was worth, and over which a footway should be completed for the use of the people. The court at New Castle was directed by the governor to name four good men to value this land, and on June 8, 1675, they named Peter Alricks and three others for that purpose, who, having viewed the land, returned that it was not worth anything on account of the great expense for necessary repairs and the yearly charge for its maintenance.

By an order of the governor dated September 22, 1676, it was directed among other things that three courts should be held in the river and bay as formerly, one in the town of New Castle, one at Upland, and another at the Horekill; said courts to consist of justices of the peace, three to make a quorum and the oldest to preside, to have the power of a

Court of Sessions, to decide all matters under twenty
pounds without appeal, above twenty pounds and for crimes
extending to life, limbo, or banishment, to admit an appeal
to the Court of Assize.

Alricks had by this time so ingratiated himself in the
esteem of the authorities, that on September 23, 1677,
Governor Andros appointed him as one of the seven justices
of the peace in the jurisdiction of New Castle and dependencies, and on the same day instructed Captain Christopher Billop, commander on the Delaware, to administer the
usual oath.

Billop was also a sub-collector of customs on the Delaware, and the ship Wi^{lli}ng Mind having arrived and anchored at Elsinburg, near the mouth of Salem Creek, he
went on board to attend to his official duties. His coming
on shore being delayed, and the justices being unable to
hold the court, for which there was urgent necessity,
Justices Moll and Alricks, who had been already sworn,
administered the oaths to the rest. On October 26, 1678,
Andros reappointed Alricks, along with six others, by a
new commission, as a justice of the same court, and again
on May 28, 1680, to the same office.

In November, 1680, Governor Andros returned to England, leaving Captain Brockholes, his lieutenant, in command.

On August 27, 1681, the Duke of York issued an order
to Lieutenant Brockholes, directing that as the commissions
of the justices of the peace and magistrates in New York
and dependencies were about expiring, the present justices
and magistrates should continue in the exercise of their re-

spective functions until further order, under which order all
the justices on the Delaware held their offices until the landing of William Penn at New Castle on October 28, 1682, to
whom letters patent for the territory on the Delaware had
been granted by the duke.

In August, 1677, Captain Christopher Billop had been
sent to Delaware by Governor Andros to relieve Captain
Collier, and was commissioned as " commander in Delaware Bay and River." His duties were to take care as
chief officer that the military in the several places were
well armed, duly exercised, and in good order and discipline.
He had authority to maintain the peace, and was authorized
to set guards in such places as occasion might require. He
was also appointed sub-collector of the customs on the
Delaware River.

Billop appears to have had a very exalted view of his
position, and, if the charges made against him are to be
believed, he behaved in the most lawless manner.

His conduct becoming unbearable, Alricks and the other
justices of the court, on July 17, 1678, prepared a minute
to be laid before Governor Andros on his return from England, where he then was, setting out what Billop had done,
and John Moll, one of the justices, was deputed to go to
New York to lay the matter before him.

As a result, Billop was, on September 13, 1678, ordered
back to New York by the governor, leaving Alricks to be
commander in chief and collector of customs in his place,
delivering, before going, to Moll and Alricks a lot of fire-
arms, ammunition, etc., belonging to the fort.

These positions Alricks held up to the arrival of Penn,

and probably to a later period. It is a matter of record
that in 1680 instructions were sent him from New York to
make no further demand for duties of persons going to
settle in West Jersey, and that in the same year, when
Samuel Jennings, a prominent emigrant to New Jersey,
arrived in the Delaware with a considerable cargo, on which
he expected to pay duties, Alricks came on board and communicated the pleasant news that he could land his goods
without paying any custom charges whatever.

A congregation of the Church of England seems to have
existed at New Castle at an early period, and to have
worshipped in a building of their own.

The first minister of whom we have knowledge was the
Rev. John Yeo, who, according to the records of New
Castle court, dated March 7, 1678, had that day come out
of Maryland, and having exhibited "his Letters of orders
and License to Read divine service, administer the Holy
Sacraments & preach ye word of God according to ye Laws
& Constitution of the Church of England," was accepted,
subject to the approbation of the governor, "hee to bee
mayntayned by the Gifts of ye free willing Givers."

Alricks had evidently connected himself with this congregation, although he belonged to another denomination.
On the records of the Dutch Reformed (now Collegiate)
Church of the city of New York, under date of September
4, 1673, the name of "Pieter Aldrichs," of New Castle,
appears as a member.

The Dutch, it is said, had not built any churches on the
Delaware, and after the erection of the Crane Hook Church,
near New Castle, in the year 1666, many of them had wor-

shipped there, as the Swedish service was not unlike their
own. When, however, the service of the Church of England was established in New Castle, which was also somewhat similar to the Dutch Reformed, Alricks and a number
of other Hollanders had evidently attended there as being
more convenient. The membership in the Reformed Church
at New York was apparently retained by the family, as in
the list of the members kept by the pastor in the year 1636,
the name of Maria Wessells, the wife of Peter Alricks,
appears.

On June 4, 1678, "the Court (at New Castle) referred the
Settling and Regulating of y° Church Affaires of this place,
unto Mr. John Moll & Mr. Peter Aldrichs, they to make
up ye acct wth y° Reader and Wardens, and to make such
further orders & Regulations, as shall bee found most
necessary," and on November 5, 1678, the court "Resolved
(In regard the Church doth mutch need Reperation) that
Mr. John Moll & Mr. Peter Alrichs, take care and order
about the same. The charge & costs to bee found and
Raysed by a Tax, if no money be more due upon the
former list of ye Reader."

The Rev. Yeo did not seem to give satisfaction to his
congregation. On July 17, 1678, a petition was adopted
requesting the governor to give them "permission to ob-
tayne and have an Orthodox minister," and in the latter
part of the month of September, 1678, Yeo was suspended
by order of Commander Billop. He petitioned the court
for leave to sue the people for his services, but it appearing that he had voluntarily surrendered the subscription
paper, this was denied.

He was very angry, and evidently incautious in his conduct. Charges were made that he had used seditious language towards the court, for which he was tried at New Castle on April 5, 1681, before Justices Peter Alricks, John D'Haas, and Will Semphill; but a doubt being shown, he was given the benefit and acquitted.

On March 5, 1679, the land on the south side of New Castle, formerly belonging to Van Sweringen and taken by Captain John Carr after the capture of the fort in 1664, extending for sixteen hundred rods along the river and back into the woods for one mile, was sold at public auction. It was put up in four parts. The first was an improved tract, and purchased by Anthony Bryant. The other three parts were bought by Alricks.

The Indians on the upper Delaware, being much dissatisfied with the manner in which certain lands sold by them had been laid out, and still claiming other rights on the west side of the river, on September 18, 1679, Alricks, in company with Captain Edward Cantwell and Israel Helm, went to Burlington, New Jersey, under orders from Governor Andros, where they held a conference with the Indians concerning their complaints. Although little progress was made at that interview, the matter was finally adjusted in a satisfactory manner.

On November 1, 1680, the chief sachem of the Cohansey Indians conveyed to Ephraim Herman, of New Castle, a tract of land on the Delaware River extending from Cedar Creek to Bombay Hook. This deed was signed in the presence of Justice Peter Alricks and others, and his name is signed thereto as one of the witnesses as follows: "Pieter Alriches."

On October 2. 1685, the Indians made a deed to William Penn for "all the lands from Quing Quingus called Duck Creek unto Upland called Chester Creek, all along by the west side of the Delaware River, and So between the said Creeks Backwards as far as a man can ride in two days with a horse," the consideration being "gunns, 40 tomahawks, powder, lead, Juice harps, beeds, molassis, tobacco, beer, etc." It was executed at New Castle, and the name of "Pieter Alricks" appears as the first witness.

Several years afterwards, for a purpose which is not shown, the following attestation of the signature was made:

"Harmanus Alricks of the city of Philadelphia gent. grandson of Pieter Alricks, late of the County of New Castle on Delaware, gent, dece^d. maketh oath on the Holy Evangelists of Almighty God, that he having viewed this writing indented, doth verily believe that the name Pieter Alricks, thereon endorsed as a witness to the signing, sealing and delivering thereof, by the several Indians within named, is the proper handwriting of him the said Pieter Alricks, for that the same appeareth exactly to agree with other of his handwriting in this deponent's custody.

"Sworn at Philadelphia, the 21st day of April A.D. 1735.

"(Signed)   HARM^S. ALRICKS."

On the day William Penn landed at New Castle, then a place of not more than fifty houses, the inhabitants made a pledge of obedience, solemnly promising to live quietly and peaceably under his government; and on the same day he commissioned "John Moll, Peter Alricks, Johannes DeHaes, William Simple, Arnoldus de la Grange and John Cann, to be Justices of the Peace and a Court of Judicature for the town of New Castle upon Delaware, and twelve miles north

and west of same, to the north side of Duck Creek, whereof any four of you shall make a quorum, to act in the said employment and trust, for the preservation of the peace and justice of the province according to law," all of whom signed the acceptance, solemnly promising that they would, by the help of God, be just and true, and faithfully discharge their trust in obedience to the same commission, and act therein according to the best of their understandings.

This court held its first meeting at New Castle, November 2, 1682, at which Penn was present, together with Markham and others of the Provincial Council. Penn made an address, directed to the inhabitants in general, requesting them to bring in at the next court, to be held at New Castle, all patents, surveys, and evidences of title, so that the same might be confirmed and adjusted.

On November 18, 1682, Penn issued writs for the election of deputies to a General Assembly to be held at Upland (now Chester) on December 6, "to consult with him for the common good of the province, and adjacent counties of New Castle, St. Jones and Whorekill, alias Deal, under his charge and jurisdiction."

This assembly met on the date mentioned, and enacted, among other things, that the three lower counties, or Delaware Hundreds, should be annexed to the Province of Pennsylvania, and passed a form of naturalization, which at a court held at New Castle, on February 21 and 22, 1683, Penn being present, was adopted, and a number of persons were naturalized, the first two being "Peter Alrichs" and "Arnold De Lagrange," two members of the court, presenting the strange anomaly of two justices of a court of

judicature being made citizens by the act of their own body.

On December 8, 1682, the assembly was prorogued by Penn for twenty-one days, but never met again. But few of the members are known, as no list was preserved.

Early in 1683 Penn directed the sheriffs of the several counties to issue writs for a new election of members of the Provincial Council and General Assembly of the province.

Peter Alricks was elected one of the members of the assembly from New Castle County, and was present at its first meeting in Philadelphia, on March 12, 1683, where Penn was present.

The session of the assembly continued until April 3, on which day it took a recess until October 24, when, after a session of two days, it was adjourned by order of the governor. The members appear to have been very slack in their attendance, and during the March session a resolution was passed providing for a fine on all absentees. Just before the adjournment on April 3, a fine was imposed on Peter Alricks, John Cann, and two others for non-attendance during the whole session of the assembly.

When William Penn took possession of the fort at New Castle, on October 28, 1682, he found on hand a meagre supply of munitions of war, but he was without soldiers.

As a man of peace, he probably thought none were needed, but the restiveness of the Indians near by, and the demands as to territory made by the adherents of Lord Baltimore, may have caused him to change his mind. Alricks had been a soldier under the Dutch and had seen conflict. He was a fearless man and knew well the habits of

the Indians, and no doubt Penn turned to him as a proper person to take charge of his military affairs.

Penn therefore appointed him commander at New Castle, with authority to enlist a company, which he appears to have done. The minutes of the Provincial Council, at a meeting held at New Castle on March 13' 1690, read as follows: "Capt. Peter Alricks came into ye council room. and presented to this board a commission from Governor Penn himself, bearing date ye 18th 8-ber 1683, Constituting him Lieft and Comdr in Chief of ye Towne and ffort at New Castle, etc., which was read, and likewise he produced a paper of subscription of several persons that had listed themselves to serve ye country upon any occasion of an enemies' approach, which was likewise read." Why these documents were produced and read at that particular time does not appear.

The appointment of Alricks and others as justices in 1682 was for the town of New Castle and twelve miles around, under which they probably acted until October 22, 1684, when at a meeting of the Provincial Council held at Philadelphia, Peter Alricks and three others were commissioned as justices of the peace for the county of New Castle.

On that same day the return of the sheriff of New Castle County was read and attested by the council, showing that Peter Alricks had been chosen a member of the council from that county for the term of three years.

At a meeting of the council held at Philadelphia on February 2, 1685, he was unanimously chosen "Rainger" for the county of New Castle for one year. From a copy of general instructions to be followed by rangers within the

province we gather that his duties were to look after horses, cattle, swine, etc., running loose, and to take up such as were not properly marked and registered, and he may possibly have added to his duties the functions of the Dutch *bos-loper*, who in the seventeenth century scoured the forests and Indian villages for trade.

At a meeting of the same council held on February 3, 1685, he with nine others were commissioned to be justices of the peace for the county of New Castle for one year.

The commissioners appointed by the court at New Castle to consider the most convenient place for a ferry over Christiana Creek having reported, the court on April 23, 1685, ordered "that the land limited by law for the accommodation of a ferry, be laid by the surveyors, at the appointment of James Walliam and Peter Alrichs."

James, Duke of York and Albany, having succeeded to the throne of England on the decease of his brother, Charles II., the Provincial Council, at a meeting held on March 12, 1685, at which Alricks was present, caused to be read an official publication of James as sovereign, "To whom Wee acknowledge faithful and Constant Obedience hartily Wishing him a happy Raign, in health, peace and prosperity."

On the same day Alricks asked and obtained "leave of this board to go to Burlington."

At a meeting of the council held July 28, 1685, it was ordered that upon Edward Green, one of the members, paying to William Phillips the amount of a certain judgment, which he had obtained against Green as part purchase

money for certain real estate, he, Phillips, should execute a
conveyance to Green for the same. Green seems to have
performed his part of the order, but not getting the deed
from Phillips, entered complaint at a meeting of the council held on February 3, 1686, when it was ordered that
the differences between the two men should be heard
before Peter Alricks and John Cann, who should report.
The records do not show what was the final conclusion of
the matter.

At a meeting of the council held January 31, 1687,
Alricks was returned as having been elected to serve as a
member of that body from New Castle for another term of
three years, and was duly admitted and sworn.

At the same meeting Major William Dyer was returned
as having been elected a member for three years from
Sussex County. He was objected to as not having discharged the office of king's collector of customs, which he
had formerly held, with faithfulness and good report. Dyer
pressed for a more particular reason for his non-admission
to the council as a member, whereupon William Clark, John
Cann, Peter Alricks, and Griffith Jones were appointed a
committee to inquire into the matter and to reduce to
writing the reasons given and report the same to the
council.

On February 2, 1687, the committee brought in their report in writing, with the reasons as taken from other persons, all of which were read "and unanimously allowed of
by the Council as a sufficient Reasons for his non-admission."

A suspicion having arisen that John Blackwell, the then

governor of the province, and some of the members of the
Provincial Council had a design to subvert and overturn
the frame of government, and to make void the charter of
liberties and privileges which the chief governor and
proprietor had granted, the governor and all the members
of the council present (one being Alricks), excepting Samuel
Carpenter, at a meeting held on March 23, 1689, signed a
public declaration, " That all the Laws past and agreed upon
by the Proprietor and Chief Governor and Freeman in Provincial Councill and Assembly made before the Proprietors
going for England shall be, Continue and Remayne in the
Same force, as they now are, until We shall Receive orders
out of England about or Concerning that matter."

At a meeting of the council held on June 29, 1689, the
governor stated that he had called them together on account of rumors of danger from the French and Indians,
" Whereupon Peter Alrichs gave an historicall accot of y⁰
proceedings of y⁰ Mohawks in the year 1685, concluding he
did not think they were in any great number, or that there
was any cause to be affrayed of them."

At another meeting of the council held on September 1,
1689, the governor called their attention to a communication
received from the secretary of state as to threatened danger
from the French, and requested advice and counsel as to
what answer should be made. Some of the members advocated holding back until they should know as to who
was king, but Alricks advocated immediate action, whereupon a committee was appointed to prepare a declaration
of William and Mary as the king and queen of England, to
be presented to the council at a meeting to be held the next

day, at which time the committee reported, which report was accepted and adopted, and fealty to those sovereigns proclaimed.

At a meeting of the council held on November 11, 1689, Alricks was again commissioned as one of the justices of the peace for New Castle County.

On March 13, 1690, he was again commissioned by the council for the same office.

By the royal charter, Penn was empowered to establish such courts and tribunals as might be found necessary. In pursuance of this authority, the Provincial Council at a meeting held on February 1, 1684, ordered "that there shall be a Provll Court, consisting of five Judges to Try all Criminalls & Titles of land, and to be a Court of Equity, to deside all Differences upon appeals from the County Courts."

This was the origin of the present Supreme Court of Pennsylvania.

On July 7, 1690, the Provincial Council appointed and commissioned Peter Alricks as one of the judges of this court.

As Alricks was actively engaged in trade, it was impossible for him to give proper attention to the duties of the new position, which would require him to be absent from his home a considerable portion of the time. Some of the other appointees were situated in like manner, and it therefore became necessary to reorganize the court. Accordingly, on September 21, 1690, the commissions which had been issued were revoked, and the council "Thought ffitt to make a new Choyce of Judges," which was done.

On May 2, 1693, Alricks was again appointed a justice of the peace for New Castle County, and took the oath of office in the presence of the Provincial Council.

Nothing more is shown by the records as to his public career until May 13, 1697, when at a meeting of the Provincial Council held at Philadelphia his name is recorded as one of the members present.

This was the beginning of a new session of the council and assembly, the former one having been dissolved on November 7, 1696, and Alricks had undoubtedly been elected as a member from New Castle County for another term.

At meetings of the council held on May 15 and 20 his name is mentioned as one *not* present, but after that time it does not appear upon the records. He was evidently in failing health, and probably died in the year 1697.

In his will, executed at New Castle, dated January 25, 1694, he refers to himself as sick in body.

Thus closed a busy and eventful life. From the numerous and varied positions which Peter Alricks filled and the duties he performed we may safely infer that he was a man of active habits, keen business insight, great personal courage, and sound common sense. Always ready for duty, he carried out with alacrity whatever his superiors directed.

His wife had evidently died prior to 1694, as her name is not mentioned in his will, but she was living in 1679. The place of their burial is not known, and is only a matter of conjecture.

The name of his wife was Maria Wessells. She came

from Utrecht, in Holland. The date is not known, but she probably reached this country before Peter Alricks, as persons of her family name were in New Amsterdam as early as 1654. One Warnaer Wessells was an excise officer in New Amsterdam, Breucklen, Midout, and Amesfort in 1654, and held the same office in New Amsterdam and the Dutch towns of Long Island in 1655. He was a small burgher of New Amsterdam in 1657, and held other offices there in 1657, 1658, 1661, and 1662.

He is frequently mentioned in the records of the earlier days of New Amsterdam, and was evidently a person of considerable prominence.

One Allard Anthony, also prominent there in colonial days, is recorded as having married Henrica Wessells, of Utrecht, at New Amsterdam on March 25, 1656.

The names of several other females of the Wessells family are mentioned in the records of the Dutch Reformed (now Collegiate) Church in New York in the years 1666, 1667, 1669, 1671, and 1675.

It is altogether probable that Warnaer Wessells was the head of the family, and that Maria was his daughter.

Peter Alricks and Maria Wessells were married in the church named. The record still in existence is in the Dutch language, and, translated, reads as follows: " Married, 1664, February 9, Peter Alricks, young man of Nykerck in Groningerlandt, and Maria Wessells, young woman of Uytrecht."

They had four children, all of whom survived their father, to wit: Peter Sigfridus, who was baptized in the same church on October 3, 1666; Harmanus; Jacobus, who

was baptized in the church named on September 10, 1671, and Wessells.

He left a large estate, the most of which was in land. In addition to what has been heretofore mentioned, he seems to have died seized of a tract of land in St. George's Hundred, extending from the Delaware River to the King's Road, and from St. Augustine Creek to St. George's Creek containing, according to a subsequent survey, about three thousand acres. A portion of this land, located on the river and next north of St. Augustine Creek, containing five hundred and sixty acres, was patented to him by Governor Andros on July 24, 1676, and named Groningen by Alricks, after the district from which he came.

By his will he made four specific devises to his sons, which, however, are difficult to trace on account of the meagre description given. To his eldest son, Sigfridus, he gave the plantation where Sigfridus then lived, "next to the Town," bounded with "a branch of the plantation where Cornelius Post now dwelleth," with grist mill, rolling mill, and tobacco engine. To his son Harmanus he gave "that plantation at Read Island." To his son Jacob he gave "that plantation called by the name of Naamans Point, where he now dwelleth;" and to his son Wessells he gave "that plantation where Cornelius Post now dwelleth, and all the smith tools whatsoever."

His personal estate consisted of ordinary household goods, cattle, horses, mares, hogs, sheep, the smith tools before mentioned, and eighteen negroes.

The negroes and some of the cattle and hogs were specifically bequeathed to his four sons, and with a humanity

that does him credit he provided in his will "that no one of my said sons shall dispose of any of said negroes but unto one another."

The remainder of his estate, both real and personal, he divided equally among his four sons.

Peter Sigfridus married and left one child, a son, Peter Sigfridus, who married Susanna Stidham at the Old Swedes' Church in Wilmington, Delaware, on May 25, 1740, and died in 1764, leaving numerous children whose descendants are scattered all over the country.

Harmanus married and left three children, Peter, Abigail, and Mary.

Jacobus married and had four children, in order of age as follows: Peter, Sigfridus, Jacobus, and Hannah. Peter, the son of Jacobus, married Dorcas Land, the daughter of Francis and Christian Land. They had five children,— one son, Samuel, and four daughters, to wit: Ann, who married Alexander Porter; Elizabeth, who married, first, John Stalcop, and after his death John Price; Sarah, who married James Dunning; and Esther, who married John Stewart.

Wessells married and left five children, Peter, Harmanus, Ann, Mary, and Martha.

Harmanus, the son of Wessells, removed to Philadelphia for a short time, and then settled at Carlisle, in the Cumberland Valley, in Pennsylvania. He had a son, James, who had two sons, Herman and Hamilton. These men were prominent lawyers at Harrisburg, Pennsylvania. Some of their descendants are still prominent there, and retain the original spelling of the name, Alricks. Most of the de-

scendants of Peter spell it Alrich, a few Aldrich.   In preparing this sketch the writer has found it spelled in twenty different ways.

As this sketch is historical rather than genealogical, the line of descent will not be further traced.

It is to be hoped that some hand, better fitted than mine, will take up that branch of research and carry it to a successful conclusion.

N. B. Smithers

PAPERS OF THE HISTORICAL SOCIETY OF DELAⱮ

XXIII.

MEMOIR

OF

NATHANIEL B. SMITHE

BY

WILLIAM T. SMITHERS.

Read before the Historical Society of Delaware, November 2

THE HISTORICAL SOCIETY OF DELAWARE,

WILMINGTON.

1899.

PREFACE.

In the preparation of this memoir I have necessarily been confined within a very narrow compass. While all about me lay a wealth of material, yet, from the very nature of my task, I have been obliged to use but a very small portion of it. I have, therefore, frequently found myself more embarrassed than if there had been a greater lack of it. The problem with me was what to use and what to reject. That I have chosen wisely, I do not pretend to say, but I have selected that which, in my judgment, seemed best suited to my purpose. I leave untouched a store of interesting anecdote, rich personal experience, and profitable instruction. I make little mention of the golden words that fell ever from his lips, many of which are treasured in my memory; nor of the sublime thoughts that came from his pen, much of which manuscript is in my possession. All this may find its place when, some day, the story of Nathaniel B. Smithers's life shall be more fully told.

W. T. S.

Dover, Delaware, August 17, 1898.

3-4

MEMOIR

OF

NATHANIEL B. SMITHERS.

NATHANIEL BARRATT SMITHERS was born in Dover, Delaware, October 8, 1818, in the house which is now the dwelling of Chancellor John R. Nicholson. His parents were Nathaniel Smithers and Susan Fisher Barratt. Of this marriage there were eight children born, all of whom died in infancy, except the subject of this memoir, and a younger brother, Edward F. Smithers, who became a prominent physician, and settled at Vienna, in Dorchester County, Maryland, where he died in 1862. His father, a gentleman of sterling integrity and dignified manners, held the offices of Prothonotary and Clerk of the Peace in Kent County. His grandfather, also named Nathaniel, was Register of Wills in Kent County. He was an influential and Christian gentleman, and, as one of the early Methodists, introduced Freeborn Garrettson. His paternal grandmother was Esther Beauchamp, whose brother, William Beauchamp, is distinguished in the annals of Western Methodism. His ancestors on his father's side, before the Revolution, came into the " Lower Counties on Delaware" from Kent County,

5

Maryland, into which colony they had emigrated from England.

His mother was the daughter of Dr. Elijah Barratt, of Camden, Delaware. She was a most estimable woman, whose nobility of character, gentleness of disposition, and grace of mind, endeared her to all who knew her. Dr. Barratt, his maternal grandfather, was a polished and courteous gentleman, and was of high repute as a physician. He was the son of Philip Barratt, who resided near Frederica, and owned the tract of land on which Barratt's Chapel was built, and in testimony of whose liberality it was named. In this chapel was the first meeting of Coke and Asbury, from which impetus was given to the advancement of Methodism. Andrew Barratt, another son of Philip Barratt, was one of the judges of the State, and a member of the convention which ordained the Constitution of 1792.

His maternal grandmother was Margaret, daughter of Edward Fisher and Susanna Bowman, and through her father lineally descended from John Fisher, who came from England with William Penn in 1682. He settled at Lewes, and his son Thomas married Margery Maud, daughter of Joshua Maud, of Yorkshire, England. They were of the persuasion of Friends, and many of their descendants still adhere to and exemplify its habits and principles.

Nathaniel B. Smithers was early sent to school in Dover, and his first teacher was one Ezra Scovell. His advancement in his books was marked and rapid from the start. He was both studious and quick to learn. At an age when few children have mastered the primer, he was dealing with the higher branches of education, and was fully launched

upon a life of systematic study, which he quietly and unob-
trusively pursued to the end. At the age of five years we
find him being instructed in Latin, and repeating passages
from Virgil, when most children are prattling nursery
rhymes.

It was about this time that the first cloud floated across
the pathway of his life,—the death of his mother. Young
as he was, he felt the loss keenly, and to his dying day he
remembered the gloom that pervaded that household, and
the grief that filled his heart on that evening in March,
1824, when death entered the home, and took away, in the
thirtieth year of her age, his tender, devoted mother. In
the course of time his father married again, the lady being
Rachel E. Clayton, the daughter of Dr. James L. Clayton,
to whom Nathaniel B. Smithers became very much attached,
and who died at her home in Elkton, Maryland, only a few
years prior to his own death.

When he was about eleven years old he removed with
his father to Bohemia Manor, in Cecil County, Maryland,
and soon afterwards was placed in West Nottingham Academy, then under the direction of Dr. James Magraw, an
eminent Presbyterian minister. Here he made rapid progress, and in the spring of 1834, being but little more than
fifteen years old, he was matriculated at Lafayette College,
Easton, Pennsylvania, which had just been founded, under
the presidency of the Rev. George Junkin, a learned and
distinguished Presbyterian minister. Here his progress was
so great that it was not long before one of the faculty of
that institution publicly declared that he was no longer able
to teach the young student any more Latin. From this

college he was graduated in 1836, at the age of seventeen
years. School-life was now ended. Real life was beginning. He was standing at the threshold of something earnest and practical. He was obliged to make his own way
in the world, and at once. In giving him an education his
father had done all he was able to do for him. True, his
father's house held out to him a cordial welcome, where he
might rest a moment before entering upon a career, but such
rest meant idleness, and that was out of the question; besides, it held out to him none of the allurements of home.
He was almost a stranger to life at the Manor. All the
tender memories of his heart clustered round the old home
in Dover, and that was long ago broken up. Of real home-
life, its influence and sweet impression, his childhood had
known but little. From the age of eleven years he had
lived within the walls of some institution of learning. He
had gained greatly on the one hand; he had lost sorely on
the other. I have heard him more than once speak with
feeling on the subject. "I was absolutely robbed," he said,
"of the fragrance of home. Home influence was sacrificed
to school discipline; the glow of the fireside to the light
of the student's lamp; heart training to mind training. It
is a grave mistake." The summer of 1836, immediately
following his graduation at Lafayette, we find him for a
brief season at his father's house.

THE LAWYER.

He had now arrived at the point where he must choose
a calling in life. During his college days he had thought
the matter over seriously, and had gradually come up to

that epoch with the cherished design to enter the profession of the law. He had looked the field over,—surveyed it with that care and deliberation so characteristic of him. He fully realized how much depends upon a proper decision; that abilities, however splendid they may be, bear but dwarfed and tasteless fruit when misdirected and misapplied. He saw all round him men obscure in a profession who might have been prominent elsewhere; men unnoted in trade who might have adorned a profession. He could not afford to make that mistake, and to that end he reasoned calmly and earnestly with himself, but ever with the same result,—the law. Yet, in almost any calling to which his genius might have led him, he would have succeeded nobly. His fondness for letters would have won him fame as an author. His predilection for divine subjects and affairs, coupled with his matchless eloquence, would have made him powerful as a pulpit orator. His profound learning and his peculiar ability to impart knowledge would have brought him renown as a teacher. But any one of these would have been chosen with great personal sacrifice. He would not have found in them that scope which his abilities demanded, and which his own profession so amply afforded. That he chose wisely, his course has fully shown. Indeed, we can hardly think of Mr. Smithers outside the profession of the law.

Having fully determined as to the course he should pursue, he now informed his father of his purpose. This determination on the part of the youth gave the father no little concern. While he fully appreciated the ability and mental capacity of his son, yet, unless he were sure that the young man was adapted to the law, he was not willing that he

should enter upon the study of it. After seriously deliberating upon the subject, he wrote a letter to the president of Lafayette College, asking his advice as to whether in his judgment the young man had the ability to make a lawyer. To that letter he received the following reply:

" His talents appear to fit him for the profession you mention. He has quickness, ingenuity, taste, and vivacity. Acuteness, strength of conception, comprehensiveness of view, and accuracy of judgment he possesses as far as they are usually possessed by persons of his age and circumstances, and from his conduct here he may be expected to cultivate diligently his natural parts, and avail himself of whatever opportunities of improvement lie within his reach."

That determined the matter with the father, and soon afterwards Mr. Smithers entered the law school of Judge Reed, at Carlisle, Pennsylvania. By a rule of the court regulating the admission of attorneys, a student who was a college graduate was required to study only two years. Both on account of his age and because money was desirable, Mr. Smithers spent one year in teaching a classical school at Snow Hill, Maryland, after which he resumed his professional studies. In 1840 he was duly admitted to the bar of Cumberland County, Pennsylvania, and in the spring of 1841 was admitted to the bar of Kent County, Delaware.

The Delaware bar, always celebrated for its learning, was exceptionally strong at this time. The magnetic Clayton was still at the zenith of his power, although he had in a great measure given up the practice of law for public life. Bayard, Frame, Bates, Hall, Gilpin, and others, all legal giants, were in the full vigor of their intellectual powers.

The people of Kent were wont to look upon the bar of their county with a feeling akin to reverence,—a sort of charmed circle, into which it was little less than sacrilege for the average man to seek to enter. Few kindly hands were held out to young practitioners in those days; on the contrary, clients clung the more closely to their old and favorite counsel, and viewed with mild contempt the young attorneys who were struggling for recognition. But surrounded even by these conditions, and amid such a glittering array of talent, Mr. Smithers was not slow in gaining recognition as a lawyer. He soon took the conspicuous place in the front rank of his profession to which his ability entitled him. But clients came slowly. Indeed, judged by the practitioner of to-day, in his feverish chase after business, his nervous struggle in the maelstrom of intense competition, Mr. Smithers did little to secure clients. He opened a plain, poorly-furnished office, and sat down with his books. No flaming "shingle" informed the public that a lawyer inside desired a share of its patronage; nor in the whole course of his long practice did he ever own one. The little business that came to him in the first months of his practice, although fees were now very necessary to his comfort, came entirely unsolicited. He wrapped about him the garb of professional dignity, and neither the allurements of fortune nor the pinch of poverty could induce him to resort to the shirt-sleeves of trade.

But he did not long remain a briefless lawyer. So wise a counsellor and powerful an advocate could not long remain unrecognized. Such service as he was able to render was invaluable, and must needs meet a constant demand.

Business now began to pour in upon him.   Clients came
daily, and the profitable ones came to stay, until Mr.
Smithers enjoyed one of the best practices at the Kent bar.

The time had now arrived when his means were such
that he could think seriously about matrimony.   From
early youth his fondest admiration had been bestowed upon
his pretty, vivacious cousin, Mary Lizzie, daughter of his
uncle Joseph, which admiration, as youth ripened into
manhood, changed into love for the accomplished, intelligent, and charming woman.   He proposed for her hand,
and was accepted by her; but the proposition did not meet
with the unqualified favor of her father.   Joseph Smithers
was a strict and positive man, and his notion was that the
young couple were too nearly related by blood to admit
of a proper matrimonial alliance.   His scruples, however,
were finally overcome, and on the 22d day of March,
1853, Nathaniel B. Smithers and Mary Elizabeth Smithers
were married at Dover, by the Rev. H. E. Gilroy.   Of this
marriage four children were born, two of whom died in
infancy.

Soon after his marriage Mr. Smithers erected a large
brick mansion in Dover, as a family residence, which, with
its successive additions and improvements, is to-day one of
the handsomest residences in the State, and is owned by
George V. Massey, Esq.   In this house he lived happily
with his family for several years.   Then there came another
cloud to cast its shadow across his pathway,—the health of
his wife began to fail.   Consumption laid its pallid hand
upon her, and she fell into a hopeless decline.   Having
now become a confirmed invalid, she grew tired of the large

house. She could not look after it properly, and things in
and about it were being sadly neglected. She prevailed
upon Mr. Smithers to dispose of it. He did so, and purchased the house on State Street, into which they moved,
and where he resided the rest of his days. On the 21st
day of February, 1867, she died, leaving him with two
little children. These were sad days for Mr. Smithers. In
referring to his life at that time, he once said to me, "No
one knows what I went through. Many a time I have tried
a case in court all day and nursed my poor wife all night."
On another occasion, when speaking of his Congressional
life, he said, "I knew no peace of mind. My wife was rapidly wasting away, and my place was by her side; yet duty
compelled me to stay at my post. I do not know how I
ever bore up under the burden."

Mr. Smithers was now the foremost man in his profession
in the State. He possessed that quality of mind which
attracts lawyers as well as clients. No great question
seemed to be thoroughly settled in the minds of the legal
fraternity until N. B. Smithers's opinion was obtained, and
to that end he was constantly consulted by both bench and
bar. The public had absolute confidence in him. It knew
his opinion to be reliable, his advice sound, and his word
as good as his bond. It knew, besides, that to employ him
in a case was to have everything done for it that could be
done, and clients who placed their interests in his hands
never worried for fear they would be neglected or made to
suffer.

The preparation of a case was, with him, an all-absorbing
task. He studied it until he became the master of it in all

its details. He carefully weighed every point in his favor, and closely scrutinized every point against him. With patient deliberation and mental debate he properly adjusted the whole, and turned upon it the fierce light of his cold criticism. Thus equipped, he entered into the trial,—his case mastered in all its aspects, and robbed of all its surprises. On the eve of some very important case I have known him to walk the floor all night long, and I could usually tell at breakfast the result of his mental wrestling. He excelled in the statement of his case, and in his argument before the court. In addressing juries he was clear and forceful. No one could misunderstand him; no one fail to be impressed by his earnestness or resist the flow of his matchless eloquence, when the occasion called it forth. No one who ever observed him in the progress of a trial can ever wholly forget it. The intelligence of his countenance, the quickness of his eye, the vivacity of his whole manner, made a lasting impression. Nor was any lawyer more successful in winning cases. That was partly because he never knowingly took an unjust one. Men soon learned that it was useless to approach Mr. Smithers with a case that was tainted with fraud. On one occasion a man, who, by taking advantage of the law, was enabled to defraud his creditors, came to Mr. Smithers and offered him a good fee to take the case. Looking the man squarely in the face for a moment, he said, "My friend, don't do that."

"But the law is with me," said the man.

"The law may be with you in this instance," said Mr. Smithers, "but every principle of honesty and right is against you." The man sought other counsel.

In the course of time he began to reduce his practice, and to take only such cases as interested him, or which were forced upon him. He very rarely now appeared in court, confining himself almost wholly to his office practice. His means, while not large, were ample for his purpose, and he turned clients away whenever he could do so. Had he looked closely after the dollar he could have been a wealthy man, but he cared nothing for money beyond a competency. His fees were invariably far too small, and in many instances never paid at all. It was frequently said of him that the only thing he did not know about his profession was how to charge. Had he desired national prominence as a lawyer he had but to assert himself to attain it. A few years ago, during the progress of a great trial which attracted the attention of the whole country and in which he was one of counsel, a New York newspaper, in commenting upon the case, asked the question why a man possessed of such great legal ability as Mr. Smithers should bury himself in a little Delaware town. There was but one answer,—he preferred to.

He now turned his attention to literary pursuits, and in 1879 published the first volume of his translation of Latin Hymns. He was an excellent Latin scholar and richly endowed with the poetic faculty, and the publication of this work brought forth the unstinted praise of scholars and college professors throughout the country, not a few of them assuring him that his translation of Dies Iræ was the best ever made. While engaged in this work Bret Harte's poem, " The Heathen Chinee," appeared. The poem pleased Mr. Smithers, and he translated it into Latin.

When it was finished, he, in a waggish mood, sent it to the professor of Latin at a certain college, with a statement that it had been found amid some ancient ruins, and that evidently Bret Harte had simply translated it and was guilty of plagiarism. At the same time, a prominent member of the Kent bar was so impressed with the story that he wrote to the *New York Herald* calling Bret Harte a plagiarist, and offering to furnish the proof of the charge. The delusion was complete, and the affair created quite a sensation. The wise men decided that the Latin translation was the original poem. After he had enjoyed the joke long enough he wrote to them, acknowledging the authorship of the translation, much to their astonishment and chagrin. The following is the translation, with its explanatory note, and Bret Harte's poem, exactly as they appeared in Mr. Smithers's manuscript:

The following is from manuscript in Lib. Duhren, entitled " Frag. ex Operibus Icti Fabricii."

FABRICIUS, SELENIO SUO S.

Mihi videtur ad te scribere, non solum, pro saluti quod tibi esse censeo, gratias agere, sed .etiam quosdam versiculos dare. Hoc est argumentum. Pompeii Nig. sub decessum ex Egypto, quidam barbarus, Calphurnio Pisone inductus, ad urbem venit et in domo Pisonis mansit. Ultima in parte Orientis natus est, in regione nobis incognita, nomine Sina. Vir, etsi incultus, tamen est vultus ingenui et, ut videtur, bonæ indolis. Propria in lingua appellatur Loo Sin et quanquam frequenter visus, mihi nomine tantum notus est.

Hesterno, mihi accidit Pisonem visere et apud illum prandere. Piso, ut mos est, pignora proposuit et cum chartis pictis certatur. Me, Divæ Fortunæ cultorem esse infrequentem scis, sed Calphurnium aleæ addictum. Barbarum esse ignorantum censemus. Quod cecidit, lege et ride. Vale.

(In Monte Palatino. Postridie Kalendas Sextas. A. U. C., 720.)

BARBARUS SINENSIS.

Quod narrare volo—
Et mi sermo simplex—
Ut vafer latro
Et doli artifex,
Est princeps Barbarus Sinensis,
Me teste—esto judex.

Ei nomen, Loo Sin—
Neç negandum, ei
Quod pertinet, quin
Patefactum mihi ;
Sed mæste subridens et blande,
In vultu distat nomini.

Sext. Calendis, quod fit
Et permollis æther,
Ex quo licitum sit
Quod Loo Sin pariter ;
Sed, ad nauseam, perlusit Pisonem
Et me, sicuti trifur.

Quod ludebamus quiddam—
Tulit partem Loo Sin—
Erat euchre—Quanquam
Inexpertus·illin,
Subridens, in banco sedebat,
Ut solet ridere, Loo Sin.

Sed me pudet, ut chartas
Compositas clam ;
Et videtur nefas,
Ut Piso, manicam
Anchoris et monis impleret,
Et id, perpetrare falsam.

**

Sed quas sortes luderet
Is incultus Sinæ,
Et quas partes faceret,
Mirum nobis esse;
Tum demum, protulit anchoram
Quam Piso dederat ad me.

Intuebar Pisonem—
Intuebatur in me—
Et assiliens—" An rem?"
Ex imo, inquit ille,
"Nulli sumus labore Sinense"
Et instanter invasit Sinæ.

Proximoque ludo
Non introibam;
Sed, ut foliis, omnino
Perstratam terram
Chartis, a Loo Sin celatis
In sortem, nunc primum notam.

In utramque manicam
Sunt biblia bissena—
Quod est magnum quiddam—
Atqui dico revera—
Et in digitos, pares candelis,
Quæ sæpe candelis—est cera.

Quod est cur enarro—
Et mi sermo simplex—
Ut vafer latro
Et doli artifex,
Est princeps Barbarus Sinensis,
Mehercle, in nullo mendax.

PLAIN LANGUAGE FROM TRUTHFUL JAMES.

BY BRET HARTE.

Which I wish to remark,—
  And my language is plain,—
That for ways that are dark
  And for tricks that are vain
The heathen Chinee is peculiar,
  Which the same I would rise to explain.

Ah Sin was his name;
  And I shall not deny
In regard to the same
  What that name might imply;
But his smile it was pensive and childlike
  As I frequent remarked to Bill Nye.

It was August the third;
  And quite soft was the skies;
Which it might be inferred
  That Ah Sin was likewise;
Yet he played it that day upon William
  And me in a way I despise.

Which we had a small game,
  And Ah Sin took a hand;
It was Euchre. The same
  He did not understand;
But he smiled as he sat by the table,
  With the smile that was childlike and bland.

Yet the cards they were stocked
  In a way that I grieve,
And my feelings were shocked
  At the state of Nye's sleeve,
Which was stuffed full of aces and bowers,
  And the same with intent to deceive.

But the hands that were played
   By that heathen Chinee,
And the points that he made
   Were quite frightful to see,—
Till at last he put down a right bower,
   Which the same Nye had dealt unto me.

Then I looked up at Nye,
   And he gazed up at me;
And he rose with a sigh,
   And he said, "Can this be?
We are ruined by Chinese cheap labor?"
   And he went for the heathen Chinee.

In the scene that ensued
   I did not take a hand,
But the floor it was strewed
   Like the leaves on the strand
With the cards that Ah Sin had been hiding,
   In the game "he did not understand."

In his sleeves, which were long,
   He had twenty-four packs,—
Which was coming it strong,
   Yet I state but the facts;
And we found on his nails which were taper,
   What is frequent in tapers,—that's wax.

Which is why I remark,
   And my language is plain,
That for ways that are dark,
   And for tricks that are vain,
The heathen Chinee is peculiar,
   Which the same I am free to maintain.

arly and middle life Mr. Smithers was a frequent vis-
Lafayette College, attending reunions, and making
ses to students. This college conferred the degree of

Doctor of Laws on him several years ago; and subsequently the same degree was conferred on him by Dickinson College.

I might dwell longer upon his professional life, so full of interest, and so profitable in its lesson, but this simple memoir is designed only as a sketch. I leave the more perfect picture to the future biographer. Let us now pass to a brief consideration of his public life.

POLITICAL LIFE.

The ancestors of Mr. Smithers were Federalists and Whigs. He cast his lot with the latter, and in 1844, three years after his return to the State, and when he was but twenty-six years of age, he was offered the Whig nomination for Congress, and declined it. In our frequent intercourse, I once asked him why the nomination was offered him at that time, and his reason for declining it. His reply was, "In 1844, in addition to the interest of a Presidential election, there was a close and exciting contest for the gubernatorial nomination. There were three gentlemen, whose names were prominently before the convention, and I was a warm friend of one of the defeated candidates. From prudential considerations, I presume, rather than from any merit of mine, friends of the nominee tendered me the nomination of Representative in Congress. I declined the offer because I had my living to make, and did not deem it wise to be diverted from my profession."

In 1845 he was elected clerk of the House of Representatives of the State Assembly, and was re-elected to the same position in 1847. In 1848 he was chosen a delegate to the

Whig National Convention, which met in Philadelphia, and, dissenting from his associates, voted for Scott and Fillmore. The State convention, which met the same year at Lewes, again tendered him the Congressional nomination, and he again declined the offer.

These years mark a transition period in the life of Nathaniel B. Smithers. The moral elements of his character were rapidly developing and forcing him to take his place among the radical political reformers of his time The anti-slavery agitation had already divided the country into two great parties. The Democratic party was fairly the party of slavery. The Whig party was going to pieces because its leaders were halting between righteousness and expediency,—admitting the wrong, they were too anxious for political power to jeopardize it by advocating the right. The great temperance reform movement of that era was at its height, and on both these questions Mr. Smithers had decided opinions, and the courage to advocate them. He was an anti-slavery man, and a prohibitionist.

Soon after the convention of 1848, a series of events occurred which placed him in a position apparently antagonistic to the party from which the tender of the Congressional nomination had twice come to him. At the session of the General Assembly of 1847 two measures were proposed, with both of which he was in entire accord. One, for the gradual abolition of slavery, which passed the House of Representatives, but was defeated in the Senate by the vote of the Speaker; the other, providing for submitting the question of granting licenses for the sale of intoxicating liquors to the decision of the voters of the several

counties, and which would now be termed a local option law. This bill became a law, and at all elections held throughout the State the county of New Castle voted for no license ; the other two counties·giving adverse majorities. This act was assailed in the courts, and Mr. Smithers assisted in its defence, but the Court of Errors and Appeals decided that it was a delegation of legislative power, and therefore unconstitutional. With this decision Mr. Smithers did not then, nor did he ever, concur. But it was made, and, as a lawyer, he loyally submitted to it.

At the next election, as usual, the Whig party was successful in electing a majority of the General Assembly. In utter abandonment of the cardinal principles of the Whig party, as Mr. Smithers had been taught them, its representatives not only determined not to further oppose these great questions, but so far retrograded from the action of the previous legislature as to enact a law which was, in effect, an invitation to the kidnapping of free negroes ; and to contemptuously refuse to legislate laws in restriction of the sale of intoxicating liquors. This was too much for Mr. Smithers. The Whig party was dominant in the State, and the responsibility was thrown upon it. It shirked the responsibility, and repudiated its ancient doctrine. Mr. Smithers looked upon its now wavering policy with sorrow and disgust, and, with the determination to be true to his teachings, withdrew from the Whig party.

In conjunction with others, who were of like mind, a third party was organized, mainly drawn from the disgusted Whig element. Into this organization Mr. Smithers entered heartily. The first result was the defeat of the Whig party,

which had been in control for twenty years. The third party was maintained unbroken for three successive campaigns; meanwhile the Whig party of the nation was in a state of collapse, and upon its ruins arose the Know-Nothing organization. Into this association he declined to enter, as he deemed its methods incongruous with the proper ordering of American politics. He declared that no party could or ought to .be permanent which would not bear the light of public observation, or the test of public discussion.

In 1854 this third or independent party was successful in carrying the State, and as one of the results, a prohibitory law, which was drafted by Mr. Smithers, was enacted. As before, it was subjected to a legal contest, and, as before, Mr. Smithers took part with its defenders. The court, at the May term, 1856, in New Castle County, adjudged it to be constitutional and valid. This was the year of the Presidential election, and the Democratic party prevailed in the State and nation. Of course, the law was repealed, but its legality had been vindicated, and still more, a lesson had been taught that it was not always safe to discard cherished principles and ancient traditions.

Great events were now hastening, which absorbed minor considerations. The struggle of 1860 was impending. The crisis in the anti-slavery contest was rapidly approaching. Men of all parties, whether influenced by calm judgment or led by inflamed passions, were taking a decided stand. There was but one place for Mr. Smithers. He unhesitatingly cast his lot with the Republican party, and was sent as a delegate to the Chicago Convention. As

chairman of the delegation, he cast the vote of Delaware first for Edward Bates, and afterwards for Lincoln, and was placed on the National Committee. As a member of that committee, he promised that there would be five hundred Republicans in Delaware at the ensuing election. After an open and unflinching canvass, this promise was redeemed by a vote of fifteen hundred, and it was particularly gratifying to him that relatively the largest gain was in Kent and Sussex Counties, because in 1856 almost all of the very small Republican vote was cast in New Castle County. Fidelity to principle had lost nothing in its appeal to the people.

At this election George P. Fisher, who had received the united support of the Bell and Lincoln votes, was elected as Representative to the national Congress. Soon after this campaign the supporters of Mr. Bell coalesced with the Republicans, and in 1862 William Cannon was elected governor. He had been a stanch Democrat, but in the perilous crisis through which the nation was passing had parted from his former associates. He offered Mr. Smithers the appointment of Secretary of State, and at his earnest solicitation, and with the assurance that the administration should be in perfect accord with the national government, he accepted the tender. Governor Cannon was true to his pledge. Although the Republicans had elected their governor, the Democrats had elected William Temple as Representative in Congress. He died before taking his seat. A special election became necessary, and in November, 1863, Mr. Smithers was elected to fill the vacancy caused

by the death of Mr. Temple, and in December took his seat as a member of the Thirty-eighth Congress.

In personal appearance he was at this time very striking. He was about five feet seven inches high and of rather slender build. His features were all good,—dark, deep-set, penetrating eyes, indicative of great kindness, great spirit, and great quickness of apprehension; an unusually high forehead; a mouth firm and expressive, upon the upper lip of which he wore a well-trimmed moustache. His step was slow, and his whole bearing dignified and reserved, giving to strangers the impression that he was cold and difficult of approach. But such was not the case. He was ever ready to receive with kindness all who came to him,—to give them a word of counsel, to listen to their troubles, and to render them pecuniary aid. Indeed, his kindness and generosity often caused him to be imposed upon.

He was now in the full strength of his physical and mental powers, and in the most trying time in the history of the nation, when it appeared as if Providence, in caring for the Union, had concentrated all the intellectual power and patriotic enthusiasm of the people in its legislative assembly, Mr. Smithers was apparently easily the equal of the best in the most notable of American Congresses. He was a member of the Committee on Elections and of the Special Committee on Reconstruction of the Union. These committees were very important ones, and exceptionally strongly constituted. In this latter committee he won a signal victory. The States of Louisiana and Arkansas sent delegates to Congress. It was well known that in very high quarters, for political considerations, there was a desire that they

should be admitted, and a majority of the committee reported in favor of seating them. Mr. Smithers opposed it, and succeeded in defeating them.

During this session of Congress the question of the relation of the seceded States to the national government was discussed, and Mr. Smithers was largely instrumental in directing the decision of the question. He held that while it was possible for the people of those States to dissolve and change their State government, they could not alter their relation to the nation. Its sovereignty over them was uninterrupted and unimpaired. A bill embodying this idea passed both Houses of Congress, but the President quietly pocketed it. This created bad feeling with a few of its advocates, and Messrs. Wade and Davis joined in a paper containing a somewhat acrimonious arraignment of the President. They submitted the paper to Mr. Smithers, but he refused to have anything to do with it.

On one occasion he had the good fortune to carry out the views of the administration in a matter which it deemed of vital consequence. The War Department, under Secretary Stanton, appealed to Congress for aid in securing recruits for the army. The provision of the conscription law allowing drafted men to pay a money consideration in lieu of military service was preventing the proper strengthening of the army. Several bills were proposed by the Military Committee of the House, but were rejected as impracticable. Walking towards the Capitol one day, in conversation with Judge Beaman, of Michigan, Mr. Smithers expressed his opinion as to why the several bills had failed, and ventured to say that he believed he could draft some-

thing which would be acceptable. When he reached his seat he hurriedly made his draft, and as the matter was pending offered it as an amendment. It was defeated at this time by a few votes, but the next day it passed. The dispatch with which it was drawn rendered it necessarily imperfect in its details, but the object was accomplished. After being put into shape, it became a law. The relief was immediate and effective, and Mr. Smithers was personally congratulated and warmly thanked by Secretary Stanton for his timely and efficient help.

In 1864 the national convention of the Republican party was held in Baltimore, and Mr. Smithers was chairman of the delegation from Delaware. Of course, his vote was cast for Lincoln, but for second place he voted for Daniel L. Dickinson. He was not willing to trust the possible fate of the nation in the hands of a man of such antecedents as Andrew Johnson. He knew too well the influence of educational prejudice to be deceived by the glamour of Southern loyalty at that time. But Johnson was nominated, and his subsequent career was a matter of no surprise to Mr. Smithers.

At the State convention held this year Mr. Smithers came forward again for the Congressional nomination. It was well known that there was some opposition to him in his party. This opposition grew entirely out of his action in Congress concerning the fugitive slave laws. A bill was introduced repealing these laws, and Mr. Smithers was the only Republican in the House who voted against it. He held that slavery was organic, and could only be abolished by constitutional amendment, and therefore considered the measure an idle farce, and devoid of all practical utility.

thing which would be acceptable. When he reached his seat he hurriedly made his draft, and as the matter was pending offered it as an amendment. It was defeated at this time by a few votes, but the next day it passed. The dispatch with which it was drawn rendered it necessarily imperfect in its details, but the object was accomplished. After being put into shape, it became a law. The relief was immediate and effective, and Mr. Smithers was personally congratulated and warmly thanked by Secretary Stanton for his timely and efficient help.

In 1864 the national convention of the Republican party was held in Baltimore, and Mr. Smithers was chairman of the delegation from Delaware. Of course, his vote was cast for Lincoln, but for second place he voted for Daniel L. Dickinson. He was not willing to trust the possible fate of the nation in the hands of a man of such antecedents as Andrew Johnson. He knew too well the influence of educational prejudice to be deceived by the glamour of Southern loyalty at that time. But Johnson was nominated, and his subsequent career was a matter of no surprise to Mr. Smithers.

At the State convention held this year Mr. Smithers came forward again for the Congressional nomination. It was well known that there was some opposition to him in his party. This opposition grew entirely out of his action in Congress concerning the fugitive slave laws. A bill was introduced repealing these laws, and Mr. Smithers was the only Republican in the House who voted against it. He held that slavery was organic, and could only be abolished by constitutional amendment, and therefore considered the measure an idle farce, and devoid of all practical utility.

His action caused considerable comment, and was used
against his renomination, but the attempt failed. He was
renominated, and the action of the convention was hailed
with delight by his friends both at home and abroad. His
friends in Congress were eager for his return. To show
the feeling which existed there I clip the following from a
letter written to him October 15, 1864, by Justin S. Morrill,
now United States Senator from Vermont, who was then a
member of the House of Representatives :

"I see with pleasure that you are unanimously renominated, and now you
must not be defeated. Our friend Davis, I fear, cannot be returned from his
district. There are too many there that hate him, and his eccentric cutting
loose from 'Old Abe' will mar his prospects. Still, he is a noble soul, and I
hope his star cannot be blotted out, even in Baltimore. Our friends should
bestir themselves to make sure of your election. We need all the genius,
wisdom, and statesmanship we can group together to steer safely through the
present stormy seas."

But he was not elected. The combined influence of the
opposing party, negro equality, and the draft defeated him
at the polls. I asked him, upon one occasion, if he did not
feel his defeat very keenly at that time, when his services
seemed so useful to the nation, and his own particular star
was in the ascendency. His reply was, " I did not. I
assure you that, as I assumed these responsibilities only in
obedience to a sense of duty, I laid them down, however so
pleasant the associations, without regret."

And, indeed, this is not to be wondered at, when we come
to inquire into it. Grave personal considerations demanded
his attention. He felt that his only place now was in the
bosom of his family,—near the children that so needed his

care, and beside the invalid wife who was fast drifting out
into the silent shadows that curtain the portals of eternity.
So far did these things influence him that when, after his
failure of re-election, Hon. Thomas A. Jenkins, of Rhode
Island, invited him to a conference, and stated that he was
deputed by Republicans, whose recommendations would
have been potential, to inquire what position at home or
abroad would gratify him, his reply was, " While my feelings are touched by this mark of regard, I must decline
your proffer, for reasons of a personal and domestic nature."

This session ended Mr. Smithers's Congressional career.
He retired from Congress, having made a marked impression upon that body, and having secured a national reputation as a patriotic and wise legislator.

In 1868 he was a delegate to the national convention
that nominated General Grant for the Presidency, and here
happened a little incident which illustrated the gathering
after many days of bread cast upon the waters. John D.
Deprees was Secretary of the National Committee, but as
he was deeply interested in the nomination of his friend
Colfax, Mr. Smithers volunteered to take charge of his
department, in addition to his own State duties. Among
the members of the committee was B. R. Cowan, of Ohio,
and that State being in proximity to Chicago, his supply of
tickets to the convention had become exhausted. In the
mean time, one whom he felt under the highest obligation
to serve, had come on with entire confidence in Cowan's
capacity to do anything. Cowan hunted in vain for a pass,
and in his emergency applied to Mr. Smithers, stating that
his reputation was at stake, and imploring Mr. Smithers to

assist him, if only with a standing ticket. As Delaware
had comparatively few visitors, Mr. Smithers was not only
able to accommodate him, so far as the admission of his
friend was concerned, but secured him one of the best seats
in the building. Several years afterwards Mr. Smithers was
in Washington, engaged in watching the interests of Colonel
McComb, in the Credit Mobilier investigation, and Cowan
was the Assistant Secretary of the Interior. It became exceedingly important to fix the date of a certain certificate.
Inquiries had been made by both sides, and always with the
same result,—the date was not satisfactory. Mr. Smithers
was confident that there was a prior one, but how to get it
was the trouble. He called upon Cowan, and was assured
that a thorough search should be instituted; that every
paper in relation to the matter should be overhauled. This
was done, and the next day the desired date was certified
to him. He always thought that the courtesy shown to
Cowan at Chicago had its influence in inducing a more ex-
haustive examination than would otherwise have been made
by the clerk.

Mr. Smithers's first experience in Washington was somewhat out of the common order. It will be remembered
that at the meeting of the Thirty-eighth Congress a number
of motions were made before organization to add representatives to the roll of the House. It came about in this way:
By law, the clerk of the House is required to make up the
roll from the certificates received by him, and this roll, so
made, is *prima facie* evidence of those entitled to organize.
Emerson Etheridge had been clerk of the House in the
preceding Congress. He was a thorough Unionist, and of

unquestioned reputation for integrity, but it became whispered about in certain quarters that he desired to be continued, and to this end he was willing to construct the roll in such a manner as to give the Democratic party the ascendency in the matter of Speaker, in return for which he was to secure the clerkship. Independently of the injustice of attributing such treachery to an honorable man, the futility of the proceeding should have been sufficient proof of its falsity. But in the excitement of those days men did not reason with calmness. The suggestion was made, and even among members was to some extent accepted. Of course, speculation was rife, and anxious consultations were held. Naturally, these rumors caused Mr. Smithers no little anxiety with regard to his own credentials. He therefore determined to call upon Mr. Etheridge in relation to them. Being a comparative stranger, he was accompanied by a friend to the lodgings of Mr. Etheridge, whom he found in an animated and not very amicable conversation with two members-elect from Connecticut. He presented to him his credentials, and inquired of him if they were correct. Mr. Etheridge looked over the paper, and replied that it was entirely satisfactory, and added that it was one of the few that strictly conformed to the law. Relieved by this assurance, Mr. Smithers inquired whether he would give him the names that he felt compelled to exclude. Etheridge unhesitatingly wrote down the list of those whose certificates were informal, and handed it to him, and upon asking whether he might be permitted to retain it, Etheridge replied that he most certainly could; that he had nothing to conceal; that he was only doing his duty as he understood it, and that

any one could have had the same information by asking for it.

With that paper Mr. Smithers went to the room of Colfax, where a large number of Republicans were assembled in somewhat excited colloquy over the situation. He showed them the list, some of them doubted its genuineness, but Colfax and others assured them that it was in the handwriting of Etheridge, and the bubble burst. The wonder was how he had managed to obtain the evidence. There was no mystery. He had simply assumed Mr. Etheridge to be honest, and treated him as a gentleman. After careful counting, it was found that there was still a sufficient Republican majority, and a number of gentlemen were designated who, the next day, should consecutively move, before organization, to add to the roll the omitted representative. This was done, and the House organized.

In 1880, Mr. Smithers was again chairman of the State delegation to the National Republican Convention, and cast the vote of Delaware for James G. Blaine. His admiration for Blaine's ability was unbounded, and, furthermore, they were warm personal friends,—a friendship which was formed in Congress and which lasted through life. In 1889, Mr. Smithers was prominent among the men mentioned for the United States senatorship, when ex-Senator Higgins was elected. His last public service was in the office in which he began his public career. He was appointed Secretary of State in January, 1895, by the late Governor Marvil, and retired from that office in the following April, upon the death of the governor.

HOME LIFE.

For fifteen years after the death of his wife Mr. Smithers remained a widower. He continued to reside in the State Street house with his family, which consisted of himself, his two children, and the housekeeper. His interest seemed to be centred solely in his children; and his only ambition to do well whatever came to him unsought and in the line of duty. There were no longings for a repetition of public life; no aspirations to break away from the quiet environment in which he was reposing. His home, his books, and his friends seemed to fill up his life so completely as to leave no room for outside ambitions or aspirations. So perfectly suited to his taste was his mode of life at this time that when his friend, the late Chief Justice Gilpin, implored him to remove to Wilmington, assuring him of a large and lucrative practice in his profession, he declined by saying that he preferred to remain where he was.

Let us not imagine that this condition was brought about by the approach of old age. Mr. Smithers was still in the prime of life,—strong, masterly, magnetic. He was the same Nathaniel B. Smithers who, for twenty years, had thrilled the people with his eloquence, and whom they had learned to look up to and to honor. Neither let it be thought that he had ceased to take any interest in public affairs. He was fully alive to all the questions of the day. With high ideals, clear insight, and sound judgment, he grappled with the social, political, and economic problems of his time, and solved them for himself. While his solution of them did not always coincide with the views of

others, yet when men could not understand why Nathaniel B. Smithers did as he did, they were always sure that he had weighed the matter well, and was acting upon conscientious judgment. In his word the people had the utmost confidence. They flocked to hear him on the hustings, and received his utterances in perfect faith. ·It was for this reason that the opposite party so feared his power, and invariably followed him around in a campaign for the purpose of building up that which he had torn down.

It often required both moral and physical courage, in no small degree, for him to advocate what he believed to be right, and to denounce what he considered to be wrong Of his moral courage I have spoken. Of his physical courage, the following incident will serve as an illustration: The campaign of 1860 was a hotly contested one. The Republican party in Delaware was regarded with the utmost contempt by its enemies, and its members subjected to the grossest criticism. During this campaign Mr. Smithers was exceedingly active in the Republican cause. Open-air meetings were held nightly, and he stumped the State from one end to the other. At one of these meetings a disturbance occurred. Indeed, it had been whispered about early in the evening, and it came to the ears of Mr. Smithers, that the enemies of the Republicans had determined to break up the meeting. When the hour for the meeting arrived the street was thronged with people. The meeting was organized, and Mr. Smithers was introduced to speak. As he stepped to the front of the platform he was greeted with a shower of stones and brickbats.

Some of those upon the platform, becoming alarmed, were in favor of retiring at once; others, incensed at the outrage, advocated a free fight. But Mr. Smithers, raising his hand with a commanding gesture, and in that clear, penetrating voice of his, said, "Gentlemen, you may proceed with your missiles; you cannot intimidate me. I came here to talk about Republicanism, and, unless you slay me, I shall do so." His words and manner had a magical effect, order was restored at once, and he delivered his speech unmolested.

In 1875 there came to him the keenest sorrow, perhaps, of his life,—the death of Sadie, his only daughter. She had been in failing health for some time, and he was much distressed about her, yet he was hardly prepared for her death, and the blow came upon him with terrible force. His life seemed bound up in this lovely daughter. Apart from the fatherly tenderness he felt for her, he adored her for her loftiness of character and lustre of mind. She, in turn, lavished upon him her admiration and affection. She placed him on a height far above all other mortals; amid a halo of goodness and grandeur, and her devotion, her idolatry never faltered. No two lives were ever in more perfect accord than these two. No two people ever understood one another better than did this father and daughter. Time was slow, indeed, in blunting the sharp edge of his grief occasioned by her death.

In 1882, Mr. Smithers was again married. His second wife was Mrs. Mary T. Smithers, *née* Mary Townsend, daughter of William Townsend, Esq., of Frederica. This marriage was an exceptionally happy one, and brought into

Mr. Smithers' somewhat gloomy and despondent life that light and cheer which it so needed. The old home-life was re-established, and a fresh interest in his surroundings awakened. There was a peacefulness, a tranquillity, about his life at this time that was indeed enviable. But it was destined to be disturbed by the same fell destroyer that had more than once before brought him sorrow. This time it was the death of his only son, Nathaniel B. Smithers, Jr., a very bright and promising young man of thirty years, a member of the bar of Kent County, and who left to survive him a wife and one child. The death of this son left Mr. Smithers childless, but in quiet submission to the will of Providence he bowed his head humbly and said, " It is all right."

He now, more seriously than ever, turned his thoughts towards religious matters. All his life he had been a student of theology, and was familiar with all the great religions of the world. He studied them as if determined to find out for himself the truth. Books of this description filled a large space in his library, while upon his office-table, within easy reach, lay the little Greek Bible, which had been his companion for years. A Methodist by birth and inclination, his name for many years had been upon the assessment list of that church, and he had been one of its heaviest contributors. He had attended its public service with regularity, and conformed strictly to its discipline, but had never formally entered into membership. One Sabbath morning, at the close of the sermon, he rose quietly from his seat in the congregation, walked down the aisle to the chancel-rail of the church, and, standing reverently at the altar of God, he, full of years and honors, testified to the truth of the gospel,

and in childlike simplicity offered his name to the church in testimony of his faith. " May I be permitted to speak?" he asked, and, lifting his eyes amid the deep solemnity of the scene, he said, " I am convinced that the way of my salvation is through Jesus Christ, the Saviour of the world."

During the last year of Mr. Smithers's life he became very infirm physically. So great was the inroad of disease upon him that he became a tottering old man, yet his mind remained ever firm and vigorous. But the end was fast approaching. It came almost with the coming of the new year. He died on Thursday, the 16th day of January, 1896, at about two o'clock in the morning, in the seventy-eighth year of his age. He had been seriously ill only a few days. On the Saturday preceding his death he had been transacting some business in the Orphans' Court, but, not feeling as well as usual, went home and to bed. On Sunday and Monday he felt better, but remained in bed. On Tuesday he grew worse, and during the day fell into a comatose state, from which he never recovered. The immediate cause of his death was Bright's disease, but the end came very quietly, and he passed away without any visible signs of suffering.

When such a man withdraws from among the living, and is seen no more among men, he does not die. To sublime characters there is no death. It is but the decay of a flower, the fading of a summer cloud, the fleeting of a sunbeam, so beautiful in their transition that they can never be forgotten. What Nathaniel B. Smithers accomplished no man can measure. His worth no man can fully estimate. The impress which he left upon the community, the State, the

nation, of which he was a part, will deepen with the flight of years, and for generations to come his name will be the synonym of all that is manly, wise, and good.

At a special meeting of the Directors of the First National Bank of Dover, of which he was president, among the resolutions adopted was the following:

"That the directors of said bank, in common with the many friends of the deceased, recognize the fact that in the death of Mr. Smithers the State has lost one of its foremost and ablest citizens, and this community one of its best and most useful members; that by reason of his splendid talents, remarkable intellectual force, and sterling integrity, he was a credit to his State and an honor to the community in which he lived so long. He was a man of strong convictions and fearless in their expression, but of kindly nature, and exceedingly generous and kind to those in need."

The bar of the State mourned his loss deeply, and gave expression to their feelings in fitting speeches and resolutions.

At a special meeting of the Board of Education of the Dover public schools, of which he was president, resolutions were adopted, from which I copy the following sentence:

"All classes and conditions of men will miss his aid and assistance in the various perplexities of life."

No greater truth than that was ever told; no grander eulogy ever written; no nobler epitaph could be graven on his tomb.

And now my grateful task is done. I lay this humble but heartfelt tribute at the foot of the mound where sleeps this scholar, statesman, patriot, as a slight token of my admiration and esteem.

PAPERS OF THE HISTORICAL SOCIETY OF DELA

XXIV.

WILLIAM PEN

AND HIS PROVINCE.

BY

MANLOVE HAYES,

OF DOVER, DELAWARE.

Read before the Historical Society of Delaware, December 2,

THE HISTORICAL SOCIETY OF DELAWARE,

WILMINGTON.

1899.

WILLIAM PENN AND HIS PROVINCE.

[THE authorities consulted in the preparation of this address are :
"The Life and Writings of William Penn," compiled and pub-
lished in 1722 ; Sewel's "History of the Quakers," translated from
the Dutch and published in Burlington, New Jersey, A.D. 1774;
"Life of Penn," by S. M. Janney ; Bancroft's "History of the
United States ;" Pepys's "Diary ;" Scharf's "History of Delaware ;"
Macaulay's "History of England ;" "Pennsylvania Archives," etc.]

MR. PRESIDENT AND FELLOW-MEMBERS OF THE DELAWARE
HISTORICAL SOCIETY.

In the selection of a subject for an address before this intelligent audience, I have not been unmindful that we live in
an age when almost every topic in which the public is supposed to be interested has been in one form or another
largely discussed.

I do not therefore expect, in presenting to you a sketch
or short biographical account of the illustrious founder of
Pennsylvania and the territory now constituting the State
of Delaware, to increase your store of knowledge by the
introduction of original information, but will venture in my
own way to relate such incidents in his life as will best
elucidate his character and the high motives by which he
was influenced in colonizing a wilderness with emigrants of

a different type and training from those of any settlement that had preceded this adventure.

Of the first settlers of Pennsylvania, it was said, "that all, or nearly all, were members of the Society of Friends, mostly from England and Wales, some from Scotland, Ireland, and Germany; the younger class had been educated in habits of industry, economy, and strict morality." Upon the integrity of such a people rested the hopes of the founder.

William Penn was born in the Parish of St. Catherine, near the Tower of London, on the fourteenth day of October, 1644. He was the eldest son of Admiral Sir William Penn, a distinguished commander in the British navy, and Margaret his wife, daughter of John Jasper of Rotterdam; his early life was spent in or near the great city, then the seat of government of the Lord Protector of the English commonwealth. After the death of Cromwell, which occurred in 1658, and the utter failure of his son and heir to administer the government as his successor, in 1660 the throne of England was restored to the Stuarts, and Charles II., who had been crowned nine years before at Scone, Scotland, was proclaimed King of England. In the year of the restoration of the Stuarts, Admiral Penn was knighted and appointed a Vice-Admiral of England. He subsequently commanded the fleet under James, Duke of York, in the victory over the Dutch in 1665, and was ever after held in high esteem by James, who, as it will be seen, became the generous friend and patron of his son.

Young Penn gave early promise of remarkable talents. At the age of sixteen he entered Oxford, and was dis-

tinguished alike for his love of learning and fondness for
athletic exercises and manly sports, though, in the third
year of college life, he seems to have chosen for his companions young men of serious thought and of a religious
turn, who were dissatisfied with the forms and ceremonies
of the Established Church, and had discontinued their attendance. They had listened to the preaching of a dissenter,
Thomas Lowe, and were holding meetings among themselves for divine worship; for this offence they were at first
fined by the college authorities; still persisting in their
course, Penn and his associates were charged with in-
subordination and rebellious conduct, and were summarily
expelled. Penn's acquirements during his three years at
Oxford give evidence of studious habits and close application. His aptness in the acquisition of ancient and modern languages was remarkable. "He had read the most
noted writers of Greece and Italy in their native tongue,
and possessed, moreover, a knowledge of French and German," and could speak his mother's native language, the
Dutch. He is also said to have acquired a good knowledge
of "history and theology." Thus well equipped he was a
fit companion of his fellow-students, the celebrated John
Locke and Robert Spencer, and he would have doubtless
ranked with the distinguished writers of his time had his
mind been turned solely to contemplative or literary work;
but the world would have lost the grand result of the application of his mental strength and abilities in other engagements for the good of mankind, in his long and active
career as a public benefactor. On returning home from
Oxford under the unfavorable circumstances of his ex-

pulsion, Penn met the stern rebuke of a deeply offended
father. The admiral had no sympathy with the young
man's religious convictions, mistaking his firmness in adhering to his religious views for obstinacy, and finding his
remonstrances of no avail, it is said he resorted to blows,
and for some time treated his son with much harshness.
Finally, in the hope of eradicating the false notions, as he
deemed them, by which his son's mind had been perverted,
he sent him abroad in company with several young men of
rank, and in Paris and other gay cities which they visited,
Penn was well received and introduced into fashionable if
not frivolous society, and doubtless indulged in the pleasures
of such companionship, though it is known that a considerable part of his time was spent at the famous Calvinistic
divinity school at Saumur, in historical research, especially
in relation to the early Christian writers. He also perfected
his study of the French language, and returned to London
much improved both in knowledge of the world, and, what
was deemed quite indispensable at court, he had acquired
the ease and polished courtesy for which the French were
distinguished. About this time we have a glimpse of Penn
in Pepys's entertaining diary, a work that affords a rare insight into the social and domestic life in London during the
reign of Charles II. The admiral's wife, Mrs. Margaret, or
Peggy Penn, as she was called, was an intimate friend of
Mrs. Pepys; though Pepys at this time cordially hated the
admiral, and in his diary takes no pains to conceal it. Of
his son, he writes, that " Mr. Penn, Sir William's son, is come
back from France; he came to see my wife; a most modish
person, grown, she says, a fine gentleman." Young Penn,

however, had but little relish for the licentious depravity of
the court of Charles; he had entered upon the study of
law in Lincoln's Inn, but in a year or two fell back into his
old habit of serious meditation. His father, perceiving the
change in his demeanor and anxious to divert his mind, as
well as to have him leave. London, where the plague was
spreading, sent him to Ireland, ostensibly to look after the
family interest in an estate in the county of Cork, but really
in the hope that his depression would be dispelled by intercourse and companionship with the gentry whose presence
gave brilliancy to the Viceregal court. He was received by
the $D_u{}^{ke}$ of Ormond, Viceroy of Ireland, with much kindness; endowed with all the accomplishments of a well-bred
gentleman he soon became a favorite in the gay circle of the
viceroy's court. In the vigor of youth, just twenty-one
years of age, it is not surprising that he joined in their
festivities and, as it is said, "gave himself up entirely to
pleasure," so much so, indeed, as to cause his father some
uneasiness. He wrote to him, July 17, 1666, "Son William,
I have received two or three letters from you since I wrote
to you; beside my former advice I can add nothing, but advise to sobriety and all those things that will bespeak you a
Christian and a gentleman."

The admiral at the same time refused to second the Lord
Lieutenant's wish to appoint William to a captaincy in the
army, as a reward or promotion for brave conduct and distinguished services in quelling a mutiny at the fort of Car-
rickfergus, when acting as millitary aid to the Lord of Arran,
second son of the Duke of Ormond. Penn's courage had
been tried on a previous occasion, as well as his dexterity

and skill as a swordsman.   When in Paris, he was attacked
on the street at night by an armed Frenchman, who charged
him with some trifling offence or slight of his quality.   Penn
defended himself with so much skill that he not only parried
the savage thrusts of his antagonist, but disarmed him, and
when the man was at his mercy showed his nobleness of
character by permitting him to depart uninjured.

This incident, as related by Janney, is followed by
Penn's reflections in after years on this episode in his life.
" Suppose," he said, " he had killed me, for he made several
passes at me, or that I in my defence had killed him, I ask
any man of understanding or conscience if the whole round
of ceremony were worth the life of a man, with respect to
God, himself, and the benefit of civil society."   There is a
portrait of Penn, painted at the time he was playing courtier
and soldier at the Viceregal court.   He is taken in the
costume of a young cavalier of the time, with head un-
covered, otherwise than with a profusion of dark hair curled
on his neck and shoulders; his fine features and mild expression are indicative of a gentle nature and not fully in
keeping with his costume as a soldier.   A copy of this portrait was presented by his grandson, Granville Penn, to the
Pennsylvania Historical Society, and from it many copies
have been made.   It is said to be the only likeness of the
founder taken during his life.

After Penn's disappointment, by his father's refusal to
aid or approve his promotion to the captaincy, he applied
himself diligently to the improvement of his father's Irish
estate, which he managed judiciously, and at this time his
conduct gave the admiral entire satisfaction.   When thus

engaged, Penn learned that his old friend of Oxford, Thomas Lowe, had an appointment to attend a Friends' (Quaker) meeting in Cork; his personal regard for this minister, who was the instrument of his conviction and change of heart at "Christ Church College," led him to attend the meeting. So much was he interested in the sermon of the eloquent preacher, and his treatment of the theme of his discourse, that he felt convinced of the errors of his past life, and believing in the soundness of the doctrine of Friends, he became a constant attendant of their meetings of worship, thus cutting loose from his young companions at court, and uniting with a sect of dissenters from the Established Church, whose religious principles and simple mode of worship had brought upon them the scorn and reproach not of churchmen alone, but of the large and more influential dissenting sects.

In Bancroft's "History of the United States," volume ii., page 337, we have in a concise form the doctrine of George Fox, the founder of the Society of Friends, as developed by Barclay and Penn. I will quote the passage.

"The Quaker has but one word, the Inner Light, the voice of God in the soul; that Light is a reality, and therefore in its freedom the highest revelation of truth; it is kindred with the spirit of God, and therefore merits dominion as the guide to virtue; it shines in every man's breast, and therefore joins the whole human race in the unity of equal rights."

"Intellectual freedom, the supremacy of mind, universal enfranchisement,—these three points include the whole of Quakerism so far as it belongs to civil history."

Those who feel interested in the subject will find in the sixteenth chapter of Bancroft's "History" (old edition) an impartial presentation of the principles and the civil and religious doctrines of this sect. "They are a people," said Cromwell, "whom I cannot win with gifts, honors, offices, or places." .

Penn, having adopted the tenets of the religious society of Friends, was soon made to share with others the persecution to which they had long been subjected by a suspicious and tyrannical magistracy. When attending a religious meeting at Cork, there came, said Penn, "several constables, backed with soldiers, rudely and arbitrarily requiring every man's appearance before the mayor, and amongst others violently haled me with them." The charge against them was for holding a "tumultuous and riotous assembly." For this he was committed to prison with eighteen others, all denying the charge, but refusing to give bond for good behavior, claiming that they were innocent. This was the first but not the only time Penn suffered imprisonment for the advocacy of his religious convictions.

On writing a clear statement of the case to the Earl of Orrery, Lord President of Munster, an order was given for his immediate discharge. These matters being made known to the admiral, he was greatly displeased, and William was at once recalled. Their meeting was a painful one; the father using every argument, and offering every inducement of personal advancement that he could command, to influence and persuade his son to leave off the peculiar manners of the dissenting sect to which he now belonged; and the son, though perfectly respectful, and in all other things obedient,

adhering strictly and firmly to what he in his conscience believed to be right. Thus differing, after an exciting interview, the old seaman, losing command of his temper, indignantly forbade him the house. In this great trouble, William received from his friends such consolation and entertainment as they could give; his father's wrath at last in a measure subsided, and his mother's appeal in behalf of her son resulted in his being again received at their home. Penn was now twenty-three years of age, and, as there was no special claim upon his time in any secular employment, he devoted his whole attention to the study and advancement of the cause for which he had suffered, and which was to bring upon him, as upon others of his religious order, the most rigorous and intolerant persecution that could be instituted under the forms of law. At a meeting of worship held in front of Grace Church Street Meeting House, which had been closed by authority of the mayor of London, Penn and Captain William Mead, an old soldier, but now a Quaker, were arrested for speaking to an assembly in violation of an intolerant Act, passed in the time of Queen Elizabeth, "for the suppression of seditious conventicles," which had been revived and enforced against the Quakers. (The full text of this Act will be found in Sewel's "History of the Quakers," copied from an old volume of Penn's "Life and Writings," compiled and published in 1722.)

The prisoners were brought before the mayor and recorder, and were called to plead to the indictment, which charged them and divers other persons with having "unlawfully and tumultuously met, with force and arms, etc." They made a general denial of the charges brought against

them, and on receiving a promise from the court that no advantage would be taken of them, and that they should have a fair hearing and liberty to make their own defence (as they had employed no counsel), they plead "not guilty in manner and form indicted."

The jury having been sworn and witnesses examined, the recorder, finding the evidence insufficient to convict, turned to Captain Mead, saying, " What say you, Mr. Mead ? Were you there ?" To whom the captain replied, "It is a maxim in your own law that no man is bound to accuse himself, and why dost thou offer to ensnare me with such a question ?" The recorder answered, " Hold your tongue ; I did not go about to ensnare you."

Penn took advantage of a moment's silence to address the court. " I will affirm," said he, "that I have broken no law, nor am I guilty of the indictment that is laid to my charge, and to the end that the bench, the jury, and myself, and those who hear us, may have a direct understanding of this procedure, I desire you would let me know by what law it is you prosecute me, and upon what law you ground my indictment ?"

To which the recorder replied, " It is the common law."

Then said Penn, " What is that common law ?"

The recorder replied, " I will not go over so many adjudged cases, which we call common law, to answer your curiosity."

"Well," said Penn, "this answer I am sure is very far short of my question, for if it be common it should not be so hard to produce. If the Lord Coke in his ' Institutes' be of any consideration, he tells us ' that common law is com-

mon right,'. and that common right is the great Charter privileges confirmed by 9 Henry III., 29; 25 Edward I., etc."

"Sir," said the recorder, "you are an impertinent, troublesome fellow, and it is not for the honor of the court to suffer you to go on."

Penn. "I have asked but one question, and you have not answered me, though the rights and privileges of every Englishman are concerned in it."

Recorder. "If I should suffer you to ask questions till to-morrow morning, you would never be the wiser."

Penn was not easily disconcerted, and quickly replied, "That's according as the answers are. I do not design to affront the court, but to plainly tell you that in denying me the oyer of the law you say I have broken, is to deny me the right of every Englishman."

Recorder. "We must not stand to hear you all night; take him to the Bale dock!" and into the Bale dock he was rudely removed.

Captain Mead then attempted to address the jury in his defence, denying that the meeting was either a riot or unlawful assembly, when he was interrupted by the mayor, who roughly declared, "that he was an enemy to the law, and deserved to have his tongue cut out;" he was also sent to the Bale dock, and the court proceeded to charge the jury in their absence; this they both openly declared to be arbitrary and not in accordance with law, whereupon the bailiff was ordered to confine them in a foul cell called the "Stink hole," where they remained until recalled to hear the jury's verdict. The charge of the court, it seems, had

little weight with the jury. Penn "was found guilty of speaking in Gracious Street."

Mayor. " Is that all ? Was it not an unlawful assembly ?"

Foreman. " My lord, that is all I have in commission."

Mayor. " You had as well say nothing."

Penn demanded that the clerk be required to record the verdict. To the jury he said, " You are Englishmen ; mind your privileges, give not away your rights."

The mayor ordered the bailiff "to stop his mouth ; bring fetters and stake him to the ground."

Penn replied, " Do your pleasure ; I matter not your fetters."

The mayor and recorder then took occasion to vilify the jury in the most violent and offensive language. They were threatened with confinement without meat, drink, fire, or tobacco. The recorder declaring, "it will never be well with us till something like the Spanish Inquisition be in England."

After being locked up two days and nights, the jury rendered a verdict acquitting both Penn and Mead from the charge, "as in manner and form indicted." This gave great satisfaction to the assembly. The prisoners then demanded their liberty, but were ordered to be confined in prison for the non-payment of the fines for contempt of court, and it is stated the jury were also sent to Newgate on a similar charge.

This remarkable trial is given in full in Penn's " Life and Writings," before referred to. I have been obliged to omit the most of it, and abridge the passages I have quoted, by which it has lost much of its force.

Penn was at this time greatly distressed on account of the illness of his father, who had been confined to his house for some months. He had become entirely reconciled to his son, and on receiving an affectionate letter from him, written in Newgate prison, he would at once have paid the fine imposed and set him free, but Penn would not permit that to be done. He wrote to the admiral, " I entreat thee not to purchase my liberty; they have so overshot themselves, that the generality of people must detest them, and they will repent of their proceedings. I am a prisoner notoriously against law."

The admiral's condition growing much worse, and feeling he had not long to live, his desire to see his son so worried him that he sent money privately, by a friend, to pay the fines of William and his companion, Captain Mead, and they were informed they were free to leave the prison.

From Newgate Penn hastened to the bedside of his father, who commended the course he had taken, and exhorted him to let nothing in this world tempt him to wrong his conscience, " which will give peace at home and be a feast in the day of trouble." Said he, " Afflictions make wise." The admiral knew well the temper of the times, and that his son's firm determination to suffer persecution rather than yield to the arbitrary and illegal usage of a bigoted and subservient magistracy would bring him into trouble; and, though exhorting him not to wrong his conscience, he had sent to his friend, the Duke of York, his dying request, that he would use his influence with the king in his son's behalf.

After the death of his father Penn came into possession

of a good estate, affording him an ample income, a large part of which was used in relieving the necessities of the poor, as his personal wants were few and his habits inexpensive.

During the troublous times that followed through the intrigues of Charles, England, in alliance with France, its natural enemy, engaged in an unholy war with Holland, in which the Dutch proved more than a match for them. De Ruyter and Tromp attacked and destroyed the allied fleets, and William of Orange, the young Stadtholder, outmanœuvred the wily French king. The alliance was soon broken and the war ended ingloriously for England.

Charles thus lost favor with Parliament, and the proposed marriage of his brother, the Duke of York, with the Catholic Princess of Modena, which had been vainly opposed, was an additional cause of dissension, and during the next seven years, says Bancroft, "the king and Parliament were in a continual contest, the troubles at home and abroad kept the nation in a constant turmoil. Plots and conspiracies, some real, others imaginary, created universal alarm and suspicion."

The persecution of the Quakers was by no means relieved by these diversions; the commotion seemed to have excited in their enemies a desire for fresh attacks. Penn was kept busily engaged in controversial writing, or speaking in defence of the principles of his sect, which was subjected to the most absurd and malignant misrepresentations. The Friends believing that war was wholly at variance with the spirit of the gospel of peace, could not conscientiously bear arms; holding, also, that the words of Christ, "Swear not

at all," were applicable to all oaths,—even the " oath of allegiance,"—they insisted that their solemn affirmation should be taken and considered as binding in law on them, as an oath on those who were not conscientiously scrupulous as to swearing.

Penn, being again arrested and having refused to take the oath of allegiance, which he knew was offered by the court to entrap him, was again thrown into prison. During his imprisonment, which continued for six months, under the most unfavorable circumstances, as all prisons at that time were notoriously foul and loathsome, he wrote several religious works, which established his reputation not only as an able writer, but as an upright and loyal citizen. Among his most important publications, soon after his release, was a " Treatise on Oaths," addressed to the king and Parliament, in which he introduced many passages from the testimonies of Christian fathers, doctors, confessors, and martyrs, in dislike of swearing.

In pursuance of his great purpose, we next find him at the head of a delegation of Friends chosen to meet a committee of Parliament, which had been appointed to consider their application to be relieved from this and other grievances. At length the House of Commons, being convinced that the refusal of " Friends" to take the oath was owing entirely to their religious scruples, in the year 1678 inserted a clause for their relief in a bill that passed the House of Commons ; but before it was acted on by the House of Lords, Parliament was suddenly prorogued, and the bill thus defeated. About this time, Penn, in company with George Fox, Robert Barclay, and one or two other Friends, visited Germany and

Holland on a religious mission. A very interesting account of their travels on foot and by boat is given in Janney's "Life of Penn," especially of his reception at Herwarden by the Princess Elizabeth of the Rhine, who with her friend, the Countess de Hornes, became disciples of his simple faith and form of worship, and with whom he afterwards kept up a correspondence on religious subjects.

In the year 1675, Penn seems to have first become interested in American affairs, when he consented to act as referee between John Fenwick and Edward Byllinge, the former having acquired by purchase, as trustee for Byllinge and his assigns, a half-interest in the province of New Jersey. After a thorough examination of the case, Penn rendered an award allotting to Fenwick a part of the territory in dispute in West New Jersey, with which he was not at first satisfied, but the matter was adjusted by Penn without an appeal to court. Fenwick embarked with his family and some of their friends and took possession of the land assigned him, making a settlement at a pleasant place on the Delaware River, which he named Salem. This was the first English ship that came to the west shore of New Jersey, and for a long time, says Janney, no other followed.

Byllinge became involved in financial difficulties, and offered to transfer his interest in West New Jersey to his creditors, and by an agreement the assignment was made to William Penn, Gowen Laurie, and Nicholas Lucas, trustees. In 1676, a deed of partition and settlement between Sir George Carteret, one of the assignees of the Duke of York, the proprietor of the province, and the trustees above named, was executed, by which Carteret retained his title to East New

Jersey, including the settled parts on the Passaic and Rari-
tan Rivers; and to Penn and his coadjutors, trustees of
Byllinge, was assigned the unsettled part of the province
extending to the Delaware River, called West New Jersey.
Proposals for the settlement of this territory were published,
and in the years 1677–78 five vessels, with about eight hundred emigrants, many of them Quakers, sailed for the province, and with them commissioners having authority to buy
land from the Indians and to organize a government. The
commissioners, halting at New Castle to renew supplies, engaged interpreters from among the Swedes, and proceeded
up the Delaware as far as Chygoes Island, and laid out a
town on the east bank of the Delaware River, now called
Burlington, but named by them "Bridlington."

It is said that "ten years before, when proposals were
issued for settlement in this province, each emigrant was
required to provide himself with a good musket, powder,
and ball" (conquest by peaceful methods was not characteristic of the Anglo-Saxon race); but the Quakers, coming
among the Indians in quite a different spirit, were met without fear or suspicion.

The colonists made it their first care on landing to establish a place for meetings of worship and for Christian instruction. The ill effect of the traffic in ardent spirits with
the Indians was apparent, and the colony resolved to put an
end to it. The Indians admitted the traffic was hurtful to
them. "When we drink," said one of their kings, "it
makes us mad, and we know not what we do. Strong
liquor was first sold to us by the Dutch; and they were
blind. They had no eyes, but this people have eyes; they

can see, and we are glad such a people have come among us." By faithfully following their convictions of duty in this and other respects, the settlers were blessed with an unusual degree of prosperity.

Penn became subsequently one of the proprietors of East New Jersey (Janney, p. 162), and his participation in the affairs of this province and his intercourse with his countrymen who had travelled in America, added greatly to his knowledge of the country, which was further increased by his friendly relations with George Fox after his return in 1673 from a religious mission to Barbadoes and to the "Friends in Maryland," thence travelling northward through the forests near the sea-coast to New England and back again, going as far south as Carolina, preaching in many places, and keeping a faithful journal of his travels. This journal was afterwards published with a preface by Penn.

With all this information from reliable sources, he was well prepared to open negotiations with the king and his brother, the Duke of York, for a grant of territory in exchange for a debt of the government to the estate of his father of £15,000. This claim was admitted to be just, and Charles II., always in straitened circumstances, doubtless readily consented to settle it in the way proposed.

The west bank of the Delaware River was held to be a part of the territory already granted with the Jerseys to the Duke of York by the king, and the duke's consent having been first obtained, other objections caused further delay in the settlement: Lord Baltimore claimed that the southern boundary encroached upon his province. This question was referred to Lord Chief-Justice North. Finally, on his

rendering a decision as to the boundary between the provinces of Pennsylvania and Maryland, the king affixed his
signature to the patent which granted to Penn "all the land
west of the Delaware River from 12 Miles North of New
Castle to the 43° of North Latitude, the said land to extend
westward 5° in Longitude." This document, dated March
4, 1681, is preserved in the office of the Secretary of State
at Harrisburg, Pennsylvania. (Janney, pages 164, 165.)

On receiving his patent, Penn, as proprietor and governor
of the province, at once issued proposals for its colonization,
The following letter was addressed to the Swedes, Dutch,
and English inhabitants of the province :

"MY FRIENDS,—I wish you all happiness here and hereafter.
These are to let you know that it has pleased God in his Providence
to cast you within my lot and care ; it is a business though I never
undertook before. God has given me an understanding of my duty
and an honest mind to do it uprightly. I hope you will not be troubled at your change and the King's choice, for you are now fixed at
the mercy of no Governor that comes to make his fortune great.
You shall be governed by Laws of your own making and live a free
and, if you will, a sober and industrious people. I shall not usurp
the right of any, or oppress his person ; God has furnished me a
better resolution, and has given me his grace to keep it. In short,
whatever sober and free men can reasonably desire for the security
and improvement of their own happiness, I shall heartily comply
with. God direct you in the way of righteousness and therein pros-
per you and your children after you. I am your true friend,

"WM. PENN.

"2d Mo. (called April, old style), 1681."

"Such," says Bancroft, "were the pledges of the Quaker
sovereign on assuming the government. It is the duty of

history to state that during his long reign these pledges
were redeemed; he never refused the freemen of Pennsylvania a reasonable desire."

The Duke of York desired to retain the three lower
counties (now the State of Delaware), which he claimed
had been granted to him as an appendage to the Dutch colony of New York. The title to this territory was in dispute; Lord Baltimore, the proprietor of Maryland, claiming
the entire peninsula from the fortieth degree of north latitude to the Virginia line as a part of his province. His
agents had on several occasions attempted by force to dis-
possess the Dutch and Swedes of their settlements both at
Lewes and at New Castle. Baltimore's claim was not admitted, and, after much negotiation, the Duke of York con-
senting to grant the lower counties to Penn, these were
conveyed to him by two deeds of feoffment, thus giving him
title to all the territory south of the forty-third degree of
north latitude, on the western and southern banks of the
Delaware River and Bay to the Atlantic.

Soon after this settlement was completed, the proprietor
made his arrangements to visit his colony. He had the year
before sent with the first emigrants his cousin, Captain William Markham, to act as his deputy. Markham's commission was dated April 10, 1681; he was charged with instructions to call a council to consist of nine members, to set
bounds between him and his neighbors, to establish courts,
appoint justices and a sheriff for the suppression of tumults,
etc., in short, to organize a government under the proprietary. Penn, with one hundred others, mostly Friends, embarked at Deal, August 30, 1682, on the ship "Welcome,"

three hundred tons burden. During the long passage of nearly two months the small-pox made its appearance on board, and of this loathsome disease thirty persons died at sea. Penn did everything possible in a crowded ship for the relief of the sufferers, and contributed much to their comfort.

The "Welcome" arrived at New Castle on the 28th of October. The sad incidents of the voyage gave Penn but little time to prepare for the reception that awaited him. The population of New Castle, consisting of three distinct nationalities, were united in resisting the claim of Lord Baltimore to their territory, and equally unanimous in extending an enthusiastic welcome to the new proprietor.

Upon his landing, the deeds of feoffment from the Duke of York were exhibited, and Penn was conducted to the courthouse, where he delivered a short address, explaining to the people his purpose in coming, and the nature and principles of the government he proposed to establish. On the following day he received formally from the magistracy and people possession of the town and country, " by delivery of turf, twig and water, and soil of the River."

He next went to Upland, changing the name to Chester, to gratify his friend Pearson, in remembrance of his native city. Penn appointed a time for meeting the Indians and prominent residents of New Castle and the adjoining territory, and on November 2 he held court at that place, the first over which he presided as governor.

After transacting other business he addressed the assemblage, assuring them they should enjoy the same privileges as those of the province of Pennsylvania, and would be

governed by such laws as they or their representatives would consent to, and promised at an early time to call an Assembly. Soon after this Penn received by his deputy, Markham, formal possession of the lower counties on the Delaware as far south as the Atlantic.

From Chester, the governor, accompanied by some of his friends, went in a barge to the site of the new city at the mouth of the Schuylkill River. He had given written instructions to commissioners, a year before his arrival, "to lay out a city at a convenient place on the Delaware River at the mouth of a creek navigable well inland, and at such place to lay off ten thousand acres, contiguous, affording ample space for houses and side lots for grass and shade trees, making a green country town," etc. To this city he gave the name Philadelphia, called, appropriately, "the city of brotherly love."

The site for the city had been fixed by the commissioners, but little progress had been made in building, or in laying out streets, and many changes were made in the city plan under Penn's personal supervision. There was a larger settlement at Shackamaxon, a short distance above, where meetings of worship were held, which he attended; and at this place he met a large multitude of Indians, as well as white people, all desirous of offering him the best entertainment the country would afford. Though Penn had obtained from the king letters patent, and from the Duke of York deeds of feoffment, conveying to him a territory of vast dimensions, he felt in his conscience that the land was not theirs to give. He had taken the same view when appointed one of the trustees of Byllinge, in West New Jersey, who

held under the grant of the Duke of York. His words were, " The soil is not his to give, 'tis the natives by the jus gentium, the law of nations." In pursuance of these just views, after settling the Swedish claim, he desired a meeting with the Indians, and the neighboring tribes were invited to meet him in council about the last of November. The place fixed upon for the council was under the famous elm tree that stood in Kensington. The assemblage was notably striking and picturesque, as represented by the great American painter, Benjamin West. The ceremonies were conducted in a decorous manner suitable to the occasion. Taminend, the noted chief, decorated with the emblems of kingly power, standing near the council fire, announced through his interpreter to Penn that they were assembled to hear him. In his address Penn reiterated the sentiments he had before expressed in letters and messages sent by his agents to the heads of the tribes : " The people who come with me are a just, plain, and honest people, that neither make war upon others, nor fear war from others, because they will be just. It is not our custom to use hostile weapons against our fellow-creatures, for which reason we have come unarmed. The Great Spirit, who knows the inmost thoughts of men, knows that I and my friends have a hearty desire to live in peace and friendship with you, so that no advantage is to be taken on either side, but all to be openness, brotherhood, and love." Such were the words of the new law-giver.

The Indian orator, taking him by the hand, pledged the tribes to "kindness and good neighborhood so long as the sun and moon should endure." And this treaty, of which

there was no written record, says Voltaire, " was never sworn to and never broken."

Forty-six years after this event, Governor Gordon, in a speech to an assembly of the same tribes, told them, " their friend and father William Penn ever entertained a warm affection for them, and enjoined on the governors of his province to treat them as his children, and he so continued this love for them until his death."

Penn in his intercourse with the Indians was free and un-ceremonious ; his high principles of personal and political freedom, and respect for the rights of man, extended even to the untutored tribes. He was not unmindful of the mental and moral culture of the natives and their instincts of a Deity. " The poor savage people," said he, " believe in God and the soul without the aid of metaphysics."

Their hearts and minds were open to receive his offers of friendship and fair dealing, and for a hundred years, says the Moravian historian, Heckewelder, the speeches of their great friend " Onas" were as household words; " written on the bark of the birch-tree, they were spread out in shady places to be read over and over again."

To the student of American history it will be interest-ing to note the influence on subsequent legislation in this country of the truly republican plan of government framed by Penn, with the assistance of his not less distinguished than unfortunate friend, Algernon Sidney. In the preface to this constitution, he says, " I do not find a model in the world that time and place and some singular emergencies have not necessarily altered, nor is it easy to frame a civil government that shall serve all places alike."

"For the matter of liberty," said Penn, "I propose that which is extraordinary, to leave myself and my successors no power of doing mischief, that the will of one man may not hinder the good of the whole country."

I will here also quote Penn's law of religious toleration.

"That all persons living in this province who confess and acknowledge the one Almighty and Eternal God to be the Creator, upholder and ruler of the world, and that hold themselves obliged in conscience to live peaceably and justly in civil society, shall in nowise be molested or prejudiced for their religious persuasion or practice in matters of faith or worship."

The plan of government provided for a Governor, a Provincial Council of seventy-two persons, and a General Assembly, not to exceed two hundred, to be elected by ballot, not by "freeholders alone, but every artificer or other resident that paid 'scot and lot' to the government was entitled to vote."

Religious toleration founded on the inherent right of man to worship God according to the dictates of his conscience; murder the only crime punishable with death; the absence of any provision for the perpetuation of distinctions of rank; the abrogation of the privileges under the English law of primogeniture; prison reform; all prisons for convicts to be workhouses; the erection and order for public schools and encouragement of useful sciences, inventions, and trades, were all distinguishing features of this first truly American constitution and code of laws. Thus was a free representative government established on the soil of Pennsylvania and Delaware nearly one hundred years

before the Declaration of Independence. (See Bancroft, page 384.)

Under the mild and beneficent government of Penn the province was being rapidly peopled. On the 29th of December, 1682, he writes to a friend in England, "that of twenty-three ships none had miscarried, making swift passages, seldom longer than six weeks." These vessels discharged their living freight upon the banks of the Delaware, and with lighter hearts than most of them had ever known they shook off the shackles of the old world, and with willing hands stood ready to take part with the toiling multitude in clearing the forest and planting crops under the most unfavorable conditions. From rough exposure and a scanty living at first, they developed a character and strength of purpose aptly fitting to the race that was laying the foundation of a free nation.

Penn loved the quiet of these great forests. "Oh!" said he, "how sweet is the quiet of these parts, freed from the anxious and troublesome solicitations, hurries, and perplexities of woful Europe."

Fortunate had it been for this good man if his family had joined him in this sweet land; had he been content to remain away from the troubles and turmoil of England, disgraced by the grossly licentious and profligate reign of Charles II., from how many an anxious hour and sore disappointment he would have been spared. During the following year, 1683, the governor travelled over a large part of his province east of the Susquehanna River; he studied the character of its soils and its natural productions; he visited the Indians in their settlements and learned to con-

verse with them in their own language; he gathered much information and many facts, and he wrote a most interesting and admirable letter to "The Free Society of Traders," in which he gave a description of the country; the diversity of its soils, the varieties of nut-bearing and other forest trees, the capabilities of the province, and the habits and customs of the natives. Taking a practical view of the needs of the colonists, he suggested the introduction of new varieties of seeds and plants, and gave thought and attention to the improvement of the native products. The limits of my sketch will not permit me to dwell longer on this letter, but its perusal will richly repay any one interested in the early settlements on the Delaware. More fortunate than the "Acadians of Nova Scotia," this settlement of Quakers lived in quietude and peace, leaving to their descendants happy homes and a grand future.

At this time Philadelphia contained near three hundred houses, and the population was estimated at twenty-five hundred. "In the province there were over three thousand of Swedish and Dutch extraction, and of native Indians about six thousand, divided into ten tribes, all united by a league of amity with *all the English* in America."

The province was singularly free from the superstition which at that time had assumed the form of a popular delusion in the New England colonies as also in old England, where grave and learned men gave countenance to active persecution for witchcraft. It is recorded that but one case was brought to trial before the provincial council; the charge was against one Margaret Mattison for bewitching a cow and causing the death of a calf. The jury, after hear-

ing the evidence of Annakæ Coolin and others, brought in a verdict of "guilty of the *common fame* of being a witch, but not guilty in manner and form as she stands indicted."

The governor sat in the case; he reprimanded the woman for her turbulent behavior, and, on giving bail to keep the peace, she was set free.

Penn's earnest desire to come to an amicable agreement with Lord Baltimore on the vexed dispute in relation to the boundary lines meeting with no encouragement, and learning that Baltimore had gone to England to prosecute his claim to the three lower counties, he determined to follow him. Commissioning the provincial council to act in his stead, and leaving his personal affairs in the care of Markham and his faithful steward Harrison, he embarked on the 12th of August, 1684, taking with him the good-will and blessings of the whole people; and, after an uneventful voyage of fifty-five days, he landed in Sussex, England, near his own home. After a few days of quiet enjoyment with his family, Penn waited upon the king and the Duke of York. By the latter he was received graciously, but the king he found greatly changed, "morose and stern, especially against dissenters." With his usual disregard of his personal interests or personal safety, Penn brought to the king's attention, through the Duke of York, the barbarities and cruelties to which his subjects, innocent of any criminal act, were subjected. True to his principles, he advocated openly liberty of conscience and religious toleration. By his timely interference many were released from prison, and among others pardoned was one Richard Vickers, an honest man of good reputation and estate, under sentence of death

for disobedience to the old statute, thirty-five of Queen Elizabeth, "for the crime of worshipping God in his own way, and refusing to abjure by oath a crime he had never committed, as he could not conscientiously swear at all."

In the month of February, 1685, Charles II. died, and James succeeded to the throne. The tolerant principles professed by James, and his long personal friendship for Penn, led him very naturally to hope for clemency towards those of his belief who were yet in prison; but, alas, those who wait on princes meet with many delays.

The ill-advised rebellion of the Duke of Monmouth, a natural son of Charles, which was little more than a raid, easily quelled, was used as a pretext, by the notorious Jeffreys and a subservient magistracy, to condemn without mercy hundreds who were charged with disloyalty, and the only means of escaping the vengeance of the corrupt judge and court was "by the purchase of pardons, at an exorbitant price." In a letter from Penn to James Harrison at this time, referring to these victims of tyranny, he says, "About three hundred hanged in diverse towns in the west, and a thousand to be transported. I begged twenty of the king. Colonel Holmes, young Hays, the two Hewlings, Lark and Hix ministers executed, the Keeper dead and Lord Jeffreys Chief Justice, etc."

Penn was perhaps the only man in the realm who dared to approach the king and courageously plead the cause of a suffering people. Charlewood Lawton, an honest and independent gentleman, who would not accept a magistracy or other office though offered by the king, speaks of Penn's good offices in getting people out of trouble at this junc-

ture, saying, " Mr. Penn gave the greatest proofs as well of
his integrity as good nature, for he was not only helping
every man out of his troubles, and busy in getting particular pardons, but daily pressing for a real general one."
(" Memoirs of Historical Society of Pennsylvania," vol. iii.,
part 2.)   King James was incapable of comprehending
Penn's liberal policy, though influenced in some degree
by his arguments; but, mainly by other motives, in the
year 1685 proclaimed a general pardon to all who were
in prison on account of " conscientious dissent," by which
thousands were set at liberty, and among them fourteen
hundred Friends, many of whom had been separated from
their families twelve or fifteen years.   For this act he received the formal thanks of the Society, in an address by
Penn, which was acknowledged by the king, saying, among
other things, " It was always his principle, that conscience
ought not to be forced."   This pardon was followed by a
declaration for liberty of conscience and the suspension of
the tests.   (Text of this proclamation in Sewel's " History
of the Quakers," page 670.)   The proclamation was based
on the *dispensing power of the sovereign,* which was looked
upon with suspicion and distrust by the hierarchy, and not
only opposed on the ground of the king having exceeded
his authority in suspending the laws, but he was charged
with an attempt to overthrow the Church of England to
pave the way for the establishment of the Catholic Church,
of which he was an avowed communicant.   This brought
on a hot contention with the bishops; they refused to comply with an order of the king's council to have the declaration read in the churches after divine service.   James

became highly incensed and committed the bishops to the Tower. Penn had advised moderation and pressed the king to set them at liberty. James obstinately refused all intercession, and Penn, who was known to be a friend of the king, was looked upon with suspicion and shared his unpopularity.

The bishops were brought to trial and acquitted. A great crowd attended the trial, and the result was announced amidst the shouts and plaudits of the people.

This act of James was followed by the desertion of almost every man of consequence at court. His son-in-law, William of Orange, having been secretly invited to come to England as the protector of the Protestant religion, landed at Torbay with an army, and was joined by a part of the king's forces. James made fruitless efforts to gather support, but the defection was universal; under these trying circumstances he was said to have lost self-control, and, being told that his favorite daughter Anne, and her husband, Prince George of Denmark, had joined the invaders, he exclaimed, " God help me ; my own children have forsaken me."

In this sad plight, knowing that his only safety was in flight, he made hasty preparations, and, first sending away the queen and her infant, he soon followed them to France. A convention of the estates of the realm met, and the throne was declared vacant.

In the month of February, 1689, William, Prince of Orange, and Mary were crowned king and queen of Great Britain. After these events Penn's fortunes were greatly changed. In the absence of William, Queen Mary gave ear to the enemies of Penn ; he was charged with being a Jesuit

and with having instigated all the unpopular acts of the late king. A letter from James to Penn, which appealed to him for his assistance, had been intercepted. This was considered sufficient ground for his arrest. He desired to be taken before the king, which was granted. He was asked "why King James wrote to him." Penn replied, "It was impossible for him to prevent James writing to him if he chose; he frankly admitted he loved the late king; he had been under great obligations for favors shown him by James; though he could not agree with him in his acts concerning the state, he would be glad to do him any private service, but he had never had the wickedness to think of assisting to restore the crown which had fallen from his head."

William knew Penn, who had been sent on a mission by King James to consult with him when Prince of Orange, as James desired to have his approval of the declaration of liberty of conscience and repeal of the Test Act before that ill-fated step was taken.

He had a high respect for Penn's liberal views, and in listening to his defence on this occasion was so much impressed by his frankness and sincerity that he would have discharged him at once, but, objection being made by some members of the council, he was required to give bail for his appearance at the next term, at which time no one appeared against him and he was honorably acquitted.

King William's respect for religious toleration and for a representative government were quite as liberal as Penn could wish, and if there had been free intercourse between them they would have arrived at a good understanding and possibly a close friendship.

In the first year of his reign (1689) the Act of Toleration was *passed by Parliament* and was approved by the king. It provided that none of the penal laws should be construed to extend to dissenters who should take the oath to the present government, and a clause was inserted for the relief of members of the Society of Friends, accepting from them instead of an oath a solemn promise to be faithful to the king and queen. The king was called upon to defend the integrity of his government, which was threatened by the invasion of Ireland by James and his French allies. The queen was thus left at the head of affairs in England. Mary was not at ease on the throne of her father; she was suspicious, and the enemies of Penn, who seemed bent on his ruin, brought against him many charges, and one William Fuller accused him with being concerned with others in a conspiracy against the government. On this charge he was again arrested and thrown into prison, but when brought before the court for examination the charge was found to be groundless, and he was set at liberty. " Fuller, the accuser, was denounced in Parliament as a cheat and impostor." To avoid further annoyance Penn found it advisable to withdraw from public life, and for several years lived in seclusion. He could not be idle, but during his retirement wrote several religious works which have still great weight with the people of his faith. About this time his faithful wife died, the wife who had tenderly sympathized with him in all his troubles, and to whom he had addressed that most touching and beautiful letter, on his departure from England for America, which is often quoted. This was indeed a sore affliction and a sad bereavement.

In addition to his domestic grief, the affairs of the government of his province in America, where harmony no longer prevailed, greatly troubled him. Disagreements arose in the Assembly between the members of the Pennsylvania province and those from the territories, as the Delaware counties were called. The population of the province had greatly increased, and, either through jealousy or a feeling that their rights and privileges, especially in the appointment of judges and other officers, were not respected, the members from the territories withdrew, and in 1691 set up a separate government, choosing Markham as lieutenant-governor.

The dissensions in the colonial Assembly were greatly magnified in England, and, pending an inquiry into the state of the proprietary, the government was withdrawn from Penn by the crown, and Benjamin Fletcher, governor of New York, was made captain-general, and assumed the executive control, *reuniting the three lower counties with the province.* Governor Fletcher made a requisition on Pennsylvania for men and money to aid in defending the province of New York against the French and Indians who threatened war, but the Assembly answered that they were at peace with the Indians, and would not vote to contribute either men or money. Taminay or Taminend, the great chief of the Delawares, said, " Indians did not want to have anything to do with war, but to live in peace and concord as they had lived with their neighbors the Friends." Fletcher, finding all his efforts to persuade or control the Assembly unsuccessful, returned to New York, and in the winter of 1693–94 Penn was reinstated. This was brought

about by a change in the king's council, into which several of Penn's influential friends having been appointed, among others Henry Sidney, they lost no time in interceding for him, and when the hardship of his case was brought to the king's attention, William answered, "Mr. Penn is my old acquaintance; he may follow his business as freely as ever; I have nothing to say against him." And in August, 1694, a patent for the restoration of his province was issued. Queen Mary died in the same year.

Penn, having been freed from the vexatious charges that had caused his retirement, would have gone immediately to his province; but in the disturbance and turmoil of recent years the income from his estate at home had greatly diminished, the colony had contributed but little to his support, and his rents were paid grudgingly.

He married a second time in 1696, and spent several years travelling in Germany on a religious mission and in the management of his estate in Ireland. About the first of September, 1699, releasing himself from his affairs at home, he embarked with his wife and young daughter Letitia on board the ship "Canterbury," at Cowes, for America, and after a tedious voyage of three months, arrived safely at Chester in December. The governor brought with him as his secretary James Logan, who became afterwards distinguished in the administration of the colonial government, and for his voluminous correspondence and other writings, which form no inconsiderable part of the colonial history. The proprietor found the number of houses in his favorite city of Philadelphia increased to about seven hundred, with four thousand inhabitants. He was everywhere

greeted with demonstrations of joy by all classes of the
people. He remained in town during the winter, and then
removed to his mansion at Pennsbury, near the falls of
Delaware River, a few miles above Bristol.

This estate comprised six thousand acres of forest, not
more than ten acres cleared and planted, and here the house
was erected on the highest ground, a large building, sixty
feet front and of sufficient depth to afford ample accommo-
dations for the governor's family and guests, of whom there
were many, for he dispensed a liberal hospitality.

The Indians assembled here, and councils were held in
the great hall or on the lawn, where they performed their
canticles or wild dances and were feasted. The ground
sloped to the river, and was handsomely laid out and ter-
raced; vistas were opened through the surrounding wood-
land to give distant views.

Doubtless the governor's table was well supplied. There
was an abundance of game, and, as he wrote to his friends,
"the country was unexceptionable, the air exceeding sweet,
clear, and healthy, and provisions, both meat and drink,
good and plentiful." He had sent to his steward, Harrison,
a skilful gardener, and also a French vigneron, to train the
vines and improve the native grapes and test their quality
for making wine.

He had come prepared to remain a long time in his province, and brought with him saddles for his wife and little
daughter, and also a coach, which was but seldom used, as
travelling was either on horseback by the forest roads or on
the river by boat. He frequently made friendly visits to the
Indian chiefs and sat and talked with the natives, and, it is

said, joined in the athletic sports of the young men. He sometimes took longer journeys to visit the governors of the adjoining provinces, for he greatly desired to maintain friendly intercourse and kindly relations with all his neighbors.

Penn's gentle disposition was often sorely tried by the wrangling and dissensions between the representatives of the province and the members of the Assembly from the three lower counties. He told the latter it had cost him a large sum of money (£3000) to make them one; that it was done at their earnest solicitation, and their desire for a separation from the province at a time when Parliament had under consideration a bill for the abrogation of their charter privileges would be used, by the enemies of the colonial charter as an evidence of their incapacity to administer the government, and that it should be annexed to the crown. The members from the territories were not convinced by his argument. They answered, they were great sufferers by the Act of Union. The governor then told them "they were free to separate, but it must be on amicable terms." The members then withdrew, and at the next meeting of the Assembly, 1701, Delaware was not represented. In 1704 a separate Assembly was elected, and met at New Castle, and from that time the three lower counties continued to hold assemblies under subordinate executive officers, subject to the same proprietary as the province, until the Declaration of Independence in 1776.

The governor's return to England was urged by his friends in London, who wrote him the safety of his charter required that he should give his personal attention to

the proceedings in Parliament. Though he had not contemplated leaving his quiet home in the "wilderness,"
where he would have loved to spend the remainder of his
life, he could not permit, through neglect, his charter to
be abrogated, and he at once made his arrangements to
return.

His last acts in the colony were to grant additional privileges under the charter, and to approve laws in accordance
therewith. "Of political privileges," says Bancroft, "he
conceded all that was desired; he yielded every reasonable
demand that could be expected of his liberality, making his
interest of less consideration than the satisfaction of his
people."

As Penn intended staying in England but a short time, he
would have left his family at Pennsbury, as it was now late
in autumn and he anticipated a rough passage; but his wife
was unwilling to remain, and his little daughter "Tishe"
(Letitia) would not listen to it. Having appointed a council of ten members, which now constituted a branch of the
executive government, he commissioned Colonel Andrew
Hamilton, formerly governor of West New Jersey, lieutenant-governor, and James Logan provincial secretary and
clerk of the council. The management of his estate and
personal affairs he left also with Logan, in whom he had
entire confidence.

James Harrison, his trusty steward, was left in charge of
Pennsbury, and about November 1, with his wife, their
young son "Johnne," born in Philadelphia two months
after their arrival in America, and their daughter Letitia,
the governor took his departure, stopping at New Castle a

few hours to transact some important business and to take a final leave of his friends.

We can well imagine Penn's solicitude for the future of his province on leaving America; he doubtless experienced a deep sense of depression. As he stood on the deck of the "Delmehoy," when she cleared the capes of the Delaware, and the pine forests of Sussex and the sand hills of Cape Cornelius (now Henlopen) sank below the horizon, the land fading out of sight, may not the proprietor, as he turned his face from the west, have had a premonition that he would never see these shores again?

Penn's claim on the three lower counties, as has been stated, rested upon the title conveyed by the two deeds of feoffment of the Duke of York, who held under the king's patent of 1664. Lord Baltimore claimed that this territory was included under the charter which was granted by Charles I. to his ancestor as far back as 1632, and covered not only the whole Delaware and Maryland peninsula, but all the territory north thereof to the fortieth degree of latitude. This would have included the Swedish and Dutch settlements on the river to a point above the mouth of the Schuylkill. (See "Pennsylvania Archives," page 507.) Boundary lines were roughly defined on the maps of Captain John Smith and of Ogilby, to which reference was made by the contestants; in fact, Baltimore's commissioners had accepted as the northern boundary of Maryland a line from the fort at the junction of the Octoraro with the Susquehanna, to a point on the twelve-mile circle north of New Castle town (supposed to be in the fortieth degree of north latitude). (See case stated vol. xvi., "Pennsylvania Ar-

chives," page 500, and also Scharf's "History of Delaware," vol. i., page 113.)

Penn's charter, on the other hand, designated the territory
assigned to him as extending from a point on a circle twelve
miles north of New Castle town to the forty-third degree of
latitude, which, if strictly defined, would have included a
considerable part of New York.   On his first visit to his
province, Penn sought an interview with Charles Calvert,
third Lord Baltimore, and proposed an amicable settlement
of the boundaries; but he found an agreement impracticable,
Baltimore having fully determined to resist his claim, and
for that purpose, in 1684, hastily took his departure for England, and before Penn arrived, in the same year, he appealed
to the government, and the case was referred to the Lords
Commissioners of "Trades and Plantations."   It is stated by
Scharf, on the authority of the *Pennsylvania Magazine*, that
Lord Baltimore, being irritated by Penn's purchase of the
lower counties from the Duke of York, remarked to him in
one of their interviews, "Mr. Penn, you did, I remember,
once propose to me in England that you had offers made
you of that part of Delaware from his Royal Highness
which I lay claim to, but you would not accept because
you knew it was mine."   Penn, he says, "evaded the point,"
and the conference closed.   Some such remark was doubtless made by Baltimore, and elicited the following reply from
Penn in a letter *not quoted by Scharf*, "I must take leave to
refer the Lord Baltimore to his Royal Highness, who is a
prince doubtless of too much honor to keep any man's
right and too much resolution to deliver up his own, and
whose example I am resolved to follow."

Baltimore had indeed claimed the territory on the Delaware when it was held by the Dutch as an appendage of
the New Netherlands, but his claim was strenuously resisted, and the Dutch commissioners, Hermans and Wal-
dron, successfully defended their right of previous possession in a council with commissioners from Maryland that
met on the eastern shore of Maryland in 1659; and the
Dutch continued in possession of their settlements until the
New Netherlands fell into the hands of their English conquerors.

In this controversy Penn relied much on the Dutch
papers, and one of the strongest points in the argument
against Lord Baltimore's claim seems to have been found
by the Dutch commissioners in a clause contained in his
ancestor's patent of 1632 restricting his grant to lands
" uncultivated and inhabited by savages." It was shown
by the Dutch records that the land on the Delaware had
been purchased of the natives, and that settlements had
been made by Christians antecedent to Lord Baltimore's
grant, and therefore, they held, could not be included in it.

O'Callaghan, the historian of " New Netherland," says,
" They, the Dutch, in arguing the boundary question,
evinced tact and shrewdness of a high order; and it is
doubtful, in the long suit which occurred subsequently between the patentees of Maryland and Pennsylvania, if any
solid plea was brought against the Baltimore claim that was
not anticipated in the Dutch papers." This paragraph is
quoted by Scharf in his " History of Delaware."

The Lords Commissioners, after a patient hearing, rendered a decision for an equal division of the territory, and a

decree of the King's Council was issued November, 1685, "That to avoid further differences, the tract of land lying between the Bay of Delaware and Eastern Sea on the one side, and the Chesapeake Bay on the other, be divided into equal parts by a line from the Latitude of Cape Henlopen to the 40° of North Latitude, the Southern boundary of Pennsylvania by Charter, and that the one-half thereof lying toward the Bay of Delaware and the Eastern Sea be adjudged as belonging to his Majesty, and the other half to Lord Baltimore as comprised in his Charter." *

This decree proved to be the basis of a future settlement, though it was not accepted by the Maryland proprietor, whose agents made repeated attempts to obtain possession of the whole territory during this and the subsequent reign.

In 1708, Charles Calvert (third Lord Baltimore) made formal application to Queen Anne to set aside the decree of 1685; but his petition was not granted, and, in fact, resulted in the confirmation of that decree, with instructions "to draw the lines." ("Pennsylvania Archives," page 22.)

Even this did not end the contention, which was renewed from time to time until both William Penn and Charles Calvert had been long dead; then followed a suit in chancery between John, Thomas, and Richard, surviving sons of William Penn, plaintiff, and Charles Calvert (fifth Lord Baltimore), defendant, which continued during the life of Charles and into the time of his successor, Frederick, the last proprietary governor of Maryland, who, growing tired of a contention in which his ancestors had been engaged for

---

* See "Pennsylvania Archives," vol. xvi., pages 19 and 20 for the minute of this decision by the king and his council.

more than a century, came to an understanding with the heirs of Penn in 1760, and accepted as a basis of settlement the agreement that had been executed by the patentees in 1732, in which Cape Henlopen was located south of Cape Cornelius. (" Pennsylvania Archives," vol. xvi., p. 37.) This agreement was afterwards repudiated by Charles, as before stated, but in terms subsequently confirmed by the Chancellor, Lord Hardwicke, in 1750. Commissioners were appointed to determine the true position of Cape Henlopen, and surveyors were employed " to run out, settle and fix all parts of the boundary lines." Charles Mason and Jeremiah Dixon, the surveyors, came to New Castle in 1763; they entered upon the work, in which they were engaged until 1767, and in that year the completion of the survey of the famous Mason and Dixon line may be dated.

The Breviate in Chancery of the Boundary Question in the dispute between the Proprietors of Pennsylvania, John, Thomas, and Richard Penn, and Charles Calvert, of Maryland, fills an entire volume, No. 16, of the " Pennsylvania Archives," published in 1890.

In the spring following Penn's arrival with his family in England, William III. died from injuries caused by being thrown from his horse. In his premature death England lost one of her wisest rulers, doubtless the ablest statesman and soldier of his time.

William was succeeded by Queen Anne, second daughter of James II. On ascending the throne, the queen declared her intention to continue the policy of the late king and to maintain the Act of Toleration.

Penn was again in favor at court; but this was small rec-

ompense for the troubles and worriments by which he was harassed. His income reduced, he found himself straitened in his finances. He had received very little at irregular periods from the province, notwithstanding his large expenditure in its support, which he estimated at twenty thousand pounds. His estate in Ireland was unproductive, and he was charged by the heirs of his former agent in America, Philip Ford, with heavy claims for services and usurious interest on moneys advanced. Penn was not a careful business man, and had neglected to settle with Ford, allowing his account to run for many years. On examining the statements, he found the charges to be so exorbitant that he declined to pay the amount claimed, and proposed to submit the account to friends of his and their own choosing. This the Ford heirs refused to do, and a vexatious suit followed, which went against Penn. On the advice of Isaac Norris and other friends who had examined the Ford account and pronounced it both extortionate and fraudulent, he resisted payment, and, as Norris expressed it, " turned himself over to the Fleet." Penn was under restraint, though comfortably lodged within the prison bounds, for nine months. Finally a compromise was made with the Fords, by which on payment of seven thousand six hundred pounds he received from them a full acquittance of his indebtedness ; this sum was about two-thirds the amount claimed.

During Penn's absence from England his eldest son William had fallen into bad habits and had involved his father in heavy expenses. In the hope of reclaiming the young man, he gave him an interest in the province and sent him to America, at the same time writing Logan to

watch over him and advise him. This Logan did for the father's sake. At first, young Penn, who was well educated and of handsome presence, won many friends by his good deportment. As the prospective heir to the proprietary he was elected a member of the Council, as was also Roger Mompesson (Judge of the Admiralty of New York and New Jersey), whom Penn had commissioned to act as Chief Justice of the province. In a letter to Logan dated September, 1703, introducing Roger Mompesson, Penn refers to him as being held in high respect "by the Judiciary in England," and adds, "I have granted him a commission for Chief Justice in case the people will take hold of such an opportunity as Government in America has never had before of an English lawyer, and encourage him by a proper salary of at least one hundred, if not one hundred and fifty pounds per annum."

Subsequently, in a letter to this distinguished jurist, dated 12 mo. 17, 1704, Penn acknowledges he is under great obligations for good legal advice given the lieutenant-governor, Evans, in relation to bills presented in the Assembly adverse to the proprietary. He also allowed him from his private purse twenty pounds at each session he should come from New York to sit as Chief Justice in the province,—a pleasing addition to his meagre salary.

His son William's restraint was of short duration. In less than a year he resumed his former intemperate habits, and in company with the young lieutenant-governor visited a tippling house late at night and got into a disgraceful brawl. The town officers were called in, "and the lights having been extinguished, the quality of the young men did not save them from receiving a sound drubbing."

William, losing the respect of the leading men in the colony, resolved to return to England. Before doing so he sold his estate, seven thousand acres on the banks of the Schuylkill, for eight hundred and fifty pounds. This tract now constitutes Norristown Township.

The incident just related shows the wisdom of Penn's reply to those who queried why he gave to the people so much liberty in his charter. " For the matter of liberty, I purpose that which is extraordinary, to leave myself and my successors no power of doing mischief, that the will of one man may not hinder the good of a whole country."

Governor Penn had experienced so much trouble in managing the affairs of his province that he was prepared to receive with favor the advice of Logan and other friends in America to dispose of the government to the crown. The knowledge that the secretary possessed of Penn's financial troubles, and the difficulties he met with in obtaining from the Assembly the relief which the proprietor's care and services justly entitled him to, had doubtless brought him to this conclusion.

Penn had long felt that he could not live in England and retain his influence over the Assembly. The emigration to the province had greatly increased, and many of the colonists were either churchmen or dissenters of different views from the Quakers. Parties had been formed, and it would probably require the strong arm of the home government to keep in check the bitter feeling that had already been disclosed by the debates in the Assembly between the discordant elements of which it was composed. He determined to surrender the government of the province

to the queen, if liberal terms were offered and the rights and liberties of the people under the charter were not impaired.

A proposition was made through his friends and counsel which led to an offer by the crown of £12,000, which was accepted by Penn; but delay was occasioned by his efforts to secure to the colonists the privileges of the charter; upon the observance of these by the queen's government he insisted. How heavily this transaction bore upon his mind, already burdened by cares and disappointments, of which the conduct of his son and the ingratitude of a clamorous and exacting son-in-law were not the least, cannot be known.

While the negotiations with the queen's cabinet for the sale of his government were in progress, he was stricken with a fever, from which he partially recovered, and was writing a letter to the secretary of his province, James Logan, when his hand was arrested by a sudden attack of paralysis. This letter was dated 24th of 5th month, 1712, and was the last Governor Penn ever wrote. The first stroke was followed by others, which rendered him incapable of transacting any business, and arrested further proceedings for the transfer of his American government.

In the words of his faithful and affectionate wife, he became as one "translated;" troubled no more by the cares that she, poor woman, inherited, his memory of past events obliterated, his mind in repose and innocent contentment, he seemed still to enjoy the company and discourse of old friends, "as appeared by his loving deportment to all that came near him."

William Penn lived in this condition of mind, though gradually weakening, for nearly six years. The end came on the 30th day of July, 1717, and on the 5th of August his body was committed to the earth at Jordon, in Buckinghamshire, in the presence of a large concourse of Friends and others who honored his virtues and noble deeds.

It is remarkable that two distinguished authors, T. Babington Macaulay and George Bancroft, historians of the same period, born in the same year (1800), the one educated at Cambridge University, England, the other at Harvard University, Cambridge, Massachusetts, leaving their respective colleges with the highest honors and subsequently the recipients of greater honors from their respective governments, should have differed so essentially in forming their estimates of the character of William Penn.

In the second volume of his " History of England," Macaulay relates the stirring events of the time of James II. in a style as free and unrestrained as his facile pen would have delineated the characters and events of an historical novel ; his heroes are clothed in a halo of light, while those who come under his condemnation are unmercifully denounced and held up to public scorn as chargeable with moral obliquity. Unfortunately for Penn, he was a friend of the king, and shared with him this author's displeasure. Old charges against Penn, brought by his enemies, with no foundation in truth, to some of which I have alluded in this sketch, were raked up and revamped by Macaulay and published as facts, apparently because he wished them to be so, with many insidious gibes upon the personality and character of the " courtly Quaker," whom he represents as "weak-

headed" and "easily seduced." To say that the admirers
of Penn were astonished when the volume was published
is to put it mildly. Criticisms appeared in many reviews,
charging Macaulay with prejudice and inaccuracy in his
quotations, carelessness in not verifying his statements, and
with inconsistency in his conclusions. Among others, W.
E. Forster, in his preface to an edition of Clarkson's "Life
of Penn," says, "It would be hard to find any other history
where the very virtues of a man are thus twisted into
grounds for the most injurious attacks upon his character."

Bancroft, on the other hand, in the second volume of his
"History of the United States" (old edition), after passing
the highest encomiums on Penn for his self-sacrificing labor
in founding a colony, "free for all mankind, in an age which
had seen a popular revolution shipwreck popular liberty
among selfish factions," says that "England to-day con-
fesses his sagacity and is doing honor to his genius. He
came too soon for success, and he was aware of it. After
more than a century, the laws which he reproved began
gradually to be repealed, and the principle which he developed, sure of immortality, is slowly but firmly asserting its
power over the legislation of Great Britain."

"Every charge of hypocrisy, of selfishness, every form of
reproach, every ill name, from Tory and Jesuit to blasphemer
and infidel, has been used against Penn, but the candor of
his character always triumphed over calumny."

PAPERS OF THE HISTORICAL SOCIETY OF DELAⅠ

XXV.

DEDICATION

OF THE

CRANE HOOK CHURCH MONUM

OCTOBER 17, 1896.

UNDER THE AUSPICES OF THE HISTORICAL SO
OF DELAWARE.

THE HISTORICAL SOCIETY OF DELAWARE,

WILMINGTON.

1899.

DEDICATION

OF THE

CRANE HOOK CHURCH MONUMENT.

THE committee appointed for the various purposes pertaining to .the commemoration of the site of Crane Hook
Church have the honor to report the final performance of
the sundry duties with which they were charged; and, pursuant to the instructions received at the last meeting, we
present herewith a copy of the historical paper read, with
reports of the remarks of the several speakers made at the
final dedicatory exercises, which are here incorporated with
such a connected and detailed, yet brief, account of the
whole proceeding from the beginning, as is deemed a substantial compliance with the wishes expressed for a complete
record and souvenir of the whole event.

The movement originated in 1894, when, at the Society's
regular April meeting of that year, Mr. Pennock Pusey presented some fragments of brick he had found on the site of
Crane Hook Church, which he accompanied with a few
remarks expressive of regret at the rapidly perishing relics
of the unusually eventful and interesting history of which
our immediate vicinity was the scene.

The subject at once interested the meeting, and elicited a

general discussion, which terminated with the appointment of a committee, consisting of Pennock Pusey, Hon. L. E. Wales, and E. T. Canby, to confer with the present owners of the historic spot with a view to setting up some suitable mark to designate the site of the ancient place of worship.

The appointment of the committee was accompanied with a request that its chairman, Mr. Pusey, should prepare and read a paper on the subject of Crane Hook Church. In compliance with such request a paper was written embracing a summary of early ecclesiastical history on the Delaware, with a review of the times and incidents preceding and attending the building of the primitive edifice, which was read to an unusually large and attentive audience on the 18th of June, 1894, and published by the Society the following year.

With growing public interest in the subject, the committee then applied themselves anew to the performance of their duties, towards which the first requisite was to secure the right or privilege of erecting the proposed memorial on the church site, from its present owners. Here they encountered at the outset a serious obstacle. The historic spot was found to belong to the unsettled estate of Richard Jackson, some of whose heirs, dreading perhaps a possible prejudice or complication of their interests, were, for a time, reluctant to consent to the erection of the proposed stone upon their land. But through the friendly interposition and influence of one of our members, George A. Elliott, Esq., attorney for the estate, the written consent of the several heirs—viz., Samuel A. Jackson, Lucy J. Jackson, Elizabeth Jackson, and John J. Jackson—was finally obtained to the placing of the stone on the church site, for which the Society tendered

thanks by formal resolution, an attested copy whereof was duly presented to the said owners of the property.

Having thus obtained the requisite permission, your committee, at the March meeting of the present year, submitted from Mr. George L. Jones, stone-cutter, two different plans of the proposed memorial, with specifications as to character and dimensions, which Mr. Joseph Jenkins, with characteristic liberality, guaranteed should be furnished the Society at a considerable reduction from the price named.

After due examination by the members present, one of the two plans was approved, and the committee was authorized to cause the stone to be prepared and planted upon the church site. The adopted plan provided for a single shaft of Brandywine granite, fifteen inches square, with proportioned breadth and height of base, the whole to stand about four feet above ground, topped with a peaked central apex, and with a widened under-base to be sunk over two feet beneath the ground surface; three sides of the upper stone to be undressed, the fourth to be dressed and bear the inscription, "This stone marks the site of Crane Hook Church, built 1667. Erected by the Historical Society of Delaware, 1896."

Bishop Coleman suggested that there should be suitable ceremonies in formal dedication of the stone, whereupon he was added to the committee, which, thus constituted, were fully authorized to do all things necessary to consummate the matter, and to finally name a day and prepare a programme for the dedication.

But various causes seemed to conspire for further delay, among which was an exceptional and prolonged spell of op-

· pressively hot weather. Yet, late in August the stone was
put in place, and with the approach of autumnal coolness,
the 17th of October, A.D. 1896, was fixed upon, and a programme arranged for the dedicatory proceedings.   In these
a cherished idea was to recognize a sort of historic sequence.
At least there seemed a propriety in linking the past and
present in historic continuity, so far as to assign the conduct
of the strictly religious part of the exercises to the rector
and choir of the Old Swedes' Church as the direct successor
of Crane Hook Church, while with much of the same idea
a lady from one of our old historic families, who is at once
a member of our Society and of the Colonial Dames, was
selected for the ceremonial unveiling of the memorial stone.

The transportation of invited attendants was a difficult
problem; and the committee wish here to acknowledge
their indebtedness to Henry C. Conrad, Esq., for his wise
practical suggestions, and especially for the prompt and satisfactory arrangements made by him with the Wilmington
and Northern Railroad Company, by which attendants were
landed by rail within a short and pleasant walk of the
grounds.   Cards of invitation had been issued to the members and friends of the Society, and in addition to those
who took the train provided, people went in their private
vehicles and travelled afoot and on bicycles, making altogether a fine representative assemblage of one hundred and
fifty to two hundred of our most intelligent and worthy citizens, who gathered about the spot where their forefathers
had worshipped more than two and a quarter centuries before.   The audience would probably have been larger but
for threatening weather near the appointed time of meeting.

Soon, however, the clouds thinned out, and left a mild and pleasant atmosphere of hazy neutrality, which, except for a fresh river breeze, was all that could be desired for the occasion.

In accordance with the printed programmes, widely distributed among attendants, the exercises began with the singing, at about 2.30 o'clock P.M., of the hymn led by the choir of the Old Swedes' Church and joined in by the assemblage, which here follows:

O God, our help in ages past,
   Our hope for years to come,
Our shelter from the stormy blast
   And our eternal home:

Under the shadow of Thy throne
   Thy saints have dwelt secure;
Sufficient is Thine arm alone,
   And our defence is sure.

Before the hills in order stood,
   Or earth received her frame,
From everlasting Thou art God,
   To endless years the same.

A thousand ages in Thy sight
   Are like an evening gone;
Short as the watch that ends the night
   Before the rising sun.

Time, like an ever-rolling stream,
   Bears all its sons away;
They fly, forgotten, as a dream
   Dies at the opening day.

O God, our help in ages past,
Our hope for years to come,
Be Thou our guide while life shall last,
And our eternal home.

Following this opening hymn and introductory general services, Hon. Charles B. Lore, President of ciety, speaking in an explanatory way and in an appr and happy vein of congratulation, said :

"We are gathered here to-day to unveil and dec memorial stone which marks the spot on which st Crane Hook Church about two hundred and thirt ago.

"As President of the Historical Society of De under whose auspices this stone has been erected, pleasure to note that this day marks a new era Society's field of usefulness. Hitherto the work ha to gather historical treasures of every character, safe-keeping, carefully put them away in the S home in the old historic First Presbyterian Church ing, at Tenth and Market Streets, in the City c mington.

" No effort has heretofore been made by stone, ta memorial to mark within the State limits histori the birthplace of her great men, or for the preserv historic buildings or homes. Kindred societies i States have ventured in this field and accomplishec good; to-day we are following in their footsteps.

" To most of us Crane Hook Church was somewl myth, associated with our early Swede and Dutch if thought of at all. Many Delawareans did n

know that there had ever been such a church. The
scholarly historic paper of our fellow-member, Pennock
Pusey, Esq., recently read before the Society, first awakened interest in this subject. To his indefatigable labor we
are indebted mainly for the successful completion of this
first effort to mark for coming generations spots of supreme
historic interest. He as chairman of the committee of the
Society which had the erection of this stone specially in
charge, from inception to this hour of completion, has
labored unceasingly. It is a significant fact that he, like
many of the audience and those who have taken a deep
interest in this matter, is a member of the Society of
Friends, like their great leader William Penn who gave
fifty pounds sterling to the building of Old Swedes' Church.
They have been earnest workers in preserving and crystal-
lizing the religious influences and memories that marked
our early settlement. Associated with Mr. Pusey on the
committee as helpful co-workers are Bishop Coleman,
ready in every good word and work, and Judge Wales.
George A. Elliott, Esq., has been active in obtaining the
consent of the owners of the land for the erection of the
stone. Henry C. Conrad, Esq., has aided largely by his
timely advice and practical suggestions. To these gentlemen and to the owners of the soil, descendants of the
original Swede settlers, we tender our grateful thanks for
the work so well done.

"It is fitting that we should keep fresh the memory of the
godly lives of our ancestors, who in the wilderness of this
then new world laid deep and broad the foundations of free
government; basing it, as this spot proclaims, upon the

truths of God's Holy Word, and an abiding faith in human
development. The church that stood upon this spot
marked, too, a new departure in the more liberal and
Christian acceptance of those Bible truths and a deeper
faith in their practical benefit upon the public welfare; for
the attendants here so far rose above jealousies of sect and
country that two languages and two denominations here
more or less merged, and sometimes three nationalities here
joined harmoniously in one worship.

"I wish we could reverse the kaleidoscope of time and
look back upon this spot just as it was two hundred and
thirty years ago. The little log church, of which not a
vestige remains, stood on the edge of primeval forests
planted by the finger of God and untouched by the hand of
man. An occasional red-skin perchance peeped from his
covert upon the sombre but gayly-dressed mixed Swedes
and Dutch, as on Sabbath mornings, by boat and by forest
path, they came here to worship their fathers' God. The
broad Delaware, now bearing the commerce of the great
city of Penn, was then unruffled save by an occasional ba-
teau or canoe, or the small craft of the settlers; sometimes
as an object of wonder and joy, now and then a ship from
across the ocean rested on her waters, bearing messengers
of love and material help to the emigrants from the old
world. No dykes or banks kept back the tide, the water
swept up almost to our feet, and the submerged marshes
gave to the river the breadth of an inland sea. Looking
out upon the prospect to-day, how marvellously has the
scene changed! This development has been along the line
of the good old ways, of the simple, sturdy, and God-

fearing people who built this church and worshipped on this spot, and who founded for us a commonwealth upon the banks of the Delaware, the corner-stone of which was faith in God and faith in man. How fitting, then, that we should mark this spot!"

First following this introductory address by President Lore was the impressive prayer offered by the Rev. H. Ashton Henry, rector of Holy Trinity (Old Swedes') Church.

After prayer came the ceremonial presentation and unveiling of the stone. The chairman of the Memorial Committee, standing on one side of the stone, formally presented the same on behalf of the committee to the Historical Society of Delaware, through its President, standing on the other, whereupon the presented stone was deftly unveiled by Mrs. Charles G. Rumford, standing between giver and receiver, and formally accepted by the President in behalf of the Historical Society of Delaware.

The chairman of the Memorial Committee, Pennock Pusey, Esq., then read the following historical paper:

"FELLOW-MEMBERS OF THE HISTORICAL SOCIETY, LADIES AND GENTLEMEN,—I need hardly say I am glad to greet you all upon this occasion: and I congratulate you upon the charming weather and all the favoring circumstances under which we meet. The waning season, the fading aspect of nature, the struggling mellow light, and the pensive, half-sombre atmosphere encourage revery and invoke at once tender and admonitory suggestions which seem in keeping with the occasion, while surely the bright

autumned foliage, the tranquil beauty of river and sky, and
the dreamy allurement of the peaceful fields newly garbed
in grassy freshness should serve to attune our hearts to
glad content; and indeed our whole environment seems in
harmony with the worshipful traditions linked with this
quiet spot. Let us hope that these gentle influences, in
which there is ever a latent incentive to worthy effort as
well as a silent rebuke of ignoble purpose, may, on this fair
day of golden October, specially lend their kindly aid to
consecrate the modest services for which we are here assembled.

"In this busy age, with its thirst for quick results, we are
apt to underrate the slow-paced past. Amid the easeful
peace and plenty of to-day we are all too prone to take our
proud heritage as a matter of course, to somewhat confound
the relative merits of sowers and reapers,—of pursuit and
possession, and to overlook those toils, trials, and sacrifices
of an ancestral past which made possible the realization of
the present.

"It is therefore well to turn occasionally from the achieved
and vaunted results of to-day to the modest beginnings of
colonial times. We may thus at once find a just gauge
of an astounding progress, and juster cause for gratefully
recognizing the struggles of our forefathers. They indeed
laid broad and deep the foundation of our national fabric,
and taught us how to rear thereon a secure superstructure.
In their whole career—alike through their wise and unwise
deeds—we may learn an invaluable lesson, a lesson which
exemplifies the immutable law that couples duty with oppor-
-tunity, and rewards travail with triumph.

"Of such early tribulations our little State had her full share. Involved deeply with the pains of parturition, they embraced the changeful, yet formative struggles pertaining to her actual birth and start as a separate commonwealth. Perhaps, indeed, no State of our national Union has undergone so many changes of sovereignty as Delaware; and it may be doubted if any equal area is marked with more of local color and varied interest in its early history. The Puritan colonists of New England, the Dutch in New York, and the Quakers in Pennsylvania furnish a colonial history largely occupied with dealings between the native red men on the one hand and the European home governments on the other, mostly unaffected by changes in such governing powers abroad, until all alike became subject to the English crown.

"But the narrow territory now known as the State of Delaware, while not exempt from bloody experience with the Indians, was under control, first, of the Dutch in 1631; second, of the Swedes in 1638; third, of the Dutch again in 1655; fourth, of the English in 1664; fifth, of the Dutch again in 1673; sixth, of the English again in 1674; and seventh, of the Quaker government of William Penn in 1682; while during most of this long period it was also sought to be governed by Lord Baltimore, who claimed that his Maryland royal grant not only included the whole upper peninsula between the Chesapeake and Delaware Bays, but extended eastward to the Atlantic Ocean. This claim caused a prolonged controversy between the heirs of Lord Baltimore and those of William Penn, the partial compromise of which was a final agreement upon the exist-

ing western boundary line of Delaware, equally dividing
the peninsula between the respective claimants. The territory thus bounded on the west had been sold to William
Penn by the Duke of York, and as its northern limit had
been marked by the circular boundary to better define the
vaguely disputed division between Penn's granted province
and the duke's prior domain, while even its eastern water
boundary has been involved in the litigation pertaining to
the control of river pilotage, it will be seen how our little
State has been the child of contention and its limits and
shape affected by adjustments between rival claimants.

"But a more vital event—one involving the State's very
existence—was the so-called De Vries settlement near
Lewes in the year 1631. The royal grant to Lord Baltimore in 1632 included all of what is now Delaware, excepting such portion as had been settled by 'Christian' people,
so called; and the actual occupation and culture of the
land by De Vries's Dutch settlement of the preceding year
was adjudged to have exempted the Delaware shore from
absorption in the territory of Maryland, and started a first
separate existence for Delaware. Upon such foundation
a loose and wavering system of government, an odd commingling of arbitrary rule and crude paternalism succeeded
through the subsequent troubles attending changes of
ruling powers abroad, until home legislation was granted
under William Penn, when the three lower counties gradually emerged from their half-nebulous condition, and
finally gained a completed autonomy through the wel-
coming recognition of the Continental Congress, which
sought aid from every source in the ardor of the struggle

for just independence. The other colonies had an existence in some form prior to the war of the Revolution;
Delaware alone owed her full statehood to that heroic
struggle for liberty. It was a liberty coupled with sovereignty; and the State which thus achieved her maturity and
her freedom by the same great event is in a peculiar sense a
child of the Revolution. Hence it was a fitting and graceful.
acceptance of the double endowment when Delaware led
off as the first of the thirteen States to adopt that honored
Constitution which united them in one grand national
government.

" Such was the fortunate outcome of Delaware's struggle
for life. Amid the rival claims of hungry and powerful
neighbors the three counties had long maintained a pre-
carious existence, wavering between partial independence,
attempted subjection to Maryland, and voluntary union with
Pennsylvania. At the outset, except for the briefly worded
reservation in the royal grant to Lord Baltimore, our narrow area would have been absorbed in Maryland, and we
would have lacked the first requisite of a territorial foothold, while subsequently, but for Penn's order for the actual
survey and marking of the nominal circular division line
between his granted province and his purchased territory,
followed by his friendly concession of separate legislation
for the latter, we would have formed part of Pennsylvania.

" Happily, these long weary conflicts, these formative and
perhaps disciplinary struggles for birthright and growth,
have long been triumphantly over; and we are assembled
here to-day with a more restful object. The occasion is
more retrospective than prospective. Linked rather with

memory than hope, its tendency is more towards quieting thought than exciting action. Yet to venerate the worthy past is to scarcely more conserve achieved results than to incite future progress. Towards progress indeed, past or future, there has been, there can be, no more essential factor than earnest religious conviction. More than any other agency, it stimulated the country's early settlement, and it continues to promote the valid prosperity of our great nation. Religious devotion allied with public virtue has long been recognized by masterly thinkers as at once the stablest basis, the worthiest incentive, and the most conservative force in the maintenance of free popular government.

" It is this view of the subject that lends special interest to the worshipping places of our colonial forefathers. Nor perhaps should we here feel the less interest from the fact that while the earliest settlement in most of the other colonies resulted from religious persecution at home, in Delaware it resulted from religious protection and direct promotion by the pious home government in Europe. In either case most of the ancient church structures left by their immigrant builders have passed away, and not infrequently their very sites have faded from the memory of their descendants. It is to aid in the rescue from such oblivion of one of those sacred spots that we are here to-day. We unveil here a stone which marks the site of Crane Hook Church, built in the year 1667. It is a small, unpretending memorial in keeping with the rude simplicity of the primitive structure which stood on this spot; being, as you observe, of native undressed granite, as the edifice it

commemorates was of native unhewn logs. Yet humble as was the crude little structure, the time and circumstances of its erection clothe its history with peculiar interest. It should be remembered how early was this period in the then comparatively new country. The broadly clustering neighborhood settlements, of which this Crane Hook was the centre, much preceded the Quaker emigration to Pennsylvania, the first of the ten Swedish expeditions across the Atlantic having reached here over forty-four years before the arrival of William Penn in 1682, while the erection of Crane Hook Church was fifteen years before Penn's surveyors staked out the streets and squares of Philadelphia, and when only Svenson's partially cleared farm and an unbroken forest beyond jointly occupied the site of the now teeming City of Brotherly Love. Of course this was long before there was any Wilmington, which was not begun until sixty-five years later, its predecessor and nucleus, the little Swedish Christinehamn, a small cluster of rude cabins about Fort Christina, having been scattered when that post was captured by the Dutch, twelve years before. New Amstel, its name but lately changed to that of New Castle, was then a small collection chiefly of Dutch gabled houses, and the only place that could fairly be called a town or village throughout the entire westerly side of the Delaware River and Bay, while on the easterly shore few or no settlements had yet been commenced above the latitude of Chester, then known as Upland.

"Coming after the little chapel built within the walls, and as part of Fort Christina, constructed in 1638, and following the church erected on Tinicum Island in 1646, Crane

2

Hook was the third structure for regular worship erected on the river or bay. In addition, according to the historian Acrelius, there had been at an earlier date a small building used at Sandhook, afterwards New Castle, for occasional worship, which stood for a short time, while to meet growing wants soon after the building of this Crane Hook Church, the old block-house at Wicaco, in what is now lower Philadelphia, was fitted up for temporary worship. So we need not doubt the reverent, God-fearing character of the people who thus early, amid the exactions of pioneer life, made comparatively so much provision for their religious needs.

"But while the two regular churches preceding Crane Hook had received more or less aid directly from the Swedish home government, this one was built by the unaided efforts of the struggling worshippers, probably without the knowledge of their kindred in fatherland. For nearly thirty years had elapsed since they left their old homes in Europe, and with two changes in governing powers and the various vicissitudes of the time, the old country had well-nigh lost sight of its distant colony in the new.

"Moreover, there was historic significance as well as religious convenience in the building of Crane Hook Church. For the little structure was erected by the united contributions of both Swedish and Dutch settlers for their combined worship. Twelve years had elapsed since the Dutch conquest, and during this period there had been such commingling of the languages, sympathies, and habits of the two peoples as permitted of a union of their resources for

a common worship. Thus the building of Crane Hook Church was a definite way-mark in the fusion of conquerors and conquered, marking their progressive assimilation as one people. Thus far in the New World they had been more or less enemies,—thenceforth they were to be friends. On this spot stood a rude structure indeed, of only simple, primitive logs; but a very temple it was, with a beauty of its own. For it meant that brotherly enmity had given place to Christian fraternity. You observe the grassy undulations of the pleasant environment, suggesting the olden peace of pastoral beauty. But in this Christian harmony was promise of the richer peace, the deeper beauty, wherein neighborly strife is lost in the united worship of a common God of love.

"Next to New Castle, the three places most frequently mentioned in the old records are Altona, or Christine, now Wilmington, on the one hand, Swanwyck, now New Castle, on the other, and Crane Hook, midway between them; and it was this intermediate position that, pursuant to the growing desire for religious combination, led to the selection of this Crane Hook as the suitable place for the church of their united worship. For it was most convenient, not merely for the localities named, but for the more distant communities surrounding, of which this spot was nearly the exact available centre. Its water-side situation was essential; for, travelling being then done chiefly by water, the church was as available to the more distant settlements on the river and its navigable tributaries as to nearer places not immediately on the watercourses. It is not difficult to imagine the broad river enlivened with approaching boats on

a bright Sabbath morning, or to see the people trudging
hither over the fields and by inland paths skirting the les-
sening woods. To this common centre they came from
every direction. They came from many miles up and down
and across the broad Delaware. With low tide they sailed
down the Christiana and through the creek's mouth around
on the river. With high water they boated over the submerged marshes to points of fast land near the Lobdell Car-
Wheel Works and the old Garasche place, now Eden Park,
and thence walked to the church, while with the stormiest
weather or icy navigation on the Christiana attendants
crossed by the old ferry near the present Third Street bridge
and made a landward circuit to the church. From New
Castle they came both by water in front and by land in the
rear, and from Swanwyck and various inland places they
approached by winding and half-beaten roadways all con-
verging into the hedge-bordered lane you observe there
running down to the river. This passage-way bears evidence
of its ancient existence, and tradition avers that it was the
olden avenue used both for access to the ferry across the
Delaware and for inland travel to the church, and that
church boats were moored near its foot to a cluster of trees
at the water's edge, where the buttonwood now grows there.

"In the then stage of transition from primitive to more
civic life there were doubtless odd comminglings of various
animal skins with woven goods in the costumes of the people; and as thus arrayed the flaxen-haired Swedes and
broad-faced Dutch converged here from land and water,
they must have presented a pleasing and picturesque spec-
tacle, while to them church-going was probably the privi-

leged event of their rough, simple lives. Amid the isolation
and hardships of the early colonial times our forefathers
were too much engrossed with the urgent practical necessities of the situation to indulge in much or frequent personal
intercourse. With much labor and little means, with religious restraint, and the lack of modern appliances, they had
little time, taste, or opportunity for even rational amusement;.
and hence, as is usual and natural in such cases, all social
requisites were embraced in the church assemblies. These
were at once occasions for worship, entertainment, and neighborly greetings, and afforded an indispensable opportunity
for exchanging views about crops and colonial affairs, and
all the momentous concerns of frontier life. May we not,
therefore, indulge the fancy that people of various nationalities and all conditions being thus drawn with a common
purpose to this common centre, chatted in picturesque groups
on the grassy space between the rustic church and the
stately buttonwood which reared its protecting arms over
the humble edifice? That lofty tree indeed, towering in
impressive grandeur above all surrounding objects as if to
offer both secular and sacred guidance, served as a beacon
alike to mariners on the river and worshippers on the shore,
and hither from far and near flocked the sun-browned settlers in their curiously mixed garments. Here, mingled
with the fast merging Swedes and Dutch and their faster
commingling descendants, we may imagine, were a few of
the newly dominating English, apparelled in later fashion,
while even the dusky savage, in his red blanket and full
array of paint, beads and feathers, occasionally lured in
simple wonder to the pale-face's shrine of the Great Spirit,

but lurking aside in his struggle between the curiosity he
disdained and the stolid dignity he inherited, peeped for a
time upon the scene from his covert, and at last stalked
forth to join the assembled throng. And does not a more
loving and home-spun sense of those primitive days summon
before us a glowing picture of such neighborly assemblages,
suggesting that here near the church entrance, under the
grassy shade of the wide-spreading buttonwood, the talk
of colonial goodman and dame, alternating with religious
themes, was wont to grow eloquent over the prophecy of
the tobacco yield, the prospect of the beaver catch, and the
ravages of wolves, intermingled with busier and gentler reflections on sewing necessities, the cure of children's ailments, the relative merits of cookery and of domestic management generally, all giving later place to the more zealous
talk of the plans and prospects for that coveted grand new
stone edifice, then a fond dream, which their descendants have
seen realized in the nearly two hundred years' existence of
what we all lovingly know as our 'Old Swedes' Church'?

"Such were the surroundings and fancied scenes of this
ancient place of worship; and here in the centre, on the
highest swell of this gentle ridge, stood the primitive church
building. As before stated, it was constructed of logs, and
it rested upon large foundation-stones at the corners and
sides. Our memorial stone has been placed at the supposed
western wall of the church structure, at the edge of the depression marking the filled-up cellar of the sexton's house
or parsonage adjoining on the west, and there a little farther
west still lingers a portion of the stump of the majestic
buttonwood, whose wide-reaching branches afforded ample

shade alike to the church and its care-takers and to the people assembled here for divine worship. Here the settlers from a widely extended circuit gathered to a common centre with a common purpose. Such purpose the humble building subserved for a period of thirty-two years, during which divine services were conducted within its walls by three regularly ordained ministers, the Revs. Messrs. Lock, Fabricius, and Bjork. The last named was one of the three clergymen sent over by the Swedish government upon the revival of its interest in the long-neglected settlement. Here he began his American ministry on the 11th of July, 1697, one hundred and ninety-nine years ago, and here he conducted the last service in the log edifice on the fourth Sunday after Easter in 1699. From here this Rev. Mr. Bjork pushed forward the then very difficult and peculiar labors demanded for the erection of the existing stone edifice widely known as the ' Old Swedes' Church,' the direct successor of Crane Hook, and here he wrote many of those interesting church records translated by Dr. Horace Burr for the Historical Society of Delaware.

" This was the day of modest undertakings, but this Crane Hook Church was one of the beginnings of an end which is not yet. Its last results are destined to an incalculable reach in the possibilities of the future. Thus the very site of such humble beginnings is worthy of due commemoration. And surely we honor ourselves when we seek to honor the places and appliances of a past which made possible the prouder results of the present, and gives yet larger promise for the future.

"A nameless pathos lingers about a spot which has known

ncere worship. It exhales a plaintive reverence and an
npressive silence; a mute eloquence pleads its tender sanc-
ty to loyal descendants of pious ancestors; and if outward
'mbols are gone, if vanished edifice and silenced voices
·eathe sadly of the past, let us cherish the hope of a more
.orious future in the abiding and helpful faith voiced by
ιe poet Whittier, that

> ‘The world that time and sense have known
> Falls off and leaves us God alone.’ ”

After the reading of this paper the choir led the assem-
age in singing the following hymn :

> Now thank we all our God,
>   With heart and hands and voices !
> Who wondrous things hath done,
>   In Whom His world rejoices;
> Who from our mother's arms
>   Hath blessed us on our way
> With countless gifts of love,
>   And still is ours to-day.
>
> Oh, may this bounteous God
>   Through all our life be near us !
> With ever joyful hearts
>   And blessed peace to cheer us;
> And keep us in His grace
>   And guide us when perplexed,
> And free us from all ills
>   In this world and the next.

It was a source of regret that ex-President Hon. Leonard
Wales, from whom remarks were expected, was unable
be present. The other speakers announced, Bishop
ıleman and Dr. Horace Burr, spoke in a pertinent and
:tructive manner, and Rev. Frederic Doerr and Hon. I. C.

Grubb, in response to calls on the spot, made interesting addresses. The reports of the remarks of all these gentlemen follow in the order named.

REMARKS OF BISHOP COLEMAN.

" It gives to one occupying such a position as, in the Providence of God, I but too unworthily occupy, peculiar satisfaction to share in the very interesting proceedings belonging to this day and place.

" For we are here not to mark the site of some temple of business or pleasure, not even of the arts and sciences; but of a rude structure used exclusively for the worship of Almighty God.

" In this age of devotion to secular things, and of, I fear, a growing indifference on the part of many as to the duty and privilege of such worship, it is reassuring and helpful to see, at the invitation of a Society such as ours, so goodly a gathering of the best people of Wilmington and its vicinity to do honor to our forefathers, who erected here for God a house to which His name should especially belong.

" It emphasizes the fact that in this deed of theirs they did something worthy of lasting remembrance. It is an evidence of a regard for God and sacred things whose significance, I am sure, some of us are only too glad to recognize. I am glad to find, too, that this worthy assemblage is not confined to adults. It affords me pleasure to see so many young people here on this occasion. Age we necessarily associate with the venerated past, but in youth is our hope of the future, and I see promise in their presence here, while we may well feel it a source of gratification when

people of all ages and interests representing the best elements of society thus join' in honoring the memory of religious ancestors.   The builders of Crane Hook Church early realized what some nowadays are so slow to confess, —namely, how of necessity the due worship of God is intimately associated with the stability and real prosperity of every community.

"This they proved even at the point of considerable personal inconvenience, as will be evident enough to any one surveying the very spot where we are now standing.

"I wonder, if there were no place of worship to-day nearer yon fair city than could be found right here, whether or not its inhabitants would come hither to church in the same proportion of numbers and with the same regularity as did those worthy settlers of the seventeenth century whom we are now especially commemorating?

"One of the descendants of a former owner of this very ground * has written to me very feelingly of the grand old buttonwood-tree † which for more than two hundred years guarded and marked this sacred site. 'It was,' as he remarks, 'a conspicuous object from river as well as land. The navigators upon the Delaware used it to aid them in their course, and the people of the Jersey shore steered their frail barks by its outstretched branches.'

·"So, too, we cannot but believe the founders of this little unpretending church found within its walls the grace and

---

* Mr. J. Cloud Elliott, who has still in his possession a deed of gift of this plot of ground by his great-grandfather, Lucas Stidham, to his sons, one hundred and fifty-eight years ago.

† Quite nine feet in diameter.

inspiration by which they were enabled to pursue their spiritual course through the tempestuous waves of this troublesome world.

"It is well, therefore, that we should set up this memorial stone to perpetuate their faith and constancy, and to remind all who may look upon it of the ennobling and enduring character of all true worship of Him 'Who is the same yesterday, to-day, and forever.'"

REMARKS OF DR. HORACE BURR.

"As we are reminded by the waning afternoon and by the President that our remarks should be brief, and as the ground has been well covered by those who have spoken, I will not weary you by any ,extended remarks, but will answer a few questions that have been frequently asked me.

"First, why is this spot called Crane Hook or Point? If you will imagine the condition here when the church was built, before the banks and sluices were constructed, you will have a picture of a cape largely surrounded by water,— a deep inlet coming in opposite the Lambron place, and another above the Lobdell Works, running inland, making what was called the Hazeldell Farm an island, from which the sand for the building of Old Swedes' Church was obtained. I have seen water of sufficient depth to float a sloop over these marshes when the banks were broken. The name Crane may have been given the point by its resemblance to the bird, or, perhaps, from its being a favorite resort of cranes.

"The question is asked why the English word hook was substituted for the Swedish word udde, a point; the an-

swer to which is that it is not English, but Dutch. The word hook is never used in English for point, but wherever the Dutch had rule you find the word hock (pronounced hook) used for a point of land, as in New York we have Carlan's Hook, Kinderhook, etc. You will see on the Swedish map of the Delaware the word udde always used for point, but when the Hollanders conquered the country they substituted their name hock for udde, and the Swedes adopted it, but retained the given name, as Trane, Crane; Kalcon, Turkey; Kastania, Chestnut; Fahr, Sheep, etc.

"I will ask your patience while I speak a few words in remembrance of two ministers who officiated in this church before Mr. Bjork,—Carl Lock and Jacob Fabricius, and also of Carl Springer, a layman. Something of a cloud rests upon the early life of these clergymen as being somewhat mutinous against the civil authorities; but the accounts of the transactions are by the authorities, and their offences seem to have arisen from (probably a mistaken) idea that the people were treated oppressively. However faulty they may have been during their early years, as they grew older the testimony is that they were sober, peaceable, and faithful ministers, Lock being for some years the only Swedish clergyman on the Delaware, and serving both congregations for a considerable time, and this at Crane Hook until his death. Fabricius was neither a Swede nor Hollander, but a German Lutheran who could speak Swedish. He was called to the Wicaco Church at first, and after the death of Lock served both that and Crane Hook until his death, though he was blind during all except the first year.

"For several years he was the only clergyman for all this

region from Cape Henlopen to the Falls of the Delaware. Picture to yourselves the blind old man journeying up and down this river, often roughened by storms, in an open boat or log canoe, ministering to a people scattered for forty miles along its banks and up its tributaries, and you will certainly feel that his name should be held in respectful and grateful remembrance.

"Carl Springer is another name that should always be associated with this church. After the death of Fabricius he acted as lay reader and conductor of the religious services here for about five years, reading from the postilla or authorized sermon-book, with prayers and hymns, thus holding the people to their church and nursing the feeble flame of their simple piety, and preventing its total decline; and wherever the name of Springer is heard throughout our broad land it should call up grateful remembrance of the first Springer in America, the faithful lay reader of Crane Hook Church."

ADDRESS OF REV. FREDERIC DOERR,

Pastor of St. Stephen's Lutheran Church,
Wilmington, Delaware.

"Not being a member of the Historical Society of Delaware, I desire to return my sincere thanks to its members, and more especially the committee having charge of this day's exercises, for their thoughtfulness in extending to me an invitation to be present upon this very auspicious occasion. I consider it, indeed, both a privilege and a pleasure to be with you at these dedicatory services. But to me, a Lutheran, the exercise of to-day is somewhat of a mournful character. I can truthfully say that it is a great pleasure to

me to be present at this time, when a memorial stone marking the site of Crane Hook Church has been dedicated.
This day's exercise, however, directs my mind to the beginning days of American Lutheranism. It is such a retrospective look which has moved me to say that the feelings
reigning in my bosom are not altogether of a gratifying
character. Sadness does, indeed, take hold of me when I
think that the church I so very dearly love is no longer a
church of mine. Beautiful 'Old Swedes' Church' does yet
remain, but that no longer is in the possession of the church
of which I am a member. Yes, sad am I when I think that
the greatness of early Swedish Lutheranism in this country
has passed into local forgetfulness. The historian well-nigh
alone knows that the first Christians of this community, yea,
the first people also, were Swedish Lutherans. Wonder not,
therefore, that I have said that the character of this service
to me, a Lutheran, is a mournful one. Let no one, however, consider that I am finding fault by remarks such as I
have just made with those who now possess 'Old Swedes'
Church.' I am not talking of the present. I am thinking
of the past. Nothing have I to do with the transfer of the
Lutheran Church property into other hands. That transfer,
I hope, has been satisfactorily made to all concerned parties.
But, although my feelings are not altogether of a pleasurable
kind, as I stand on the spot where the first Lutherans of
this land were wont to worship, yet I am thankful that the
Historical Society of Delaware has seen fit to mark the spot
where the second Lutheran Church building in this country
stood.

"Those who worshipped here were not my forefathers, for

I am neither a Swede by birth nor am I a born child of the Commonwealth of Delaware. Though these early Swedes were no kin of mine, yet we possessed a common heritage. I am speaking of the Augsburg Confession, that grand expression of our faith. Yes, the early Swedes were my confessional forefathers. Therefore I am thankful that you, the members of Delaware's Historical Society, have seen fit to remember in a tangible manner the place wherein one common service in past days was heard.

"May this spot become a very dear one to the Lutherans of this land, for many of such there be.

"A small town of this country has risen into prominence because the standard-bearer of one of the greater national parties dwells within her borders. Pilgrimages are daily made by the thousands to the home of the Presidential candidate. Just as that town has risen into great prominence, so may our city become widely known on account of the pilgrimages which the Lutherans of this land in the coming days will make to this tangible mark of 'Crane Hook Church,' the predecessor of our present 'Old Swedes' Church,' Wilmington, Delaware. That this spot may indeed become a Lutheran Mecca I sincerely trust.

"This day is likewise not without its lesson. It tells us to be more careful and zealous in the future than we have been in the past. The buildings which the early Swedes erected manifest most obviously that they lived their Confession of Faith. May the remembrance of their activity and self-denial incite us to greater consecration. Then the dedicatory service of this day will have been observed both profitably and pleasurably."

ADDRESS OF HON. IGNATIUS C. GRUBB.

"LADIES AND GENTLEMEN,—Chief Justice Lore, who presides so efficiently over both our Historical Society and our State courts, has, with quite a Benedictine cordial warmth, commended me to your favorable consideration as his bachelor brother of the Bench. His venerable aspect, of course, suggests to you—especially the fairer portion of this assemblage—that he means that I am his brother *in law* merely, and not in any *contemporary* sense.

" Consequently I must disavow any connection with our Historical Society's 'Bureau of Antiquities'—except as a reverent admirer. Candor compels me to confess, as the printed programme shows, that I did not come here as one of the Society's 'selected specimens,' to tell you what occurred on this spot two hundred years or more ago. As I was not here at that time, the Chief Justice and the other gentlemen who have preceded me were, as you have doubtless observed, more appropriately selected to address you.

" As you all know, the evidence of credible eye-witnesses is always admitted, whilst hearsay testimony is invariably excluded by the courts. Hence I can see no reason for my being called upon, so unexpectedly, to tell you what I really do not know, unless it be to vouch for the general veracity and credibility of these venerable eye-witnesses. Inasmuch as none of the other actors of the period whose events they relate are now living to tell a different story, and as I have never heard the veracity of any of these gentlemen discussed *pro* or *con*, therefore, as a member of our Historical Society, I feel bound to stand by them and give them a good char-

acter,—at least until they are found out and the contrary appears.

"So far I have always concurred with the Chief Justice, if it was at all possible to do so.

"Bishop Coleman, being the head of my own church here, I have always, of course, regarded as infallible; whilst I certainly must take on faith what Dr. Burr has so learnedly said in the ancient Swedish tongue, which I do not understand. My only knowledge of Mr. Pusey and his credibility is derived from my very pleasurable perusal of his historical paper on Crane Hook Church when I superintended the printing of it as chairman of our Historical Society's Committee on Publications. If more sceptical readers have thought of it, as Lord Macaulay did of Herodotus's history, that it is difficult to determine where fiction ends in it and history begins, I did not so think, for, to my delighted mind, it seemed true as a fairy tale.

"Therefore I feel that we may reasonably assume from the statements of these antique narrators of ancient events that in 1667 a log church was built on this spot where we now congregate by our Swedish and Dutch predecessors. Indeed, their direct testimony seems to be supported by cogent circumstantial evidence.

"In the first place, the personal appearance of these 'oldest inhabitants' manifestly indicates to us that they belonged to that early period. Secondly, the Crane Hook point of their story—the *locus in quo*—is still here, if the log church is not, together with the almost vanished stump of the historic sycamore-tree which these 'ancient mariners' say overshaded their old house of worship. Lastly, the sage officers

and members of the Historical Society of Delaware, having
carefully investigated and maturely considered the evidence,
both oral and documentary, have adjudged and resolved
that this is the identical site of the Crane Hook Church of
1667.

"But, seriously speaking, they have fortunately done more
than merely resolve, for they have emphasized their faith by
works, in appropriating their funds to the purchase and erection of this monument to mark this spot and perpetuate the
memory of the old church and its zealous and venerated
builders.

"To co-operate in this commendable purpose we are here
to-day. The dedication of this memorial stone is a notable
occasion, and will prove, I am sure, a memorable one to each
of us. It is well to commemorate the virtues and good
deeds of earnest and useful men and women. Such efforts
tend to elevate human nature and advance mankind. They
preserve ennobling ideals, promote higher aspirations, and
encourage others to more earnest endeavor and greater usefulness in their day and generation.

"If the fleeting moments of this waning day did not forbid
me, I could dwell long and earnestly upon this and other
thoughts appropriate to this occasion and this scene. I
have to-day, for the first time in my life, visited this historic
locality. In looking from this isolated point, or hook of
land, one can yet vividly realize how it and its environment
appeared in 1667, before the Delaware River embankments
were constructed, and when ' Crane Hook' at high tide was
surrounded by a watery expanse. What a contrast, in so
many ways, between then and now ! And what teeming

thoughts rise in the brain of each of us as we now stand here and gaze upon this scene and think upon its past and present!

"Here the poor and struggling settlers, with none of the comforts and few of the necessaries of life, bravely faced a primeval forest, inhabited only by wild beasts and savage men. Now we behold a flourishing city, denizened by a thriving people enjoying the refinements and luxuries of our marvellous civilization. Then the pious Swede and Hollander came to this sacred spot on foot or by canoe. To-day we have come here by railway, by carriage, and by bicycle.

"In the midst of our numberless benefits we now do well to pay this tribute to those who founded both our religion and our civilization here amid trials and sufferings of which in actual experience, we happily know naught. For our lasting gratitude and enduring remembrance are justly due to them and their noble patron, the great champion of the Protestant Reformation, Gustavus Adolphus, who planned our early Swedish settlements, and his enlightened and faithful minister, Oxenstiern, who established them.

"Surely it behooves all of us who are their beneficiaries earnestly to strive, jealously to guard and zealously to perpetuate the faith which they planted and the free institutions which they founded here in this immediate vicinity within the narrow circle of our view to-day."

Following the several addresses, the assemblage heartily joined in singing the final hymn:

Our Fathers' God! to Thee,
Author of liberty,
    To Thee we sing;
Long may our land be bright
With freedom's holy light;
Protect us by Thy might,
    Great God, our King!

Bless Thou our native land!
Firm may she ever stand,
    Through storm and night;
When the wild tempests rave,
Ruler of wind and wave,
Do Thou our country save
    By Thy great might.

For her our prayer shall rise
To God, above the skies;
    On Him we wait;
Thou Who art ever nigh,
Guarding with watchful eye,
To Thee aloud we cry,
    God save the state!

The services concluded with a benediction, pronounced by
Bishop Coleman, whereupon most of the audience dispersed,
but many remained long enough to view the ancient ap-
proaches to the spot, yet seen in the landing place on the
river bank and in the hedge-bordered lane leading from inland localities, while others lingered fondly over the fast
perishing remains of the venerable tree which long kept
guard near the ancient church site, and whose lofty branches
served as a beacon both to mariners on the river and church-
goers on the land.

And so ended a successful and interesting occasion, which to all participants was deemed a rare combination of profit and pleasure.

All of which is respectfully submitted by your

MEMORIAL COMMITTEE.

WILMINGTON, DEL., November, 1896.

Gunning Bedford

PAPERS OF THE HISTORICAL SOCIETY OF DELAWA

XXVI.

GUNNING BEDFORD, JUNI

BY

HENRY C. CONRAD,

LIBRARIAN OF THE SOCIETY.

Read before the Historical Society of Delaware, March 20,

THE HISTORICAL SOCIETY OF DELAWARE,

WILMINGTON.

1900.

GUNNING BEDFORD, JUNIOR.

THE first Judge of the United States District Court for the District of Delaware was Gunning Bedford, Junior, he having been appointed by President George Washington in 1789, soon after the formation of the court by Act of Congress. Both the father and grandfather of Judge Bedford were named Gunning, the family coming from England, the first American branch settling at Jamestown, Virginia, in 1621. The grandfather seems to have been a resident of Cecil County, Maryland, his remains being interred at North East River in that county. The father of the Judge was a captain in the French and Indian War, followed the trade of an architect, and was a resident of Philadelphia, having been an alderman in that city for several years previous to his death in 1802, at the age of eighty-two; and the mother of the Judge was Susannah Jacquett. There were eleven children, the fifth child and second son being Gunning, Junior, the Judge, who was born in Philadelphia in 1747. At the age of twenty he entered Princeton College, then known as Nassau Hall, where he graduated in the Class of 1771. He stood at the head of the class, being the valedictorian, and made an enviable record as a college

student. Among his classmates were James Madison, who afterwards became President of the United States, and Hugh M. Brackenridge.

He studied law under Joseph Reed, an eminent Philadelphia attorney, and about 1779 moved to Delaware and settled at Dover, where he was admitted to the bar under date of August 4, 1779, in Sussex County.

After a brief residence at Dover, finding that the climate did not agree with him, he removed to Wilmington. Winning a high reputation by his scholarship and oratorical ability, he was early recognized by the people and was soon honored with official station. In 1783 he was elected a member of the Continental Congress from Delaware and served for three years. On April 26, 1784, he was appointed Attorney-General of the State of Delaware, where he served with marked ability. On June 17, 1786, he was elected, with George Read, Jacob Broom, John Dickinson, and Richard Bassett, as a commission to meet commissioners from the other States in the Union for the purpose of forming a system of commercial regulations between the States, who were to meet in Annapolis on the first Tuesday of September of that year. His high rank as a professional man is shown by his association with the most distinguished men of his time. The same men who were delegated to attend the Annapolis convention were selected a year later as delegates from Delaware to frame the first Constitution of the United States.

In this Constitutional Convention Mr. Bedford was a prominent figure. Its membership represented the master

THE CITY RESIDENCE OF GUNNING BEDFORD, JUNIOR.

NO. 606 MARKET STREET, WILMINGTON, DELAWARE.

minds of that day. Gunning Bedford, Junior, frequently took the floor and argued questions brought before the body with marked ability and force. He combated strenuously the efforts made by the members from the larger States whereby they sought to give the more populous States a representation in both houses of Congress based on population. He frequently crossed swords with Alexander Hamilton, a member from New York, and James Madison, a delegate from Virginia, and it was largely due to his personal efforts and eloquent appeals that the provision of the Constitution was adopted whereby each of the States was accorded the same representation in the United States Senate, the wisdom of which provision the experience of a century has fully vindicated.

A recent article which appeared in *Munsey's Magazine* on " The Making of the Constitution," from the pen of Hon. Thomas B. Reed, says:

" The Constitution of the United States was not the work of inspiration, or even of genius. It had its origin in the good sense of able men applied to the practical work in hand, in a keen appreciation of the dangers already existing, and the greater dangers to come, and in the spirit of conciliation forced upon its authors by the ever-present nature of the troubles to be avoided.

" A little less than four months of almost constant discussion covered the period between the 25th of May, when they began, and the 17th of September, when all but three, who were present, signed and recommended the Constitution to the people of the United States. There were

twenty-nine members present when they organized, and during the four months, from time to time, came in other members to the number of twenty-three. Fifty-two men, therefore, contributed their wisdom to the final result, though only thirty-nine certified by their signatures to the ' Unanimous Consent of the States Present.' "

Mr. Reed pays a deserved tribute to the members of the Convention and commends the faithfulness of their work in his concluding paragraphs as follows:

" Nevertheless, the reader of the debates arises from their perusal with increased respect for the wisdom and foresight of the men of whom Madison justly says, ' There never was an assembly of men charged with a great and arduous trust who were more pure in their motives, or more exclusively or more anxiously devoted to the object committed to them.' Peace to their ashes. Reverence to their memories. If their work should not be eternal, that work and its results will have educated their children to meet successfully the problem of that future into which they could not penetrate.

" How earnest they were, and how doubtful was the issue, how often they were alternately torn by doubts and difficulties, and rejoiced by successful coping with their hazardous problems, was voiced by the many-sided intellect of the great Dr. Franklin.

" Whilst the last members were signing, Dr. Franklin, looking towards the President's chair, at the back of which a rising sun happened to be painted, observed to a few members near him that painters had found it difficult to

distinguish, in their art, a rising from a setting sun. ' I have,' said he, ' often and often, in the course of the session, and in the vicissitudes of my hopes and fears as to its issue, looked at that behind the President, without being able to tell whether it was rising or setting; but now at length I have the happiness to know that it is a rising, and not a setting sun.' "

Returning from the Convention to his home, Mr. Bedford exerted himself in having his State ratify the Constitution; and to no man more than to Gunning Bedford, Junior, is the credit due for having the name of Delaware at the very head of the sisterhood of States. In 1788 he was elected a member of the State Council from New Castle County, and continued to serve until his elevation to the bench a year later.

In 1789 he was appointed by President George Washington the first District Judge of the United States for the District of Delaware, the President doubtless being fully convinced of his eminent fitness for the place by reason of the long and intimate acquaintance which had existed between them beginning during the War of the Revolution and continuing until the death of Washington.

In times past much confusion has been caused by the mixing up of two Gunning Bedfords who figured in Delaware at the same time. Judge Bedford was always known as Gunning Bedford, *Junior.* He uniformly signed his name with the Junior attached. He had a cousin whose name also was Gunning Bedford. The latter was five years the senior of the Judge, being born in 1742, and was the

son of William Bedford, a farmer, who lived in New
Castle Hundred. Gunning Bedford and not Gunning Bedford, Junior, married a sister of George Read, the signer,
was Lieutenant-Colonel in David Hall's regiment in the
Revolution, and in 1795 was elected Governor of Delaware. He also served as Prothonotary and Register of
Wills for New Castle County, and is buried in Immanuel
Church-Yard at New Castle. Even so careful a biographer
as Judge Whitely made the mistake of giving to Gunning
Bedford (the Governor) some of the credit and offices
which belonged to Gunning Bedford, Junior (the Judge).

Judge Bedford married early, so early that on the occasion of his graduation at Princeton, in 1771, his wife was
present with her first baby, and the story goes that the baby
was left in the care of the wife of Dr. Witherspoon while
Mrs. Bedford attended the commencement exercises. So
the young college student stepped from the graduating
desk to " family cares" in reality. His wife was Jane Bal-
laroux Parker, the daughter of James Parker, editor of
the *Post Boy,* published in New York, and one of the earliest American printers. Parker learned his trade as a
printer side by side with Benjamin Franklin in Boston,
and he exchanged with Franklin the first dollar he ever
made as an apprentice. That dollar, by the way, was afterwards fashioned into a punch-strainer, and is now among
the valuable relics of the Historical Society of Delaware,
having been bequeathed to the Society by Henrietta Jane
Bedford, a daughter of Judge Bedford.

Mrs. Bedford is described as a lady of rare accomplish-

"LOMBARDY," THE COUNTRY RESIDENCE OF GUNNING BEDFORD, JUNIOR.

ments and great intellect, whose grace and conversational powers contributed much to the advancement of her husband's home, and naturally gave her a leading place in the most cultured society of that day.

Judge Bedford's residence in Wilmington was at what is now known as No. 606 Market Street (now occupied by William J. Fisher, and for many years known as the Mc-Caulley house). It was built by Abijah Dawes, an early resident of Wilmington, and in the Revolution is said to have been the head-quarters of the French army. It was at that time the stateliest house in the borough. Afterwards this house was owned and occupied by Louis McLane, a distinguished Delawarean who served as United States Senator, Secretary of State, and Secretary of the Treasury under President Andrew Jackson, and twice as United States Minister to Great Britain. Judge Bedford occupied the house for some years, but in 1793 bought from the Charles Robinson estate a farm of two hundred and fifty acres on the Concord Turnpike in Brandywine Hundred, being, as described in the deed, " Pisgah, part of a larger tract called New-work." He renamed the place "Lombardy," and the present Lombardy Cemetery is a part of the same farm. The large and handsome stone mansion which he built on the farm is still standing; and there he made his home during the remainder of his life.

Elizabeth Montgomery in her " Reminiscences of Wilmington" says: "Judge Bedford and his lady were remarkably handsome persons and of noble stature. Mrs. Bedford received an accomplished education and spoke

French fluently, her mother being a native of France. When emigrants from that country crowded this town, Mrs. Bedford was their friend and patron. Her entertainments excelled in tasteful arrangement and ornamental display—so said foreigners."

Judge Bedford died on March 30, 1812, in the sixty-fifth year of his age. His wife, one son, and a daughter survived him. Mrs. Bedford lived nineteen years after her husband, dying in 1831. For several of the last years of her life she was blind, yet still retained the charming manners which had characterized her youth and prime. The son, whose name was Gunning James Bedford, and who was always of feeble mind, died in 1845. The daughter, and youngest child of Judge Bedford, was Henrietta Jane Bedford, who lived to reach her eighty-third year, having died in this city in 1871. She possessed intellectual gifts of a high order. She alone of all the children of her father's house appeared to inherit the abilities with which her parents were endowed. Her education was the best that her day afforded for women, and she was trained in all the accomplishments then in vogue. She was a passionate lover of music, performing skilfully upon piano and guitar, and having learned to play the harp when nearly seventy years old. Her conversational powers were very fine, and even in her old age she entered most vivaciously into social intercourse. Retaining full recollection of most of the famous people who had gathered at her father's fireside, she brought the past into contact with the present in a remarkable manner. Animated, witty, full of anecdote,

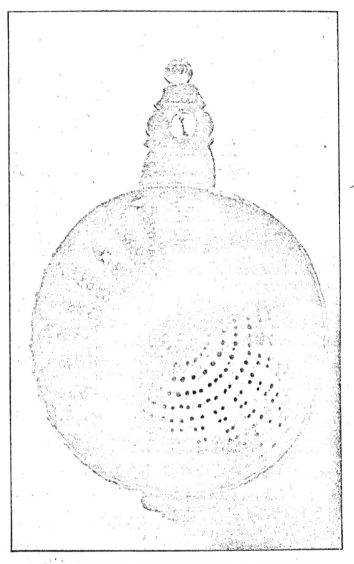

THE SILVER STRAINER MADE FROM THE FIRST DOLLAR EARNED BY
BENJAMIN FRANKLIN.

well informed in regard to current events as well as those of bygone times, she was a delightful companion, even when her life had long passed the limits of three score years and ten.

Her disposition was kindly and affectionate. To her suffering mother and afflicted brother she showed the utmost tenderness, fulfilling to the utmost every duty that devolved upon her as a daughter and sister.

Miss Bedford by her will, which was proven in this county on the 21st of August, 1871, describes herself as a daughter of " Hon. Gunning Bedford, Junior, Aide-de-Camp to General Washington in the Revolutionary war." The will provides that a portrait of her father be placed in the Capitol at Washington near that of James Madison, a room-mate of her father's and one of the framers of the Constitution. It also provides that a pair of pocket-pistols be placed in the Smithsonian Institution at Washington, or if that cannot be done, that they be delivered to the Historical Society of Delaware. The portrait of her father was sent to Washington and now hangs on the wall of the corridor, in a conspicuous place, at the head of a stairway at the Senate end of the Capitol. The pocket-pistols were delivered to the Historical Society, and now remain in its collection. Her will gives the following history of the pocket-pistols: " During the Revolutionary war General Washington, desiring my father to go from Trenton to New York on some important secret embassy at night, and fearing that he was not sufficiently armed with the pistols in his holsters, presented him with a pair of pocket-pistols with a view to his protection and greater security."

The silver punch-strainer, of which I have spoken heretofore in this sketch, came to the Historical Society by Miss Bedford's will.

I presume that Miss Bedford's allusion to the military service of her father as aide-de-camp to General Washington must be correct, although I have found nothing in the records to corroborate the statement. He did not come to Delaware until about 1779. I am satisfied that he did not serve in the Revolutionary War in any of the Delaware regiments. He may have served from Pennsylvania and been credited to that State.

Gunning Bedford, Junior, was a Presbyterian in religion, and usually worshipped in the building in which we are now assembled. His remains lie buried in the graveyard adjoining this building, the First Presbyterian Church, and I cannot more concisely and appropriately close this sketch than by quoting the epitaph which was written by William T. Read and which appears on the handsome marble monument which was erected over his remains by Henrietta Jane Bedford, his daughter, in 1858:

"In hope
of a joyful resurrection,
through faith in Jesus Christ,
here rests the mortal part
of
GUNNING BEDFORD.
Born in Philadelphia, A.D. 1747,
Graduated at Nassau Hall, New Jersey, A.D. 1771,
with great distinction.

THE BEDFORD MONUMENT

Having studied law in Philadelphia,
he practised in Delaware
with success ;
distinguished by his eloquence as an advocate,
Attorney-General, member of the Legislature of Delaware
(and of Congress)
and one of the delegates to the Convention that
framed the Constitution of the United States (by whose
efforts, with those of other delegates, two Senators were obtained
for the State of Delaware).
He received from Washington the Commission of first Judge of the
District Court of the United States for the District of Delaware
which he held till his death in 1812.
He so behaved in these high offices as to deserve and receive
the approbation of his fellow-citizens.
His form was goodly, his temper amiable,
his manners winning, and his discharge
of private duties exemplary.
Reader, may his example stimulate
you to improve the talents—be they five or
two, or one—with which God has entrusted you."

JOHN. FISHER.

JOHN FISHE

BY

HENRY C. CONRAD,

LIBRARIAN OF THE SOCIETY.

Read before the Historical Society of Delaware, March 20,

THE HISTORICAL SOCIETY OF DELAWARE,
WILMINGTON.
1900.

JOHN FISHER.

JOHN FISHER, the second Judge of the United States
Court for the District of Delaware, was born May 22,
1771. He was a descendant, in the fifth generation, from
John Fisher, who emigrated from England and landed
at Philadelphia. This first John Fisher accompanied William Penn on the "Welcome" on his first voyage to America in 1682, and is supposed to have come from Clitheroe,
Lancashire, England. He was a member of the Society of
Friends. A few years after his arrival he moved to Delaware, settling near Cape Henlopen, in Sussex County. He
bought land in Sussex County in 1685. The first John
Fisher had a son John, and he in turn had a son John, these
three Johns being the direct paternal ancestors of the subject of this sketch.

The father of John Fisher, the Judge, was Jabez Maud
Fisher (born in 1733, died 1786), and his mother was
Elizabeth Purnell (born 1730, died 1776), daughter of
Thomas and Mary Purnell, of Somerset County, Maryland. She married, first, Anthony Wright, who died about
1760, and afterwards married Jabez Maud Fisher. Of the
latter marriage there were six children, of whom John, the
subject of this sketch, was the youngest. At the age of

five his mother died, and at the age of fifteen, by the death
of his father, he was left largely to the care of his brother,
General Thomas Fisher, through whom he was enabled
to get a classical education; and afterwards he studied law
with his cousin, Joshua Fisher, at that time a leading member of the Dover bar, John Fisher being admitted as a
practising attorney under date of August 11, 1791. For
about twenty years he was an active practitioner, and was
recognized as among the leading and most influential members of the bar at the State capital.

In 1799 he was clerk of the State Senate and in 1807
clerk of the State House of Representatives. In 1802 he
was appointed Secretary of State under Governor David
Hall, and in 1811 was again made Secretary of State by
Governor Joseph Haslet. While holding the latter office
the United States judgeship for the District of Delaware
became vacant by the death of Gunning Bedford, Junior.

James Madison was at that time President, and his first
choice for the vacant judgeship was Cæsar A. Rodney, the
recognized leader at that time of the Democratic party in
New Castle County. Henry M. Ridgely was one of the
United States Senators from Delaware, and he and Fisher
were warm personal friends. The following correspondence, the originals of which are in my possession, will show
that human nature was much the same at the beginning
of the nineteenth century as at its close, and that there was
then the same anxious solicitude for public office as is prevalent among the politicians of to-day. The following letter
from John Fisher to Henry M. Ridgely explains itself:

"DOVER, 3. April, 1812.

"DEAR SIR,—The Wilmington papers which arrived the evening before last, announced the death of Judge Bedford;—this unfortunate event, unfortunate for his family, happened on Monday last. Several of my friends have urged me to an application for the vacancy occasioned by his demise. I have always thought that a *personal* application for a judgeship, was a matter of indelicacy and inconsistent with the modesty, which such a candidate ought to profess. I have, however, thought, on reflecting how the loaves and fishes are now distributed, that there can be but one rival, and but one man, on the same political side, whose pretensions are in any way superior to my own. This gentleman's legal acquirements are superior to mine; but in nothing else can I yield to him. There is one qualification of a judge in which I think him not my equal—this I shall not name, but will leave you to conjecture. Under all circumstances, and especially knowing that Mr. Rodney would not accept of the appointment, I have made up my mind to state my claims to the vacancy in such manner as is customary. May I calculate upon your friendship to me on this interesting occasion? The Chancellor, I am informed, writes on by the ensuing mail, in a friendly manner to me. Would the recommendation of Governor Haslet sent on to the President, avail any thing? If Yea, I think it can be procured by the next mail. I wrote to Mr. Bayard by the last mail, requesting him to communicate the substance of my letter to yourself and Mr. Horsey. This application is, my friend, most important to me. Such another

portunity of providing for my numerous and expensive
mily, will never occur. The very respectable representa-
m of this state, in Congress, may do much for me, if so
sposed. Their attempts to effectuate the advancement
w desired, will claim and receive the most sincere grati-
de of which the human heart is capable. I am already
der many obligations to you for your kindnesses here-
fore, and I still calculate on your benevolent disposition
this application of such high importance to my future
osperity.

"I am, Dr. Sir, with sentiments of perfect esteem and
spect

Your most obed'n. humb. servt.

"JOHN FISHER."

Four days after, no reply having been received from the
regoing letter, Mr. Fisher writes again to Mr. Ridgely
follows:

"DOVER, 7th April, 1812.

"DR. SIR,— * * * * * I hope by this time you have
ceived my communication of the 30th current. Since
en I have obtained (inter nos) the letter of Gov. Haslet
the President—will this avail any thing? It was written
the Governor on the 6th. and is full in point. I learn
m Wilmington that probably Mr. Rodney will accept Mr.
dfords place, if offered. Should this be the case, I am
st in wonder at Mr. Rodney; for he declared in Decem-
r last, that he should think himself insulted by an offer

of Mr. B's office. However, he wisely thinks, that ' half a loaf is better than no bread.' This conduct of his, if true, will lower him much in my esteem and will convince me of the fact, that twenty years intimate acquaintance with a man will give me no knowledge of him.

"I am your's devotedly,

"JOHN FISHER."

A week later the following letter was sent by Mr. Ridgely to Mr. Fisher:

(Confidential.)

"WASHINGTON, 14 April, 1812.

"MY DEAR SIR,—Your two favours of this month have been duly recd. Bayard you know is now absent from this place. Horsey and I have had several consultations on the subject of the appointment of a District Judge in Delaware, and we both feel every disposition to render you all the service in our power. He has been consulted from the department of State to know whether your nomination to the Senate would be acceptable to the Senators from Delaware. Pleasanton is anxious in your behalf and I am just now going to see him on the subject. It would I think be wise to send on the Governor's letter to the President. It is however a delicate matter and the letter if it be sent on, should be very cautiously written.

"I have not time at present to add more.

"Yours sincerely,

"H. M. RIDGELY."

Five days later Mr. Ridgely wrote again as follows:

(Confidential.)

"WASHINGTON, 19 April, 1812.

"MY DEAR SIR,—I wrote you a short letter on Tuesday last, which I hope you have received before now: and spent the evening of that day with Mr. Pleasanton.

"In the course of the evening, thinking no person except myself and his family present, Mr. P. and I had a good deal of conversation on the subject of the appointment of a District Judge for our State.

"He thinks, from a conversation he had with the President a few days before I saw him, that the office will be offered to Mr. Rodney, notwithstanding he stated to the President his firm conviction that Mr. R. would not accept it. Nothing, he thinks, but Mr. R. stands between you and the appointment, and he expressed himself quite confidentially that you would be appointed, under the *full impression* that Mr. R. would *not* accept the office. He advised the sending on the Governor's letter to the President.

"With sincere wishes for your success and a tender of my services so far as they will avail you anything, I remain, Dr. Sir,

"Yours with much regard,

"H. M. RIDGELY.

"JOHN FISHER, Esqr.

"Dover,

"Delaware."

In answer to which Mr. Fisher writes as follows:

"DOVER, 19th April, 1812.

MY DEAR SIR,—Your letters of the 14th and 19th
·ent have both been received by me. For the contents, I
you to accept my sincerest thanks. I think, after Mr.
lneys declaration, lately made, that he will not accept
appointment of Judge, if offered to him. He has deed, 'that should the commission be offered to him he
ıld not accept it, nor would he use any influence in
alf of any applicant.' This I have directly from the
;on to whom the declaration was made by Mr. Rodney.
Mr. Haslet's letter to the President must long since
e been received, as he wrote it and put it in the hands of
Postmaster on the 6th. instant at Milford, as he told
in fifteen minutes after it was done. This letter was
tiously and appropriately worded, such in every re-
:t as it ought to have been. I went down on purpose
rocure it and its purport was fixed on, some days before
·as written. I am quite astonished that after all that has
pened, it should be in contemplation to offer the ap-
ıtment in question to Mr. Rodney.
The Chancellor has written, perhaps twice, to Mr. Bay-
on the subject of Judge and I much fear that his letters
e never been received by Mr. B. He has authorized him
ıake any use of his first letter, which might advance the
ointment which it recommends. I wrote at large to
Pleasanton by the Mail of Saturday last, in answer to
tter received from him on the 13th inst, to which I beg
·e to refer you, as I am just getting ready for Sussex,
:re I am going at an early hour in the morning. The

engineer is at work relative to our canal—all Dover are out with him. He has already taken the level from the mill to Sykes's landing—fall is found to be 7½ feet. Your family are all in good health—Fine lot of timothy—good Andes grass—Every thing looks very well, Cub excepted, who declines very fast.

"When I return home will write you again,

"May Heaven bless you,

"JOHN FISHER."

This closes the correspondence on the judgeship. I have reason to believe that the President, adhering to his first inclination, offered the place to Mr. Rodney and that he declined it, although I have not been able to verify this; at all events, shortly afterwards John Fisher was appointed United States Judge for the District of Delaware, and continued as such during the remainder of his life, a period of about eleven years. Under date of Sunday, June 7, 1812, a few months later, he wrote the following friendly letter to Mr. Ridgely, which indicates that he was then in the pleasant exercise (as we will assume) of the judicial functions:

"Sunday, June 7, 1812.
"WILMINGTON.

"MY DEAR SIR,— * * * * * Mr. Duval and myself have been sitting as a Circuit Court at Newcastle since Wednesday last. I find we surprise the *natives,* by doing something like business. To-morrow the trial of the eight sailors for a revolt comes on—it will, I am told, be an ani-

mated discussion. *God send them a safe deliverance.* I
have nothing new to inform you of. Please to give me
the Washington news, when you write and remember me
affectionately to Mr. Horsey.

"I am, Dr. Sir, with the utmost sincerity

"Your friend, &c &c

"JOHN FISHER.

"HONBLE HENRY M. RIDGELY."

Under the first Act of Congress providing for the United
States Courts, the courts were held alternately at New
Castle and Dover. This continued until 1852, when by
special Act it was provided that thereafter they should be
held at New Castle only; and after the erection of the new
government building at Sixth and King Streets, in the city
of Wilmington, an Act was passed June 14, 1856, providing for the holding of the courts of this district only
at Wilmington.

In John Fisher's time, as Judge, the courts were held at
Dover and New Castle, and I presume that in those days
there was only a limited amount of business brought before
them.

John Fisher, while not a college man, was regarded as
a remarkably fine Latin and Greek scholar, and George P.
Fisher, his kinsman, who died very recently, told me that
he had a fine taste for poetry, and was withal a great wit
and humorist, and it is related that it was always a treat
for the members of the learned professions in Dover to
listen to the conversations of John Fisher and his next-

door neighbor, Dr. Arthur Johns, and to enjoy their passages in wit and pleasantry.

George P. Fisher is my authority for the following
story: It was John Fisher, the Judge, that John Vining,
not a great while before his (Vining's) death, invited to
dine at his (Vining's) home with the High Court of Errors
and Appeals on lamb and peas, when he had, in fact, neither
lamb nor peas nor money to buy them. This was on Saturday; the invitation was given for Sunday dinner. There
was no butcher then in Dover. Mrs. Vining went over to
Mrs. John Fisher to bemoan her trouble. John Fisher,
knowing Vining's thriftlessness, had in the meantime,
out of his own large garden, had the peas picked, and
while Mrs. Vining was there returned from a visit to a
farmer client with an elegant quarter of lamb. The peas
and lamb were sent over to Vining's house with such other
accompaniments as the ladies thought necessary, and the
dinner passed off pleasantly; and Vining, being ignorant
of the provision made for his feast, plumed himself on the
good time they had discussing the first lamb-and-pea dinner of the season.

Through the courtesy of Mr. Joseph Maxfield Ritter, a
grandson of Judge John Fisher, I have had the privilege
of examining a diary that was kept by Judge John Fisher
for several years. It is in the handwriting of the Judge,
who made entries at irregular periods from 1807 to 1820.
Much of the matter therein contained is too personal in its
character to be quoted. It establishes the fact that the
Judge was heir to some of the faults and frailties that have

afflicted humanity from the beginning of time, but it shows also that he was a man of deep religious feeling, and that he had the sentiments of a man of honor.

I make the following extracts from his diary to show not only that the life of a judge is sometimes beset with the same difficulties that are often the lot of those who walk on a less exalted plane, but to give an intimation of the religious feeling of which I have spoken, and which is the striking feature of his entries.

"September 5, 1814. Monday 4 o'c. P.M.

"This is a day of considerable affliction to me—my means of supporting my family have become so scanty, that I have not it in my power to provide for them the necessaries of life. My public compensation as a judge is really so very a triffle by reason of the depreciation of money, that with all the management and economy I can use, all my salary is expended before the termination of two months after I receive a quarter's compensation. I then become penniless for the other month before my salary is due. Those who owe me for business heretofore done in my late profession, will not or cannot pay me. To-day I have no dinner either for my poor little children or myself—not a particle of meat in the house—nor any money to procure that article with. Indeed if I had money, I doubt if I could get any, it has become so scarce. It is not to-day, only, that I go without dinner, but many days of late, I have been exceedingly hungry and have had nothing wherewith to make a dinner of. My babes come

in from school and ask for dinner and are told that there
is to be none—they with heavy hearts and empty stomachs
leave the house for their school—sometimes, indeed they
can get bread and milk, but that is not the case to-day for
we have no meal in the house to make bread of. This is
one of the effects of that most distressing war we are now
engaged in with G. Britain—a war commenced by the
present administration, merely because it would secure the
re-election of James Madison. What distress, what privation, what public and private affliction, what expense of
blood and treasure has this dreadful measure of our rulers
occasioned? How much reflection, how great deliberation,
what wisdom and foresight are necessary to the rulers of
a nation and how much ought they to employ these great
qualities before they commence so awful and so solemn a
work, as war! What responsibility rests upon them temporarily and here below? but how dreadful the account to
render to God for beginning the work of destruction, the
terrible calamity of war merely because it will continue
the exaltation and promote the ambitious projects of an
aspiring, but perhaps an undeserving individual? However, my present business is not to dwell upon this disa-
greeable subject, but to throw myself on the tender mercies
of my God and saviour and to thank him for the health
and strength which are enjoyed by myself and my dear
wife. and children; to thank him for the measure of grace
he imparts to us; and that our lot is not cast into a worse
condition than it is—that we are all in full life where we
may implore the mercy and grace of God and of his Christ

and may make our calling and election sure unto salvation,
through the merits of the Mediator; and finally invoke
of God, if our condition should not be ameliorated here
below, that he may receive our souls into mansions to which
the sufferings of this world are not incident; and where
only complete and uninterrupted felicity can be enjoyed.
O God may we love and adore thee forever—may we never
be unmindful of thy great goodness and loving kindness
—may our hearts be duly impressed with our obligations
to thee and O may we pour out our spirits at the foot of
thy throne forever—And though we are at present in a
state of privation we rely on thy goodness and mercy for
relief—for thou hast vouchsafed to promise that thou ' wilt
withhold no good thing from them that walk uprightly.'
Almighty father receive our hearts and make them to act
in entire subjection to thy most holy will; may they be
regenerated by the efficacy of thy divine spirit; and may
we compute all things naught in comparison with the love
of Christ Jesus. ' May our lips not speak wickedness, nor
our tongues utter deceit: till we die we will not remove
our integrity from us. Our righteousness we hold fast
and will not let it go: our hearts will not reproach us so
long as we live. Let our enemy be as the wicked and he
that riseth up against us, as the unrighteous.' O merciful
Being suffer us not to despair of thy mercy but altogether
rely upon thee and we shall do well. Blessed be thy holy
name forever, thou giver of every good and perfect gift—
Amen.

" JOHN FISHER."

John Fisher married, when twenty-three years of age, Lavinia Rodney, the only daughter of Thomas Rodney, who was a brother of Cæsar Rodney, the signer. Thomas Rodney was the colonel of the Kent County Militia in the War of the Revolution. Lavinia Rodney was the sister of Cæsar A. Rodney, one of the most brilliant lawyers that Delaware has produced, who served as Attorney-General of the United States under the administration of James Madison, and who built the large stone mansion still standing near Cool Spring Reservoir in this city. Miss Rodney was a young woman of unusual accomplishments, but died in 1802, in the twenty-seventh year of her age. The following year John Fisher was married to Elizabeth Wilson. She was the daughter of Simon Wilmer Wilson and her mother was Sarah Wilson, who was the half-sister of Cæsar Rodney, the signer. Sarah Wilson's mother was Elizabeth Crawford, being the daughter of Rev. Thomas Crawford, one of the earliest preachers of the Episcopal Church in Delaware. She was married first to Cæsar Rodney (father of the signer) and afterwards to Thomas Wilson, Sarah Wilson being the only child of the latter marriage. John Fisher's last wife outlived her husband nearly forty years.

John Fisher was the father of fourteen children, four by the first marriage and ten by the last. Several of the children died young. His youngest daughter, Louisa Fisher Ritter, is still living in Philadelphia at an advanced age. His son, Rodney Fisher, entered the navy as midshipman, but after a few years' service resigned and became interested in " the China trade." He resided for many years in

the East, and was both in China and India connected with some of the leading commercial transactions of his time. The latter years of his life were spent in Philadelphia, where he was identified with the Bank of the United States and the Bank of Commerce. He died in 1863. A daughter of John Fisher, Harriet, married Dr. Franklin W. Clement, and was for many years a resident of this city.

There is but little to show what record John Fisher made as a judge. As I have suggested, there was but little litigation before the United States Courts in this district while he was on the bench. There is nothing to indicate but that his judicial term was entirely satisfactory both to the bar and the suitors. He served in a day when Delaware had strong men at the bar. His diary, to which I have alluded, shows that Judge Fisher was a great sufferer from the gout. In several places he minutely describes the symptoms of this dread disease from the time of its first attack until his convalescence. The attacks of gout became more and more frequent, and finally, on April 22, 1823, he departed this life at his farm called Claremont, near Smyrna. His remains repose in Christ Church-Yard at Dover. Three weeks after his death, President Monroe appointed as his successor on the Bench, Willard Hall, who for nearly fifty years performed the duties of the place.

PAPERS OF THE HISTORICAL SOCIETY OF DELAWARE.

XXVIII.

BRIEF MEMOIRS

OF

HORACE BURR, M.D.,
REV. CHARLES E. MURRAY, D.D.

AND

HENRY R. BRINGHURST,

DECEASED MEMBERS OF THE SOCIETY.

BY

PENNOCK PUSEY,

HISTORIOGRAPHER.

Read before the Historical Society of Delaware, December 22, 1899

THE HISTORICAL SOCIETY OF DELAWARE,

WILMINGTON.

1900.

BRIEF MEMOIRS BY THE HISTORIOGRAPHER.

To the Historical Society of Delaware:

I beg respectfully to report that no practical duties seem heretofore to have been required of the Historiographer of this Society. The province or functions of such an office, never perhaps very well defined, have been in this case purely nominal from the practice, long followed, of finding suitable expression upon the decease of members through appointed committees or by the volunteer services of personal friends. But since the last annual meeting of this Society the death of three of its prominent members seems to afford a specially fitting occasion for a definite record or report from its Historiographer, so far, at least, as to arrange and summarize here what has been properly said by others elsewhere.

Dr. Horace Burr died on the 10th of January, Rev. Dr. Charles E. Murray on the 26th of the same month, and Henry R. Bringhurst on the 25th of October, all in the year 1899.

Of course, brief sketches must here suffice for detailed or elaborate biographies, while there will be attempted no adequate tribute to the character and services of our departed members.

3

HORACE BURR, M.D.

Of the first named, Dr. Horace Burr, indeed, little need
be added to what is well known of his long, strenuous,
and well-spent life in varied fields of usefulness. Dr.
Burr was a high type of the self-made American in the
best sense of the term.

Born at Haddam, Connecticut, on the 13th of December, 1817, he came of the sturdy stock whose ancestors
shared alike in the settlement of Hartford and in the trials
and sacrifices of the American War of Independence. On
the maternal side Dr. Burr was descended from the eminent English family of Bulkeley, one of whom, Rev. Dr.
Peter Bulkeley, having been silenced for non-conformity
by Archbishop Laud, sold his English estate and emigrated
to America, where he became one of the founders of Concord, Massachusetts.

Horace Burr's father was a farmer with seven children,
of whom Horace was the second. His elder brother had
defective eyesight and a feeble constitution, disqualifying
him for severe physical labor, on account of which his
father resolved to spare no effort or expense in fitting
him for one of the learned professions, while Horace was
to continue a farmer, obtain instruction as best he could
at the common schools of the neighborhood, and succeed
the family head in the care of the paternal acres.

Such was the irrevocable decision under which Horace
was kept at hard work on the farm, with little leisure for

DR. HORACE BURR.

reading and scant means for self-improvement. But with a keen thirst for knowledge, the lad determined to obtain for himself what had been denied him by his father. With pluck and persistence he used his small earnings in the purchase of books and his brief leisure in the careful study of them. At fourteen he had mastered Daboll's Arithmetic wholly unaided, which he followed up with rapid proficiency in grammar, geography, and other studies.

When near eighteen years of age Mr. Burr was employed in the extensive stone quarries near Haddam, where supplies of gneiss, feldspar, and red sandstone afforded him an opportunity for geological and mineralogical research. This he prosecuted with his summer work, while in the winter months he taught school in Haddam.

Mr. Burr had pursued his studies with diligent secrecy, and his father was ignorant of his aspirations and plans, but the lad made a confidante of his mother, from whom he received sympathy and encouragement. By her advice he divulged to his father his wish and purpose to seek elsewhere the means to further his education. Persisting in this object against the strong persuasions of his father, Mr. Burr left his home and opened a subscription school in the suburbs of Trenton, New Jersey, where he spent a pleasant and profitable year. Returning home, he was kindly received by his father, but was not aided or encouraged by him in his course, and later he journeyed as far south as Richmond, Virginia, but, finding no suitable opening so late in the season, returned homeward and came *en route* to New Castle, Delaware, where he

expected to take the boat for Philadelphia, when he became acquainted with the principal of the New Castle Academy, by whom he was persuaded to remain in Delaware, and who obtained for him a position in the public school at Red Lion.

The next year Mr. Burr took charge of a large school near Wilmington, Delaware, and began reading medicine with Dr. Samuel Higgins, of this city. The medical course thus begun Mr. Burr had arranged to continue in Philadelphia, when by the sudden death of his elder brother he was summoned home, where, yielding to the persuasions of his afflicted parents, he remained, and after pursuing his preparatory studies in Haddam entered the Medical Department of Yale College.

While attending the regular lectures Mr. Burr was a private pupil of Professor William Tully, an enthusiastic scientist, with whom he formed a close and life-long friendship which proved a keen incentive to the scientific pursuits of the young student. Mr. Burr graduated from Yale College in the class of 1842, and immediately began the practice of his profession in Southern Middlesex County, Connecticut. This grew so rapidly that he was soon weakened by overwork, and when in his twenty-eighth year was attacked by scarlet fever, which was followed by lingering diseases terminating in typhoid fever. During these repeated ailments Mr. Burr's devoted friend, Professor Tully, left his business and watched for weeks day and night at his bedside.

After his recovery Dr. Burr, while still unable to re-

sume his practice, was elected to the State Legislature of Connecticut. But he needed fewer rather than more cares, and, finding his large practice too great a tax upon his strength, he procured a young assistant, and at length was persuaded into an unlucky partnership in a publishing house, by the failure of which his entire earnings were swept away.

Resuming his largely extended practice, Dr. Burr's strength soon proved unequal to the growing demands upon it, and at the end of fourteen years, having found it impossible to curtail his labors, he felt that he must have relief and change of climate or die. With a view to such change he considered the advantages of various localities, and his love for Delaware induced the purchase of his late home, near this city, to which he removed in the year 1867 and soon began to practise in Wilmington. The change proved very beneficial, and his varied and earnest pursuits will long be gratefully remembered by the community that welcomed his advent here and experienced the benefits derived therefrom.

Dr. Burr was not a proficient in science alone: he was master of many languages, and made a valuable collection of European classics, which he bequeathed to Trinity College, Hartford, Connecticut, while his own writings and various translations have commanded the attention of high literary and historic authorities. He was examiner for the State of Connecticut of the graduating classes in medicine in Yale College for 1861 and 1862, and delivered the address to the graduating class in 1863.

Dr. Burr wrote much on social and scientific subjects; he translated the records of the early Swedish church in Delaware published by this Society, and also the early church records of the Swedes in New Jersey for the Pennsylvania Historical Society, with other manuscript documents. He, moreover, translated the "History of the Swedish Settlements on the Delaware," published in Stockholm in 1894 in Swedish, German, and Latin, and left a valuable history of Trinity Church from the first Swedish settlement to this day.

Dr. Burr was a member of the Protestant Episcopal Church, and ever evinced a zealous and practical interest in its affairs. In his native State he was several times a delegate to the Diocesan Convention, and upon his removal to Delaware he soon became one of the vestrymen of Trinity Parish, of which for the greater part of the time he was senior warden. Holding for many years various positions of trust in his church, he was for a long period its chosen delegate to the Triennial Convention of the Episcopal Church in the United States.

The scientific and scholarly attainments of Dr. Burr, his character as a citizen, his reputation as a skilful physician, his intelligent interest in this Society, and his assiduous and invaluable services in historical research are too well known to be here dwelt upon. He was emphatically the architect of his own fortune. Perhaps no man was ever less indebted to adventitious aid for his advancement, and few have exhibited a more indomitable will in overcoming obstacles to the end sought. It is

REV. CHARLES E. MURRAY.

said that he had no knowledge of the Swedish language until he came to Wilmington, in ill-health, at fifty years of age, when, becoming deeply interested in the annals of the early Swedes, he taught himself their language without assistance, not as an end or a mere accomplishment, but expressly to qualify himself for translating and rewriting the early church records and history of the colonial Swedes. Had he done nothing more than leave to us the revealed particulars attending the erection of our Old Swedes' Church, the linking of his name with that venerated structure would have assured his lasting and grateful remembrance, not only in this community, but among lovers of historic and sacred relics throughout the country.

Dr. Burr was, as you know, a man of plain manners, concerned less with the semblance than substance of things. In this, as in other matters, his was not unlike the national character of the sturdy people whose early church history he revealed to us. His honest simplicity of purpose and his unassuming worth won the kindly confidence of his fellows, while his strenuous and useful career amid besetting difficulties should prove a fresh incentive to all worthy and noble aspirations in life.

REV. CHARLES E. MURRAY, D.D.

During the same month that witnessed the decease of Dr. Burr, our Society was summoned to mourn the loss of another of its valued members by the death of Rev. Dr. Charles E. Murray, long rector of St. Andrew's Protestant

Episcopal Church, of this city, who was an associate with Dr. Burr in the services of the diocese.

Dr. Murray, while a younger, and from feeble health less active, member of our Society, manifested always such a discerning and sympathetic interest in its proceedings as to render his simple presence to many of us a source of inspiration. To refined and scholarly tastes he added an instinctive appreciation of the true historic spirit, and while not a constant attendant at our meetings, his helpful presence was ever welcomed among us.

Dr. Murray was born at Chestnut Hill, Pennsylvania, May 17, 1838. He was the son of Issachar and Mary Murray, whose parents came from England to America in the year 1789 and settled at Chestnut Hill, where his maternal grandfather became a large property holder and manufacturer. At an early date the parents of Mr. Murray removed to Philadelphia, where he attended James Academy, and at the age of fifteen years graduated from the Philadelphia High School. He then attended Pennsylvania College at Gettysburg, from which he received the degree of B.A. in 1861 and of M.A. in 1862. Later he became a student in the Theological Seminary of Kenyon College, Ohio, from which he graduated in 1864 and the same year was ordained to the diaconate in the Church of the Epiphany, Philadelphia, and in 1896 received the degree of D.D. from Pennsylvania College.

Dr. Murray's first charge was the Zion Episcopal Church in Philadelphia. Afterwards he became rector of the Church of the Covenant in that city. In 1881 he became

assistant minister of St. Andrew's Church, of Wilmington, Delaware, and upon the death of Bishop Alfred Lee in 1887 was elected its rector. He held that position until near the time of his death, when impaired and failing eyesight compelled his resignation. This was to have taken effect upon the election of his successor, when, by the decision of the vestry, he would have become rector emeritus.

At the time of his death Dr. Murray was chairman of the Standing Committee of the Diocese of Delaware, one of the chaplains to examine young candidates for the Episcopal ministry, registrar of the diocese of Delaware, secretary in Delaware for the office of the Church House in London, member of the Clerical Brotherhoods of Philadelphia and Wilmington, a trustee of the Divinity School of Philadelphia, and a member of the Board of Managers of the Evangelical Educational Society of Philadelphia. He was for seven years president of the Delaware Bible Society, and when failing health forced him to relinquish this position he received a feeling testimonial appreciative of his services by resolution of the Bible Society at their ensuing annual meeting.

Of the general character of Dr. Murray in the various relations of life there seems to have been but one opinion among all who knew him. Bishop Coleman in a touching tribute said of him:

"Older friends may have known Dr. Murray longer and better; but I will not allow to any one a warmer love

or stronger confidence. . . . Dr. Murray was always a scholar. To study was as natural to him as to breathe. By reason of his mental constitution investigation and reflection were delightful and compensating. Realizing the ever-widening field of other men's reading, and the necessity laid upon the clergy to cope in some large measure with their intellectual attainments, he pursued a liberal course of research, always having due regard to the queenly excellency of theology. . . . To some who knew him chiefly by his wide and accurate scholarship and by the highly-finished character of his discourses, it may be a surprise to learn how much of his time was devoted to strictly pastoral work. In an extended visitation of the poorer members recently made by one of the devoted parishioners, the frequency of his calls upon them came as a matter of astonishment, as also the amount of relief afforded them—so quietly and unostentatiously was it all done. The testimony borne to his kindness and practical sympathy by those whom he had thus comforted and re- lieved was most touching in its grateful words of affection- ate grief at the loss of one who had been so truly their friend."

Of like spirit an' tenor come numerous testimonials from the classmates of Dr. Murray and from friends and comrades of other days and places. One of these, as quoted by Bishop Coleman in his memorial sermon, de- picts our lamented friend in a glowing and truthful sum- mary thus:

HENRY R. BRINGHURST.

" I knew him in his seminary days, and what he was then he was to the last day of his life, simple-hearted, pureminded, kindly affectionate towards all men, adorning the doctrine of God our Saviour both by faith and love, as well as good works. A scholar without pretension, a saint without affectation, a lovable man and humble disciple of his Lord."

The compiler of this brief sketch had not the pleasure of a long or intimate acquaintance with Dr. Murray; but it was long and close enough to leave a deep impression of the beautiful symmetry of his character. He seemed to combine in nice proportion the gentle Christian spirit with the quiet, virile force of the olden heroism which dared to practise not less than profess the steadfast Christian life.

HENRY R. BRINGHURST.

At the regular September meeting of this Society following its midsummer vacation our Treasurer, Mr. Henry R. Bringhurst, did not make his appearance. So unusual a thing as the absence of that notably punctual and zealous officer led to inquiries, followed by the tidings that Mr. Bringhurst was detained at home by illness; and when upon his repeated absence at the October meeting his attending physician, Dr. John P. Wales, announced that his malady had grown so serious that Mr. Bringhurst would probably never more be with us, an impressive silence pervaded the meeting, broken by murmurs of sym-

pathetic and unfeigned sorrow. His death following within ten days, on the 25th of October last, realized the saddest apprehensions and brought sincere sorrow alike to his fellow-members here and to a large circle of life-long friends throughout the community.

Henry R. Bringhurst was emphatically a Wilmington-ian. Here he was born on the 20th of September, 1825, and here he died on the 25th of October, 1899. Here he grew to manhood, carried on business, and always resided without interruption for more than threescore and ten years. But notwithstanding so geographically restricted a field for action, Mr. Bringhurst was by no means an inactive man. With an ardent and energetic temperament, he took a warm interest in many of the early movements for promoting the social improvement and industrial development of his native city. He was an early and active member of the Delaware Pharmaceutical Society, of which he was president a long period. For sixty years he was a druggist at the same stand, 317 Market Street. He served for several years as president and also as secretary of the Water Witch Fire Company, and was noted for his rare efficiency in raising the requisite funds for, and zeal in maintaining the standard of, the volunteer fire department. He was connected with various literary and other societies in former years, and in recent years was specially known for his long and faithful service as treasurer of the Historical Society of Delaware.

When a young man Mr. Bringhurst took an active part in the political affairs of city and State. He was a close and

trusted friend of Hon. John M. Clayton, with whom he often consulted; and later, during the Civil War, he shared in the trials and secret councils involved in the momentous border problem of keeping Delaware in the Union and resisting the disruption of the government.

Mr. Bringhurst never held nor sought a political office for himself, and few men were ever more disinterested in the faithful political support of others. He was cousin to Joseph Bringhurst, whom he succeeded in business while yet in his teens; their ancestors were among the early Quaker families that settled in Philadelphia and thence came later to Wilmington.

Following Mr. Bringhurst's death kindly and respectful reference to the event was made by the Pharmaceutical Society, of which he had been president, while a special meeting of our Society was called to take suitable action October 27, 1899, when George W. Bush was called to the chair, and the following resolutions were passed:

"WHEREAS, The late treasurer of this Society, Henry R. Bringhurst, having departed this life on Wednesday, October 25th, it is deemed fitting and proper that this Society should place upon record this testimonial of his worth as a citizen, his long and active interest as a member, and his faithful and prudent management of the affairs of the office of treasurer of the Society.

"As a citizen he was patriotic and public-spirited; as a member of the Historical Society he constantly sought to promote its aims and objects; and as treasurer he guarded with zealous care the financial concerns of the Society; therefore, be it

"*Resolved*, That a committee of five members be appointed to attend the funeral of Mr. Bringhurst as representatives of this Society, and that a copy of these resolutions be sent to the family of the deceased and also be spread upon the minutes of the Society."

Pursuant to the foregoing a committee was appointed to represent the Society at the funeral services. These proceedings will be seen in the minutes of the special meeting duly recorded; but as these do not detail the touching and appreciative remarks made by the several speakers upon the occasion, it is deemed proper to fully set forth here the glowing tributes paid to the character and services of the deceased by friends and fellow-members who had known him longest and best.

Colonel William A. LaMotte, upon reporting the resolutions prepared by the committee, added a few pertinent and feeling remarks, in the course of which he stated that Mr. Bringhurst had been a member of the Society for twenty-seven years and its treasurer for eighteen years; and he warmly invoked the kindly and grateful remembrance by the Society of one who had served it so long and faithfully.

Henry C. Conrad, the librarian of the Society, said:

"MR. PRESIDENT:—In seconding the motion for the adoption of the resolutions I am sure that I voice the sentiment of every member present when I say that we all had a profound respect for our friend whose loss we mourn to-day. Mr. Bringhurst has been treasurer of the Society ever since I have been connected with it. As such he was most prudent and faithful in the management of the Society's finances. He was one of the most regular of the members in attendance at its meetings, and no one took a livelier interest in the proceedings. I doubt whether our Society had a truer or more loyal friend.

"As a citizen, he had the highest respect of this community. His whole life had been spent here. He made no attempt to attract attention; on the contrary, was of a quiet, retiring disposition. I shall always remember him as about the last representative we had left of the 'old-school gentleman.' Of dignified bearing and correct deportment, his striking characteristics were the vigor and strength of mind and the individuality of his opinions. He was not afraid to take a stand and assert himself in its favor, although every one else should oppose him. I never knew a man who had a higher ideal of honesty and integrity. We shall miss him. He has been a faithful member and officer of this Society. I am reminded that Mr. Bringhurst at the time of his death was the oldest merchant on Market Street in point of length of years in which he had been engaged in business.

" His life work is ended. The memory of his honorable career as a business man, his devotion to duty, his loyalty to his friends, and his faithful services to this Society will linger in the hearts of some of us for years to come."

Remarks of Lewis C. Vandegrift:

" MR. PRESIDENT :—It is an unusual thing for the members of this Society to meet here at this hour of the day, but the occasion that calls us together is of such overshadowing sadness to us all as to cause us to stop for a time, even in the midst of engrossing duties, and give heed once again to the summons which as years go by we become more accustomed to hear.

"This time it is our honored and respected treasurer, Henry R. Bringhurst, upon whom the hand of death has fallen.

"When I entered this Society, now nearly twenty years ago, he was then its treasurer, always careful, honest, trustworthy.

"On occasions such as this, our memories turn to the earlier days, when the friend and companion we loved and now miss was with us,—when the body now lifeless was full of activity, when the eye now closed had in it the sunshine of life, of friendship, of affection.

"With our years, our sorrows keep pace. My earliest recollection of our meetings here takes me back to the evenings in the room above. As the members would gather there about the table, four figures stand out prominently in my memory, and the last of the four has gone to join the others. Judge Wales, who usually presided over our meetings, although somewhat slight of form, was erect and active to the last. There was about him a certain precision of expression, but the tone and manner of his address and conversation were always affable and pleasant.

"Dr. Bush would be near by, and at the proper time, in his kindly, benignant, and lovable way, would sooner or later present some book or letter or other matter of interest to the Society.

"Dr. Johnson, for so many years our librarian, would probably be moving quietly about the edges of the room, reverently examining here and there the treasures he had through many years been so instrumental in collecting.

"Then our good friend, Mr. Bringhurst, in whose memory we are now here in sadness gathered, genial of face and of pleasant speech, would usually be at the other end of the table from Judge Wales, prepared on the instant to tell us just what our small balance was, and to stop, so far as he could, any inclination to spend it.

"Then, after our formal duties were over, how delightful to adjust one's self in a comfortable attitude in the environment and atmosphere of this quaint old building, so dear to each of us, and hear these men interchange reminiscences of our city and State. They had been lifelong friends and companions, and each knew much of the joys and sorrows, the struggles and successes, interwoven in the lives of the others. Each stood in his sphere as an anchor about which were gathered those good influences which make for the uprightness, morality, and honor of a community.

"They could, through those who were old when our friends were young, reach far back into the early days, and, being men who from boyhood had been fond of those things this Society was founded to preserve, their minds had always been receptive to the history and traditions of our State and its people.

"Each in his way had been a considerable part of the public life of the State. They had known and been in personal contact with the leading men of all professions and businesses for fifty years past, and by report knew almost as well those of an hundred years preceding.

"Hardly any conspicuous figure of a century past, or

any matter of local history, could be recalled for discussion that one or the other of them had not preserved some unique story by which a glimpse could be gotten of the past. How delightful to sit by in the mellow light of that upper room, with its books and records of earlier days, and listen to those good comrades recall to each other how things were in the long ago. They hardly realized that to some of us they filled the same position relatively as to them did those whose lives and actions they were recalling.

"One thus listening would have opened to his views such glimpses of the past as would take it out of its habitual half-light and give a realizing appreciation of the fact that the sun shone then with the same brightness as to-day, and that our grandparents and great-grandparents moved about in its warmth then as now, hampered less by the exactions and conventionalities of our day and generation, more dependent upon each other for their pleasures, and bound closer together in their sorrows and adversities.

"The last of the four has departed. In our association here we shall miss him sadly as we have missed the others. We are ourselves moving closer up to the waiting ferry-man, and our turn will not be long delayed. If we shall have performed our part somewhere near so well as these four good comrades and friends, I believe that when upon this theatre of our activities the curtain shall fall for us we will hear, as sweet music, the welcome words, 'Well done.'"

Francis H. Hoffecker, Esq., said:

"Mr. President:—Were I to yield to the impulse of my own feelings, I would be silent on this occasion. It is not with flattery to soothe the cold ear of death that those who have preceded me have spoken beautiful and touching words of our deceased friend and fellow-member of this Society. I feel that I must add my imperfect but sincere tribute to the memory of one whom I have ever loved and respected. In the death of Mr. Bringhurst I have sustained a double loss,—one who was a warm personal friend of my own father and mother, who have but recently passed into eternity, and one who was to me ever interesting, kind, and loyal.

"I cannot realize the great personal loss as a friend that his death will be to me. He was a man of unblemished character and pure mind, one of the strictest integrity.

"In his death the Society has lost one of the oldest and most valued members. It was truly said by one of the preceding speakers that Mr. Bringhurst belonged to the 'Old School' of gentlemen, a school that is, I fear, too rapidly being decimated in numbers. He was a gentleman, ever gentle, kindly, and courteous; one with sympathy and generosity sufficient to include those who might claim his aid simply in the name of humanity.

"But he has gone. His life-work is done. His good deeds 'can chant the requiem of a life well spent,' and the tomb, the environment of his mortality,—'the silver

cord is loosed, the golden bowl broken, the dust has returned to the earth, as it was, and the spirit has returned to God who gave it.'"

To these kindly and touching expressions the undersigned, with sadly tender memories, adds that he well knew the deceased in boyhood and in youth. We were companions in fishing, swimming, and skating sports along the Brandywine; we were members of the same youthful clubs and societies; we belonged to the same fire company, and we shared in much of the common experiences of the young people of early modern Wilmington. Later on a separation of thirty years could do little to cement, yet still less to sever, our friendship. Our renewed intercourse proved that the boy had been father to the man,—the old comrade was the same genial Harry Bringhurst, the same true friend, a broad-minded, whole-souled man—a plain man uniting a gentle spirit with the positive fibre of a hearty nature, buttressed always with the quiet courage of his convictions,—a hater of shams, and a lover of life's wholesome verities, whom it was ever pleasant and helpful to meet.

It has been beneficently ordered that no honest human striving shall ever be wholly in vain; and hence the world will be the better for these three men having lived in it, while their memory will be specially cherished as well by the community as by the historical society of which they were honored members.

All of which is respectfully submitted.

PENNOCK PUSEY,
Historiographer.

RICHARD BASSETT.

1735-1815.

Captain Continental Army. State Council of Delaware. 1776-1786. United States Constitutional Convention, 1787. State Convention to ratify Constitution, 1787. United States Senator, 1789-1793. Chief Justice Court of Common Pleas, 1793-1798. Governor of Delaware. 1797-1801.

PAPERS OF THE HISTORICAL SOCIETY OF DEl

XXIX.

THE LIFE AND CHARACT

OF

RICHARD BASSE

BY

HON. ROBERT E. PATTISON,

EX-GOVERNOR OF PENNSYLVANIA.

Read before the Historical Society of Delaware, Novemt

THE HISTORICAL SOCIETY OF DELAWA

WILMINGTON.

1900.

PAPERS OF THE HISTORICAL SOCIETY OF DELAW

XXIX.

THE LIFE AND CHARACTER

OF

RICHARD BASSET

BY

HON. ROBERT E. PATTISON,

EX-GOVERNOR OF PENNSYLVANIA.

Read before the Historical Society of Delaware, November 1

THE HISTORICAL SOCIETY OF DELAWARE,
WILMINGTON.
1900.

THE LIFE AND CHARACTER

OF

RICHARD BASSETT.

WHEN I was first brought under the magnetic influence
of your distinguished chief justice I received from him an
invitation to visit the Historical Society of Delaware and
talk on the life and character of Richard Bassett; I was
over-persuaded to treat the invitation as a command. In
obedience to this order, I am here to-night.

If an unfortunate dispute had not taken place in our
early colonial history as to appointments, I might now be
addressing you as citizens of Pennsylvania. Nevertheless,
our loss then became the nation's gain. The Commonwealth of Delaware vindicated her right to independence
by her firm patriotism and the magnificent record of her
troops in the war of the Revolution. The services of her
distinguished statesmen will always have a place in the
annals of our country. The roll of honor would not be
complete without the names of Bassett, Bayard, Clayton,
and Saulsbury.

Some years ago a beautiful Methodist church was built
in Philadelphia, under the ministry of the late Dr. Chas. W.
Buoy, a clergyman distinguished for his scholarly attain-

3

ments as well as great pulpit ability. It was adorned upon the interior with four handsome Corinthian columns. They stand in the four corners of the audience room, and reach from the floor to the ceiling. At his suggestion, upon each was carved a bust of a representative character of early Methodism. The learned Bishop Coke speaking for English Methodism; the pious and indefatigable Bishop Asbury for American Methodism; the brave old soldier, Captain Webb, for Methodism in the army; and the wise and conservative Richard Bassett, of Delaware, for the statesman in Methodism.

Upon different occasions I have spoken of the histories of these distinguished men, and also have had the pleasure of listening to addresses delivered by the Hon. Thomas Bayard and Chief Justice Lore in the church so honored.

While appreciating the services of Senator Bassett as a citizen and a lawyer, a statesman and a patriot, yet my inquiry has largely been directed to his associations with the early history of Methodism.

Dr. Buckley opens his history of Methodism with a very apt quotation to the end that " In the infancy of society, the chiefs of state formed the institutions; afterwards, the institutions formed the chiefs of state." Emerson declared " that an institution is the lengthened shadow of one man"—as the Reformation of Luther, Quakerism of Fox, Methodism of Wesley. Scipio, Milton called " the height of Rome"; and all history resolves itself very easily into the biography of a few stout and earnest persons.

Methodism far outstripped the highest anticipation of

its founder. As a chief of State, he had formed his institution, and it, in turn, developed the chiefs of State, who have so successfully enlarged its boundaries and extended its influence.

Wesley was as dependent upon his preachers as was Napoleon upon his marshals: neither would have succeeded without the other. The decline of Napoleon in his military triumphs began with the loss of his marshals; their successors either failed in loyalty or ability.

The rise of Methodism is due to a well-chosen ministry and their unswerving fidelity to the institution to which they had given their services. No better test of Mr. Wesley's ability in the selection of men could be found than in his choice of Francis Asbury at the Bristol Conference in 1771. Mr. Asbury began his career in this country as an itinerant, which was only to terminate with his death in 1816. In 1771 he was simply a missionary. In 1816 he was a full-fledged Bishop, with a well-organized ministry and church. "Can his career be paralleled? In his American ministry alone he preached sixteen thousand five hundred sermons, ordained more than four thousand preachers, travelled on horseback or in carriages two hundred and seventy thousand miles." Well does Stevens say, that with "Wesley, Whitefield, and Coke he ranks as one of the four greatest representative men of the Methodist movement." So fine was his discrimination that his estimate of men was almost infallible, and such his self-restraint that one could never discern his thoughts before he was disposed to declare them.

Bishop Asbury pronounced Dr. Coke a man of blessed mind and will; of the third branch of Oxonian Methodists; and as a minister of Christ in zeal, in labors, and in services the greatest man in the last century. On the morning of the 3d of May, 1814, Coke, while on the Indian Ocean, sailing for Ceylon in company with six missionaries, was discovered lifeless in his cabin.

At one of the meetings in New York City where Embury preached in 1767, the historian records, "a stranger appeared, in military dress and wearing a sword. He was obviously an officer of the royal army, and the few Methodists seem to have been disturbed, perhaps frightened, suspecting that he might have come to question them concerning the conversion of the musicians and other members of the army. But his devout conduct allayed their fears, for he conformed to their methods. At the close, he introduced himself as Captain Thomas Webb, of the King's service, and also a soldier of the cross and a spiritual son of John Wesley," and informed Embury that he had been authorized by Wesley to preach. Webb was in the siege of Louisburg, where he lost his right eye, and at midnight on September 12, 1759, was with those who landed at the foot of the tangled ravine below the Plains of Abraham, and in the van led by Howe which scaled those heights before dawn, where he fought in the murderous battle of Quebec, in the midst of the fiercest carnage, seeing scores of his companions killed, but escaping himself with a wound in his right arm. Five years after that battle he heard John Wesley preach in Bristol, and

became a zealous Christian. In 1765 he joined the Methodist Society and was licensed to preach. Webb frequently referred to his hair-breadth escapes, and the manner in which he lost his eye has never been paralleled. A ball struck him on the bone which guards the right eye, and taking an oblique direction burst the eyeball, and passing through his palate into his mouth he swallowed it. The wounded were put into a boat, and all were assisted to the land except Webb. One of the men said, "He needs no help; he is dead enough." But he was just able to whisper, "No, I am not dead." It was three months before he could attend to his military duty. His escape was so narrow—for had the ball struck him a hair's-breadth higher or lower it would have taken his life—that he felt that in a peculiar manner he owed his life to God. Of his scars he was not ashamed, and over his eyeless socket he wore a green shade. At the breaking out of the revolutionary war he returned to England, and resided near Bristol. He died in 1796, at the age of 72.

Mr. Asbury visited Delaware for the first time in 1772. He started for Bohemia to find Richard Wright, who had come over with him from England in response to Mr. Wesley at the Bristol Conference. Before reaching Wilmington he met Mr. Wright, as he was turning off to Mr. Tussey's to stay all night. Next day he went to Mr. Stedham's in Wilmington. Without stopping to preach, he went to New Castle, and preached in Mr. Robert Furness's tavern. Mr. Furness was a Methodist at this time, and one of the first in Delaware.

During the latter part of the year 1772 he visited Bohemia Manor for the first time. After visiting Mr. Ephraim Thomson, near Back Creek, he came to Wilmington, where he preached for the first time. It was, no doubt, upon this visit that he records preaching to the "First Lord of the Manor" in Bohemia. This visit was to be the beginning of many, which were to eventuate in acquaintances and events that were to give him protection and shelter. Here, six years later, he met Richard Bassett.

Richard Bassett was born in 1745. He was the adopted son of Mr. Lawson, a lawyer, who married a Miss Inzer. The Inzer family was Herman's heir to Bohemia Manor. In this family the title of "First Lord of the Manor" existed until the Revolution abolished all titles of nobility. The Boushell or Sluyter family, one or the other, by marrying into the Inzer family, inherited a part of the Manor; so, also, the Oldham family. Mr. Bassett was educated and trained for the profession of law by Mr. Lawson, whose heir he became. By this inheritance he came into possession of six thousand acres of Bohemia Manor, which, we are informed, embraced the fairest and best portion of the Manor.

Mr. Bassett married Miss Ann Ennals, of Dorchester County, Maryland, sister of Mr. Henry Ennals and niece of Judge Ennals of the same county. Mrs. Bassett did not live many years. His second wife was Miss Bruff, a lady from Talbot County. Mr. Bassett raised but one child. She became the wife of the Hon. James Bayard, the eminent lawyer and statesman who was associated

with Messrs. Gallatin, Russell, Adams, and Clay in nego-
tiating the Treaty of Ghent in 1814.

Mr. Bayard studied law under Mr. Bassett. It is said
they frequently debated experimental Christianity. When
they met it was Greek meeting Greek, and diamond cutting diamond. Sometimes Mr. Bassett would cut him
short by saying, "All you know I taught you;" and
would be answered, "You taught me all you knew, and
all I know besides I taught myself."

Bohemia Manor, to which I have referred, is bounded
by Bohemia and Elk Rivers, Back Creek, and the Delaware State line. It takes its name from a Bohemian,
whose name was Augustine Herman; he obtained a grant
of eighteen thousand acres of land in Cecil County, Maryland, which he called Bohemia Manor. It is said that the
Dutch had him a prisoner of war at one time, under sentence of death, in New York. A short time before he was
to be executed he feigned himself to be deranged in mind,
and requested that his horse should be brought to him in
the prison. The horse was brought, finely caparisoned.
Herman mounted him and seemed to be performing military exercises, when, on the first opportunity, he bolted
through one of the large windows, which was some fifteen
feet above ground, swam the North River, ran his horse
through Jersey, and alighted on the bank of the Delaware
opposite New Castle; and thus made his escape from death
and the Dutch. The daring feat, tradition says, he had
transferred to canvas, himself represented as standing by
the side of his charger, from whose nostrils the blood was

flowing. It is said that a copy of this painting still exists. He never suffered the horse to be used afterwards; and when he died, had him buried and honored his grave with a tombstone. Herman first settled in the town of New Castle. Here he buried his horse, and here this stone, if it exists, should be.

This weird tradition was characteristic of the times out of which it came, and reminds us of the story given by Washington Irving in his sketch of a visit to Abbotsford, the home of Sir Walter Scott, when he observed to Mr. Scott that his cats seemed to have a black-letter taste in literature. "Ah," said he, "these cats are a very mysterious kind of folk. There is always more passing in their minds than we are aware of. It comes no doubt from their being so familiar with witches and warlocks." He went on to tell a little story about a "gude" man who was returning to his cottage one night, when in a lonely, out-of-the-way place, he met a funeral procession of cats all in mourning, bearing one of their race to the grave in a coffin covered with a black velvet pall. The worthy man, astonished and frightened at so strange a pageant, hastened home and told what he had seen to his wife and children. Scarce had he finished, when a great black cat that sat at the fireside raised himself up and exclaimed, "Then I am the king of cats," and vanished up the chimney. The funeral seen by the "gude" man was one of the cat dynasty. "Our grimalkin here," added Scott, "sometimes reminds me of the story, by the airs of sovereignty which he assumes; and I am apt to treat him with respect from

the idea that he may be a great prince incog., and may some time or other come to the throne."

Herman settled in Bohemia Manor prior to 1664. Herman was the great name of the region. He had his deer park: the walls of it are mentioned in 1850 as still standing. He rode in his coach, driven by liveried servants. His mansion commanded a fine view of the Bohemia River to the Chesapeake Bay. His tombstone has this inscription:

AUGUSTINE HERMAN, BOHEMIAN,

The First Founder and Seater of

Bohemia Manor, Anno. 1669.

There was in former years a house on the Manor that had been standing for more than one hundred and sixty years. The bricks, sash, and all the original materials in it were made in England.

Mr. Bassett had his first interview with Mr. Asbury in 1778, at Mr. Thomas White's. This was Judge White, who was born about 1730. He married Miss Mary Nutter, daughter of David Nutter, Esq., of Northwest Fork, Sussex County, Delaware. Of him it was written, "As to moral worth, he had no superior in his day—his house and hands were always open to relieve the needy. He was the friend of the poor and oppressed." He died in the spring of 1795, in his 63d year.

Mr. Bassett was going to Maryland on professional business, and called to pass a night with Judge White. As the family was passing through the house, and opening

and shutting the doors, he noticed one or more persons
who seemed to be occupying a private room. Inquiring
of Mrs. White who they were, dressed in sable garments,
keeping themselves so retiredly, she replied: "Oh, they
are some of the best men in the world; they are Methodist
preachers." Having heard of them before, he seemed to
be alarmed at his close proximity to them, and observed:
"Then I cannot stay here to-night." Mrs. White replied:
"Oh, yes; you must stay, they will not hurt you." Supper being ready, they all sat down at the table. Mr. Asbury had considerable conversation with Mr. Bassett, by
which he was convinced that Methodist preachers were
not so ignorant or unsociable as to make them outcasts
from civil society. On taking leave, he invited Mr. Asbury, more from custom than desire, to call on him in case
he visited Dover. When Mr. Bassett returned home and
informed his wife that he had been in company with Methodist preachers and invited one of them to his home, she
was greatly troubled, but was quieted when he told her
"It is not likely that he will come." He had not yet, evidently, become thoroughly acquainted with the Methodist
preacher, or he would have known that they never let such
an invitation pass by.

Some time in 1779, Mr. Bassett looked out of his win-
dow and saw Mr. Asbury making for his door. Wishing
to have company to help on the conversation, Mr. Bassett
stepped out and invited Dr. MaGaw, Governor Rodney,
and some others to tea. They sat down at the table and
became so deeply interested in conversation that they con-

tinued it until a late hour. This was the beginning of a friendship which lasted 36 years. Judge White had occasion soon after to visit Dover on business, and stayed all night with Mr. Bassett. Like most others who countenanced the Methodist at that day, he was marked as a Tory. Some of the rabble went in search of him, declaring their intention to inflict summary punishment upon him in case they found him. They came to Mr. Bassett's door. Mr. Bassett was at that time captain of a militia company. He took his stand in his entry, with his sword and pistols, and when the mob inquired if Thomas White was there, and asked that he might be given to them to be punished as an enemy of his country, Mr. Bassett told them that Mr. White was in his house, that he was no more a Tory than any of them, and that if they got him into their hands they would have to walk over his dead body. Well knowing the standing and influence of Mr. Bassett with the community, the raging rabble retired without their victim, and Judge White was saved through the chivalry of his friend. Under date of February, 1780, Mr. Asbury says: "Went home with Lawyer Bassett, a very conversant and affectionate man, who from his own acknowledgment, appears to be sick of sin."

Wesley's Chapel in Dover was erected in 1784, principally by Mr. Bassett's means. It was the expectation of Mr. Asbury that Mr. Bassett would become a preacher. He frequently spoke in Philadelphia at St. George's Church, and was noted as a "sweet singer."

In an exhortation, in the old log Bethesda Chapel, on

the manor where his family worshipped, in meeting the skeptic's position of doubting and disbelieving whatever he cannot test by his senses, he wishes to know, "How a man could believe, by this rule, that he had a back, as he could not see it, unless he had a neck like a crane or a goose." Quaint as this language was, it was better suited to the populace than if it smacked more of metaphysics. In 1795 he was settled on his large estate in Bohemia Manor; as he was both wealthy and liberal, his house was the principal resort for Methodist preachers. He was seldom without some of them, and often had a number of them together.

When camp-meetings were adopted, Mr. Bassett would pitch his tent near the tents of the darkies, and their music to him was, as he designated it, "his harp." While he lived in the Manor he had two camp-meetings in a beautiful grove on his land, a mile north of his mansion, at Bohemia Ferry. The First was held in 1808 and the second in 1809.

He was a member of Congress during the time the Articles of Confederation were in force. In 1786 the Legislature elected him a member of the commission which had under consideration the commercial relations of the several States, and was known as the Annapolis Convention. In 1787 he was a member of the convention which gave to the country the Constitution of the United States. Of this convention Mr. Jefferson wrote from Paris in 1787: " We promise ourselves good from the Convention holding at Philadelphia. It consists of the ablest men in

America. It will surely be the instrument of referring to Congress the regulation of our trade." Later in the year he wrote: "Our Federal Convention is likely to sit until October; there is a general disposition through the States to adopt what they shall propose, and we may be assured their propositions will be wise, as a more able assembly never sat in America. Happily for us, that when we find our constitution defective and insufficient to secure the happiness of our people, we can assemble with all the coolness of philosophers and set it to rights, while every other nation on earth must have recourse to arms to amend or restore their constitutions. With all the defects of our constitution, whether general or particular, the comparison of our government with those of Europe is like a comparison of heaven with hell; England, like the earth, may be allowed to take the intermediate station. And yet, I hear there are people among you who think the experience of our government has already proved that republican governments will not answer. Send those gentry here to count the blessings of monarchy. A king's sister, for instance, stopped on the road, and on a hostile journey, is sufficient cause for him to march immediately twenty thousand men to revenge this insult, when he had shown himself little moved by the matter of right then in question."

Writing in 1787, "The constitution, however, has been received with very general enthusiasm, and, as far as can be judged from external demonstrations, the bulk of the people are eager to adopt it. In the Eastern States, the

printers will print nothing against it unless the writer sub-
scribes his name. Massachusetts and Connecticut have
called conventions in January, to consider of it. In New
York, there is a division. The Governor is known to be
hostile to it. Jersey, it is thought, will certainly accept it.
Pennsylvania is divided; and all the bitterness of her factions has been kindled anew on it. But the party in favor
of it is strongest, both in and out of the Legislature. Delaware will do what Pennsylvania shall do."

The Constitution of the 17th of September, 1787, received the unanimous consent of the States present in convention. The signers to it for Delaware are George Reed,
Gunning Bedford, Jr., John Dickinson, Richard Bassett,
and Jacob Broom, with Washington as president and
deputy from Virginia.

George Reed was born in Cecil County, Maryland, in
1774. He became well known as a well-read lawyer, thoroughly versed in the intricacies of special pleading, and
master of the logic of law. In 1763 he succeeded John
Ross as attorney-general to the three lower counties, as
they were known in Delaware. In September, 1776, he
was president of the convention which formed the first
constitution in Delaware. In 1777 he became governor of
the State. He was Senator from Delaware immediately
after the adoption of the constitution, and remained in
this office until September, 1793, when he was appointed
chief justice of the Supreme Court of Delaware. He died
in 1798. As a lawyer, a patriot, a senator, and a judge, he
was alike unpretending, consistent, dignified, and impartial.

John Dickinson was one of those distinguished writers whose pens, in the earlier stages of the struggle between the colonies and England, proved flaming swords. He was the author of Farmer's Letters, and also of letters signed "Fabius," urging the ratification of the Constitution then before the people. Of him Mr. Jefferson wrote in 1808, when hearing of his death, "A more estimable man or truer patriot could not have left us. Among the first of the advocates for the rights of his country when assailed by Great Britain, he continued to the last the orthodox advocate of the true principles of our new government, and his name will be consecrated in history as one of the great worthies of the Revolution. We ought to be grateful for having been permitted to retain the benefit of his counsel to so good an old age; still the moment of losing it, whenever it arrives, must be a moment of deep-felt regret. For himself, perhaps, a longer period of life was less important, allowed as the feeble enjoyments of that age are with so much pain. But to his country, every addition to his moments was interesting. A junior companion of his labors in the early part of our Revolution, it has been a great comfort to me to have retained his friendship to the last moment of his life."

Gunning Bedford was born in Philadelphia in 1747. Graduated at Nassau Hall, New Jersey, in 1771, with great distinction. He studied law in Philadelphia and afterwards practised in Delaware; was distinguished for his eloquence as an advocate. He received from Washington the commission of the first judge of the district

court of the United States for the District of Delaware, which he held until his death in 1812. He so behaved in these high offices as to deserve and receive the approbation of his fellow-citizens, and the historian records of him, " His form was goodly, his temper amiable, his manners winning, and his discharge of private duties exemplary." In the Federal Convention he accused the large States of seeking to aggrandize themselves at the expense of the small. He boldly threatened an alliance of the small States with foreign power if oppressed by the larger ones, and explained the circumstances which would justify the small States in a foreign alliance.

Jacob Broom was born in Philadelphia in 1752, and died April 25, 1810. Mr. Drake in his biographical dictionary says: " At the time of his death he was aged 58 years. He filled many offices of trust in Delaware." The address to General Washington, December 17, 1783, was written by Jacob Broom, and is unrivalled as a composition. His son, James M. Broom, of the Philadelphia bar, who died in 1864, was the candidate of the Native American party for the Presidency of the United States. Jacob Broom, the member of the legislative convention, was a familiar associate of the public men of his day, and his name constantly occurs in connection with those of Bassett, Reed, Dickinson, and Bedford.

Mr. Jefferson wrote in 1788: " The President is to be elected the first Wednesday in February; the new Legislature to meet the first week in March; the place is not yet decided on." Philadelphia was first proposed, and had

six and a half votes; the half vote was Delaware, one of whose members wanted to take a vote on Wilmington. So your city had the honor of having a part in the contest for the place of meeting of the first Congress after the adoption of the Constitution.

From 1789 to 1793 Mr. Bassett served as a Senator, and was the first member to cast his vote for locating the Capitol on the Potomac. Subsequently he was governor of Delaware and judge of the United States Court for the district which included Pennsylvania, New Jersey, and Delaware; the latter office he filled at the close of his life. During this period he had three furnished houses: his old home in Dover, his principal one on the Manor, and one in Wilmington. In person he is described as a heavy-built man. The last year of his life he was rendered partially helpless by paralysis. Mr. Asbury refers to him in 1815 in touching and affectionate terms: "My long-loved friend, Judge Bassett, some time past a paralytic, is lately stricken on the other side and suffers much in his helpless state." He died in the latter part of 1815. His funeral was attended by a large concourse of people, at his mansion on the Manor. He lived to see the institutions of his country and church firmly established. He adorned every position he held. His virtues will live in the recollection of all who are brought within the knowledge of his services and character.

JOHN DICKINSON.

1732-1808.

PAPERS OF THE HISTORICAL SOCIETY OF DELAWARE.

XXX.

THE

LIFE AND CHARACTER

OF

JOHN DICKINSON.

BY

ROBERT H. RICHARDS, Esq.

Read before the Historical Society of Delaware, May 21, 1900.

THE HISTORICAL SOCIETY OF DELAWARE,

WILMINGTON.

1901.

THE LIFE AND CHARACTER

OF

JOHN DICKINSON.

THE name of Dickinson, while not a *very* common one, has been well known in various parts of the country for several generations. There are in this country two general branches of the family, one of which is found to have first appeared in the New England States and the members of which were Presbyterians, and the other immigrated to the Middle and Southern States.

Those who bear the name in the Middle and Southern States are descended from Charles Dickinson, who died in London in 1653, leaving three sons, all of whom were Quakers. In 1654 these sons emigrated to Virginia to escape imprisonment at home as Non-conformists.

There is a legendary account of the renown achieved by the English ancestors of the family as soldiers, but of this there appears to be no authentic record. It is important perhaps for us to know, however, that this family belonged to that middle class of English society which, we may safely say, has had more to do with shaping the destinies of England in modern times than any other.

The family coat of arms consisted of a shield divided horizontally by a single bar, above and below which a lion, and at the top of the shield a visored helmet surmounted by a lion rampant. The motto was *esse quam videri*, " to be rather than to seem;" and a careful study of the life of John Dickinson impels one to the belief either that the selection of this motto by the Dickinson family must have been the result of some deep-rooted, uneradicable family characteristic, or that John Dickinson made it the motto of his life.

Of the three brothers to whom I have referred, Walter, the immediate ancestor of the subject of this sketch, removed in 1659 to Talbot County, on the Eastern shore of Maryland. He there purchased a plantation, which he called " Crosia-doré," on the shores of the Choptank River, and this estate, from the day of its settlement until the present hour,—a period of over two centuries and a half,—has always been the home of the same Dickinson family, the present owner and occupant being in the direct line of descent from the original proprietor.

At Crosia-doré, on the 8th of November, 1732, John Dickinson was born. He was the second son of Samuel Dickinson, the grandson of the first proprietor of the estate, and of Mary Cadwalader, his second wife, of Philadelphia.

Samuel Dickinson was bred to the law, but, at the time of the birth of his son John, was living upon his Maryland estate the life of a country gentleman.

In 1740 Samuel Dickinson removed to Kent County,

Delaware, where he purchased an estate of about one thousand three hundred acres near Dover. It is thought that this change of residence was made because of the fact that Dover furnished better educational advantages than the locality in which Samuel Dickinson was living. At this day the descendants of Samuel Dickinson are among the largest land owners in Kent County, possessing more than three thousand acres.*

At Dover, Samuel Dickinson, who shortly after his removal was appointed first Judge of the Court of Common Pleas, secured the services of William Killen, a young Irishman, as a tutor for his son John.

We know very little about William Killen, but the fact that he subsequently became the Chief Justice and afterwards Chancellor of Delaware is sufficient testimony of his ability.

In those days the prevalent idea of an education embraced little more than a thorough knowledge of classical literature. " It is certainly not a little remarkable in the history of teaching," says Dr. Stillé, " that, under the instruction of this young Irishman, himself but fifteen years of age when he went to Dover, Dickinson should not only have early imbibed a love of classical literature, but that his studies should have taught him that comprehensiveness of view and those forms of expression which are characteristic of the ancient classical authors. If there is any truth in the saying, ' The style is the man,' it was true of

---

* The last statement is taken from Scharf's " History of Delaware."

Dickinson. It would be difficult to over-estimate the power which this style, derived from those who wrote in what is erroneously called a dead language, enabled him to exercise in the political controversies in which he was engaged."

In 1750, when John Dickinson was eighteen years old, he was entered as a student of the law in the office of John Moland, Esq., of Philadelphia, one of the leading lawyers in that city and King's Attorney in Pennsylvania. We may pause here to observe that the connotation of the term "student of the law" was vastly different in those days from now. The industry and luminous ability of Mr. Justice Blackstone had not yet blazed the way into the intricate mazes of the common law, but the road to this "perfection of human reason" led through the austere portals of the venerable Coke's Commentaries upon Littleton, and the Year-Books.

After three years in Philadelphia, Mr. Dickinson prevailed upon his father to send him to England, as was customary in those days with men of means, to finish his legal education at the Temple. He remained here at the Middle Temple for four years, having as fellow-students such men as Lord Thurlow, afterwards Lord Chancellor; Kenyon, Lord Chief Justice of the King's Bench; John Hill, afterwards Earl of Hillsborough, and William Cowper, the poet.

Let me refer here to some statistics furnished by the Historical Society of Pennsylvania. I stated above that it was customary before the Revolution for young men

who contemplated practising the profession of the law to complete their studies in England, at the fountain-head of the common law. This statement is subject to sectional restriction, for an investigation has shown that this custom was almost exclusively confined to the Middle and Southern States; the number of young men educated in England increasing as we go farther south; South Carolina possessing the greatest number, and the New England States almost none. We shall see, I think, the effect of this hereafter.

Mr. Dickinson returned to Philadelphia and began to practise his profession in 1757. Of him as a lawyer we know comparatively little. In a letter written to his mother shortly after he began to practise, he urges her to come to Philadelphia, says that he is busy, and that " the money is flowing in." In the first volume of Dallas's Reports we find that there are three cases mentioned which Mr. Dickinson argued in the Supreme Court in 1760. One of these was a case of " foreign attachment;" the second an eject-ment case, and the third a question of criminal procedure. William Rawle, the elder, speaking of Dickinson as a lawyer, says, " He possessed considerable fluency, with a sweetness of tone and agreeable modulation of voice, not well calculated, however, for a large audience. His law knowledge was respectable, although not remarkably extensive, for his attention was directed to historical and political studies. Wholly engaged in public life, he left the bar soon after the commencement of the American Revolution." Whatever may have been the depths of his

legal learning, it is quite certain that his early prominence
in public life was largely due to the reputation he had
gained as a lawyer.

In October, 1760, he was elected a member of the Assembly of the "Lower Counties," as Delaware was then
called, and upon taking his seat was made Speaker of that
body.

In 1762 he was chosen a member of the Pennsylvania
Assembly from the city of Philadelphia. He writes to his
friend, George Read, concerning this election, in the following noble strain: "I flatter myself that I came in with
the approval of all good men. I confess that I should
like to make an immense bustle in the world, if it could be
done by virtuous actions; but as there is no probability
in that, I am content if I can live innocent and beloved
by those I love." The question which almost exclusively
occupied the attention of the Pennsylvania Assembly at
the time of Dickinson's entrance into it was whether or
not the Assembly on behalf of the people should petition
the king to abrogate the Proprietary Charter and take the
government of the province into his own hands. Mr.
Dickinson opposed this measure, and led the fight for the
opposition; against him were Joseph Gallaway, the greatest lawyer of his time in Pennsylvania, and Benjamin
Franklin, the apostle of common sense, already loaded with
honors and degrees by all the universities of Europe.
Dickinson was completely successful.

Now begins Dickinson's career in that field in which
he was most successful, and in which he stands without

a peer, as the pensman of the Revolution. We know of no man in history who, by his pen, through the means of pamphleteering, exercised a greater influence upon the thought, action, and policies of his time than did John Dickinson. In 1765, during the discussion in Parliament of the " Stamp Act," he printed a pamphlet entitled " The Late Regulations respecting the British Colonies on the Continent of America considered." It is impossible to consider the contents of each of these numerous pamphlets or their influence upon events, and we can do scarcely more than enumerate them. Dickinson was a member of the Stamp Act Congress, and in that body a mighty opponent of the right of the English Parliament to tax the colonies for revenue without their consent.

On the 2d of December, 1767, in the *Pennsylvania Chronicle,* under date of November 7, the anniversary of the day upon which William of Orange had landed in England, a day of ill-omen to those who, the colonists contended, were governing them in the same arbitrary manner as that in which James II. had governed their forefathers, there appeared the first of that great series known as the " Farmer's Letters." These letters, twelve in number, have been said to contain more " practical and applied political philosophy than is to be found in many elaborate treatises." To most Americans they became, until the beginning of the war, a genuine political text-book, and their maxims were received with absolute confidence. Like the writings of Burke, which they greatly resemble, they form a great storehouse of political wisdom

with reference to the fundamental questions that were occupying the attention of Americans and Englishmen at the time of their publication. After the series was complete, they were collected and published by Richard Henry Lee, of Virginia, by Benjamin Franklin in Dublin, and at about the same time were published in Paris. Benjamin Franklin, Dickinson's ancient and continued enemy, himself secured their publication in Dublin and Paris. There were also two editions printed in Boston.

These letters were received with enthusiasm throughout the colonies, and the " Pennsylvania Farmer" found himself looked upon as the foremost patriot of America.

About this time the first cargoes of tea arrived in the colonies since the passage of the bill taxing tea in America, and it is interesting to know that the citizens of Philadelphia held a meeting, at which Dr. Thomas Cadwalader presided and Dickinson took a prominent part, to take steps to prevent the landing of tea in Philadelphia, seventeen days before the similar meeting was held in Boston which preceded the famous Boston tea-party. Such drastic measures as were resorted to in Boston were not, however, found necessary in Philadelphia.

Mr. Dickinson suffered from the position he took in the Pennsylvania Assembly upon the question of the Proprietary charter, and at the expiration of his term was not re-elected. After devoting his leisure to study and reflection, the results of which are seen in the " Farmer's Letters," he became again a member of Assembly in 1771. On the 5th of March of this year, at the request of the

Assembly, he drafted a petition to the king, which was unanimously adopted. The petition, which is in the tone of the most loyal devotion to the Crown, asks that the people of Pennsylvania may be restored to the condition they were in before 1763.

In the mean time, in 1770, Dickinson had been married to Miss Mary Norris, the only daughter of Isaac Norris, for many years Speaker of the Pennsylvania Assembly, but then deceased, and with his wife resided at Fairhill, the beautiful country home of the Norris family, where was collected one of the finest libraries in America. Dickinson was married on July 19, and the only wedding-tour we can find any record of began some time in September, the itinerary of the journey touching Reading, Bethlehem, Lancaster, York, and the frontier town of Carlisle, being, in fact, a tour of Pennsylvania. Let us stop to quote from a letter written by Dickinson to an aunt during the journey, dated September 20, 1770.

Among other things he says, " We dined at Pottsgrove, and among memorable things it may be put down as one, that after proper respect paid to a beefsteak, somebody desired an egg to be poached. It may also be added as another remarkable fact that yesterday completed *two months* of marriage without a quarrel. . . . To-morrow we proceed for Carlisle, which I expect to reach on Saturday." This journey, however, had a double purpose. It was not known what position the German and Scotch-Irish inhabitants of Pennsylvania would take upon the question of resistance to the English Parliament, and Dickinson

desired to sound them on this point. It is needless to say that he found them all the stanchest patriots.

As the hour approached when the fate of America was to be tried, Dickinson, with the wise conservatism of a man bred to the law and learned in the classics, having ever before him the precedents of history, began to shrink from the advanced course taken by the patriots of New England. He refused to endorse the measures of Massachusetts. He did not think America in the best condition for revolution at that time. Consequently in New England he fell from the high estate in the popular estimation that once he held, and, instead of the greatest American patriot, was called "timid" and "apathetic."

He was chosen a delegate from Pennsylvania to the first Congress in 1774, and was immediately placed upon a committee to draft a petition to the king, which he did personally, as well as a subsequent petition to the king passed at the next Congress. These petitions rank among the other state papers prepared by Dickinson, and he, in fact, was the author of practically all of the many issued by Congress during this period, whose ample eulogium is the tribute paid to them by Lord Chatham when he said in the House of Lords, " History, my Lords, has been my favorite study, and in the celebrated writings of antiquity I have often admired the patriotism of Greece and Rome, but I must declare and vow that in the master states of the world I know not the people nor the Senate who, in such a complication of difficult circumstances, can stand in preference to the Delegates

of America assembled in General Congress at Philadelphia."

Mr. Dickinson was also the author of the " Declaration announcing to the World our reasons for taking up arms against England."

We are now approaching the period of the Declaration of Independence. It was becoming apparent that the great object of Samuel Adams (Judas Iscariot, as Edward Tilghman called him) and the New England delegates in Congress was to precipitate open hostilities with England and secure the independence of the colonies. This the delegates from Pennsylvania, led by Dickinson, opposed, and with them, at first, were the delegates from the Southern and Middle colonies generally; but gradually the independence party gained strength until a Declaration of Independence was drafted and proposed. The continued oppression of the New England colonists and the sending of troops to New York strengthened the independence party, but at no time, either before or after the discussion of the proposed Declaration, had they enough votes in Congress to adopt the resolution, until Dickinson, seeing that the sentiment of a majority of the people appeared to be in favor of independence, together with his friend, Robert Morris, afterwards the financier of the Revolution, absented himself from Congress and allowed the vote to be taken. Unlike many of his colleagues who, with him, opposed the measure, he did not stay and vote or afterwards sign the Declaration, but with an honest consistency characteristic of the man and mindful of his

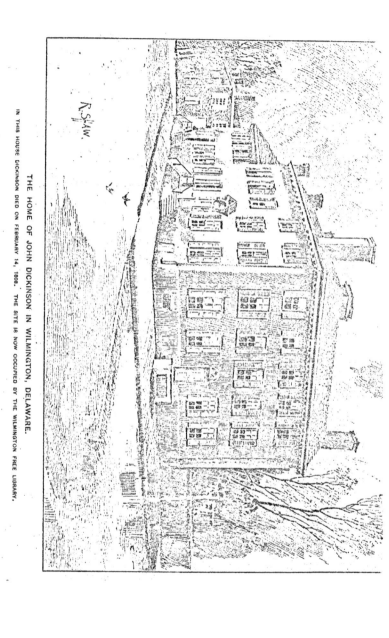

THE HOME OF JOHN DICKINSON IN WILMINGTON, DELAWARE.

IN THIS HOUSE DICKINSON DIED ON FEBRUARY 14, 1808. THE SITE IS NOW OCCUPIED BY THE WILMINGTON FREE LIBRARY.

family motto, "to be rather than to seem," he even refused to sit as a figure in the famous picture painted by
Trumbull of the "Signing of the Declaration." Giving,
as his reason, that he did not sign it, did not at the time
approve it, and had no share in the glory of the act of
signing it. Dickinson's position in this matter brought
upon him the odium of all the advanced revolutionists
in the country.

During the severe trial of the long debate in Congress
on this vital question, it is worthy of remark that Dickinson, whose views in regard to the inopportune time which
had been chosen for a final separation were well known,
should have been regarded by his fellow-members with un-
diminished trust and confidence. Special pains seem to
have been taken to meet his objections, which were chiefly
twofold,—the want of unity among the colonies, and the
want of foreign allies. For over a year before the Declaration, and after that time until the persecutions of his
political enemies drove him into retirement, Dickinson, as
colonel of the first battalion of the Pennsylvania Asso-
ciators, a State military organization, was under arms;
being among the first to promote the idea of arming to
resist British oppression, and, rather than "tame," "spirit-
less," and "apathetic," as his enemies called him, there
are but few who, after studying his career, will not agree
with Hildreth, the historian, in thinking that his course
with respect to the Declaration exhibited the "noblest
proof of moral courage ever shown by a public man in
the history of the country."

The public life of Mr. Dickinson was eclipsed, but not extinguished, by the attitude he assumed in regard to the Declaration of Independence.

Through the machinations of his enemies he was forced to resign from the army, and retired into private life on his farm near Dover, in Kent County, Delaware. Immediately, almost, the Delaware Assembly elected him to Congress, November 5, 1776, but he absolutely refused to serve, without assigning a reason. After remaining on his plantation enjoying the cultured friendship of such men as the Ridgeleys and Rodneys in Kent County, Dickinson re-entered the army as a private soldier in Captain Lewis's company of the Delaware militia, and fought through the Brandywine campaign, after which he was commissioned a Brigadier-General by Governor McKean, of Pennsylvania. In 1779 Dickinson was unanimously elected to Congress by Delaware, in 1780 he was elected to the Delaware Assembly from New Castle County, and the same year was elected President of Delaware. In 1782 he was elected President of the Supreme Executive Council of Pennsylvania, therefore being at the same time Governor of Delaware, Governor of Pennsylvania, and member of Congress from Delaware. But times have changed. Pennsylvania no longer has to come to Delaware to borrow a governor. As President of the Supreme Executive Council of Pennsylvania, Dickinson was *ex officio* Chief Justice of the High Court of Appeals, and as such, associated with the Justices of the Supreme Court; he delivered in 1785, among other opinions, one in an important cause,

—viz., Talbot *vs.* The Achilles *et al.,* reported in 1 Dallas, and involving important questions of Admiralty jurisdiction.

Thus this man whom two States vied with each other in honoring was, at the same time, the chief executive officer in them both, the highest judicial officer in one and a member of the highest legislative body in the country from the other, a combination of the legislative, executive, and judicial powers hardly compatible with the Constitution which Dickinson himself subsequently helped to make.

When in September, 1786, in pursuance to the invitation of the Legislature of Virginia, the Commissioners appointed by the various States assembled at Annapolis to devise a method of forming a more perfect union of the colonies, John Dickinson, a Commissioner from Delaware, was chosen president of the meeting. This meeting being ineffective, Dickinson was a delegate from the same State in the convention, subsequently held, which framed the Constitution of the United States. His eminent fitness for this work must have been apparent, bringing as he did to that body a broader knowledge and insight into English constitutional law than any other man on this continent could have done, and being in point of diplomatic and political experience the peer of any member. He took a very prominent position among those early American sages who builded a fabric the enduring utility and symmetrical adaptation of which they could in no sense have conceived of, and, I think we may say, if

they had been spared here for a century and a quarter longer, the apparent elasticity of which would have surprised them.

After the submission of the Constitution to the States for ratification, Dickinson wrote and published a series of essays in the form of nine letters signed *Fabius*, where he appears as an ardent champion of the ratification of the Constitution. These essays did not treat the features of the Constitution in the profound and argumentative manner in which the Federalist did; they were probably designed for a more popular audience, but they had great influence, and did much to secure the ratification of that remarkable instrument.

Politically, Mr. Dickinson became attached to what was known in that day as the Republican party, in this the Democratic party. He was a State's rights man and a warm friend and adviser of Thomas Jefferson. He was, in fact, looked upon generally as one of the political sages of the period, and his advice was often sought in difficult matters. In 1805, during the discussion of the proposed purchase of Louisiana and Florida, the advice of Dickinson was sought by Senator Logan, of Pennsylvania. On the 19th of December Dickinson replies in a letter, a quotation from which perhaps the times justify, as disclosing the writer's feeling upon the question of the acquisition of new territory by the United States. He says,—

"To rush into war at this time for the wilderness beyond the river Mexicano, or on the remote waters of the

Missouri, would be, in my opinion, madness. We want them not. We can hereafter have as much territory as we ought to desire. Nothing is so likely to prevent acquisitions as the seeking of them too eagerly, unreasonably, and contemptuously. In the natural course of things we shall, if wise, gradually become irresistible, and the people will sink into our population. Let us patiently wait for this inevitable progression, and not deprive ourselves of the golden eggs that will be laid for us by destroying in a covetous and cruel frenzy the bird that, if left to itself, will from day to day supply them."

It is natural to suppose that a man who was so deeply indebted to literature as Mr. Dickinson, and whose life had been so sedulously devoted to the application of its inestimable riches to the service of his country, would not, among his many benefactions, overlook education, the mainspring of republican greatness and stability. While President of Pennsylvania, he conceived the idea of establishing a college west of the Susquehanna, then the frontier of the colony. Consequently, with Dr. Benjamin Rush and other friends, he secured the passage of an Act of Assembly incorporating what the Assembly insisted upon naming Dickinson College, "In Memory," as the Act says, "of the great and important services rendered to his Country by his Excellency John Dickinson, Esq." Mr. Dickinson gave to the new college a plantation in Adams County of three hundred acres, and one in Cumberland County of two hundred acres, and all the books saved from the library of his father-in-law,

Isaac Norris, the Speaker, at the burning of Fair-Hill by the British during the Revolution, in all about fifteen hundred volumes.

After the expiration of his term as President of Pennsylvania, Dickinson went back to Delaware to live, and located permanently at Wilmington, where he built a fine mansion at Eighth and Market Streets, upon the site now fittingly occupied by the Wilmington Free Library building. Here, retired from the toil and anxieties of a public life; enjoying an affluent fortune, surrounded by friends who loved him, and by books which, to him, were a constant source of consolation, he spent the concluding years of his life, dispensing among others the blessings which he enjoyed himself, and receiving in return the heartfelt tribute of popular veneration.

He died on the 14th of February, 1808, at the age of seventy-five.

In a life of such manifold and varied activities, it is usually difficult to determine which of its policies and achievements are most characteristic and most important. In the career of Dickinson, however, there appear to be two periods when his most important work was done.

To the successful prosecution of the war of independence the power of the pen was almost as essential as that of the sword. To arouse and sustain a spirit of resistance, to give to the proclamations, addresses, and resolutions of Congress a tone becoming the dignity of that body, and the destiny of the country, and to command the respect and secure the support of the enlightened in

Europe, required genius and cultivation of the highest order and the most commanding influence. In this department of the patriotic contest none surpassed the subject of this paper.

Reference has been made to the fact that almost no students from the New England colonies were entered at the English Inns of Court prior to the Revolution, although all the colonies were governed mainly by the same English common law. The cause of their absence is of course referable to the peculiar circumstances under which the New Englanders left England and to their religious beliefs. To this fact, that the New England lawyers had not the solid training in English law and politics which could at that time be gotten only in England herself, we think, are to be ascribed the difference in the positions maintained by the New England colonies and the other colonies during the pre-Revolutionary controversy.

In Massachusetts, the leading colony in New England, the government was essentially a theocracy up to the time of the Revolution. In New England generally the clergy directed the course of public opinion and of the movement looking to the resistance of the English Parliament. What, then, was their position? They disdained to argue that Parliament and the ministry were exceeding their authority, or that their acts were wholly unjustified by the English theory of colonial law or by the precedents and practice under it; they refused to rest their case upon the allegation that the acts complained of were mere violations of positive written law, or even the provisions

of their own charters; but they conceived their rights to rest upon something above and beyond English law. They claimed that they possessed certain natural rights, founded, as they asserted, on the principles of what was called natural equity. They forgot their own traditions, and, disregarding all their responsibility as members of a civil society, they relied upon what the French afterwards, in their frenzy, called the rights of man. Upon this line, then, the New England colonies acted, desiring from the beginning complete independence. The Middle and Southern colonies, however, led by Dickinson, bounded the horizon of their position by the legal aspects of the situation. They looked at the dispute with Great Britain as mainly a legal question, and that up to the period of the Declaration of Independence it might be settled as any other legal questions were, if not by a judicial tribunal, then by an appeal to legal principles recognized in common by both the mother country and the colonies as the outgrowth of English history and traditions. In extremity, English precedents pointed them to armed resistance, but not to rebellion or separation. They would coerce the mother country by an appeal to law and to reason to yield to the requisitions of freedom and of justice.

John Dickinson then, with his pen and voice, was the champion of constitutional resistance, adapting the brilliant theories of Montesquieu to the conditions of the colonies, tapping all the abundant resources of his wide learning, experience, and splendid intellect to inculcate into the colonists those immortal principles of constitu-

tional liberty and civil freedom that made possible the Constitution of the United States.

This was Dickinson's great pre-Revolutionary work. " For who are a free people?" he asks. " Not those over whom government is reasonably and equitably exercised, but those who live under a government so constitutionally checked and controlled that proper provision is made against its being otherwise exercised." Has there ever been a clearer definition of constitutional rule? And, withal, his contentions were maintained with such unanswerable logical skill and nice discrimination, and his arguments set down in such a matchless classical style, as to attract the attention and win the support of many of the foremost men of Europe.

The other most enduring work of the subject of this sketch was accomplished in the Convention which framed the Constitution of the United States. The most serious controversy in the Convention arose between the delegates of the larger and those of the smaller States in regard to the number of the representatives which should be sent by each to the national Congress, and upon what basis they were to be elected. Various plans were proposed. The large majority of the delegates were evidently in favor of proportional representation, while those from the smaller States, feeling that by the adoption of such a plan they would be crushed or their influence wholly destroyed, refused, even at the risk of losing a national government, to consent to it. In fact, the delegates from Delaware had been instructed to withdraw from the Convention if

any change in the existing rule of suffrage, giving one vote to each State, should be adopted. Mr. Dickinson, as representing Delaware, was foremost in the controversy. His great object was to insure an equal representation of each State in the Senate, thus placing there at least the smaller States on a footing of equality with the larger. The Convention decided unanimously, on the 7th of June, 1787, on the motion of Mr. Dickinson, that the members of that body should be chosen, two for each State, by its Legislature. The enduring usefulness of this novel feature of the Constitution is ample testimony of its wisdom. It needs no eulogy from these pages; its continued influence through an efflux of over a hundred years has established its position as one of the strongest features of that immortal document of which it is a part. If the Senate is the permanent and conservative force in our system, we should not forget, as we are apt to do, to whose influence we are indebted for the introduction into it of this rare invention of state-craft.

Let us refer again, briefly, before bringing this paper to a close, to Dickinson's position with regard to the Declaration of Independence. His name has never been associated with it; nor does it appear that he ever recanted the opinion which he had expressed of its propriety; although he not merely acquiesced in it, but engaged with his accustomed zeal and assiduity in preparing and carrying into effect the measures necessary to sustain it. However much we may regret that his name is not enrolled on that instrument, which is now the pride and boast of

every American, it would not only be uncharitable, but it would be wantonly to dim the lustre of one of the brightest of the Revolutionary luminaries, to suspect the purity of his motives, or to diminish the gratitude of the country to him. The reasons he gave for his position bear testimony to his wise prudence and foresight. He was right in holding that the colonies were not united or prepared, and his policy gave opportunity for the organization of the colonial militia, which scarcely existed at the beginning of the controversy. The soundness of his doctrine of the necessity of foreign alliance was amply vindicated by the effect made upon the struggle by the open espousal of our cause by the French. In fact, the occasion was one in which the righteousness of the cause outweighed the hesitation of prudence, but yet the prudent man cannot be blamed for the policies which his wisdom dictated.

As there was no deficiency of men prepared and anxious to press the Revolutionary car on to its goal, it was fortunate for the country that Congress possessed one man of the peculiar constitution of John Dickinson; for through his instrumentality, whilst they were rushing with a patriotic impetuousness into the midst of a sanguinary revolution, and their country was rapidly bursting its fetters and rising into national existence, their cause was invested with dignity, moderation, and firmness; their motives were exhibited in a condition of purity; and the holy principles of civil liberty, which they were struggling to sustain, were promulgated to the world with a force

and clearness which commanded the respect of the civilized world, and have commended the conflict to the nations of the earth as an example which has been gazed at with admiration.

Mr. Dickinson has been charged with advocating a timid policy, inconsistent with the spirit which became the great cause in which he had embarked, but nothing of the sort appears in his writings. Although he did orally advise Congress to pursue a less daring course than that which was successfully adopted, when he wielded the pen he invariably made Congress speak in a manner that became its dignity, fearlessness, and exalted position, in the presence of the world and of after ages. After the Declaration he supported his associates in the execution of their most energetic measures, and devoted an undivided affection to the cause of his country, no matter by whom or in what manner directed. "Two rules I have laid down for myself throughout this contest," said he on an important occasion in Congress, in 1779, "to which I have constantly adhered, and still design to adhere. First, on all occasions where I am called upon, as a trustee for my countrymen, to deliberate on questions important to their happiness, disdaining all personal advantages to be derived from a suppression of my real sentiments, and defying all dangers to be risked by a declaration of them, openly to avow them; and, secondly, after thus discharging this duty, whenever the public resolutions are taken, to regard them, though opposite to my opinion, as sacred, because they lead to public measures in which the common

weal must be interested, and to join in supporting them as earnestly as if my voice had been given for them. . . . If the present day is too warm for me to be calmly judged, I can credit my country for justice some years hence."

Such was John Dickinson, and I would that we had more public men to-day imbued with so lofty a spirit of patriotism.

PAPERS OF THE HISTORICAL SOCIETY OF DELAWARE.

XXXI.

LETTERS

OF

JAMES ASHETON BAYARD

1802—1814.

Read before the Historical Society of Delaware, by Henry C. Conrad, Librarian, March 18, 1901.

JAMES ASHETON BAYARD.

LETTERS

OF

JAMES ASHETON BAYARD.

NOTE.—The letters from James A. Bayard to his friend Cæsar Augustus Rodney, printed herewith, were written during Bayard's service in the House of Representatives, during his retirement in 1803–1805, his service in the Senate in 1805–13, and on his diplomatic mission abroad, first, to take advantage of the offer from Russia as mediator between the United States and Great Britain, and second, as a peace commissioner at Ghent. He died soon after his return to this country. Rodney was in the House of Representatives in 1803–05, and Attorney-General in 1805–11, practicing law after his resignation from the latter office. During the war with Great Britain he raised and commanded a rifle corps. These letters are printed from Bayard's letter-book, which was presented to the New York Public Library by Mr. Philip Schuyler.— *Librarian New York Public Library.*

WASHINGTON 31 Mar 1802

MY DEAR SIR

I was surprised to find by your last letter that you had given up the project of going to Sussex, tho' you certainly assign very substantial reasons for varying your intentions. It will not be in my power to attend the Supreme court in N-Castle, but I hope my absence will not interfere with the interests of my Brethren of the Bar or occasion any material delay in business. I never was more desirous of quitting any place than I am of leaving Washington & nothing

detains me here but a sense of the impropriety of leaving the State without representation on the floor of the House. I know not what business is yet designed to be done, but I know if we go thro' all upon our table we shall have no adjournment before the 3rd of March next. We proceed intolerably slow, and I believe there is a majority of the House who without doing anything find themselves in very lucrative employment. I envy you your liberty, and am consoled only by the hope of partaking of it before long.

Your's

J. A. B——

WASHINGTON 13 Apr. 1802.

My DEAR R.

I am glad to find you are so well occupied and so much amused with your late purchase upon the hill. I can hardly expect it will be a fund of profit, but I heartily hope it may be a source of health to you. Your adulterated water will prove extremely inviting on a warm summer's afternoon & your friends will have reason to wish that the adulterating material may be as unfailing as your spring.

I cannot express too strongly my desire to leave this place. Washington is tolerable for a few days, but detestable for a winter's residence. A joint committee of the two Houses have agreed this morning upon the business to be done this session and have fixed upon the 26th Inst. as the day of adjournment. I am in some hopes of being at the Kent Common-Pleas, but I shall not be re-

leased in times for Sussex. It would have been extremely agreeable to me to have gone the whole cruise with you, I hope it may turn out lucky & profitable. I thank you for the good news and good services on the subject of the wine. If we divide it in the first instance we shall certainly subdivide it between us afterwards.

Your's &c

J. A. B——

————————

WILMINGTON Nov 11th 1803.

DEAR SIR

We have just finished the circuit of the Supreme Court & to-day I set out upon that of the pleas. The Brandywine causes are all off, the first against Mr Dickinson was tried, and the close of the 2nd day ended it in a non.pros: at Bar. Without a shadow of title it was seriously protracted to the length mentioned, by Bedford, Vandyke, & Hall. When we moved for a nonsuit upon their closing, Bedford went out of Court, Vandyke only said we ought to demur, and perhaps there was not a man in the U. S. bearing the name of lawyer but Hall who would have been stupid and impudent enough to deny that an Estate in general tail descended from a Parent to a Child in preference to a 2nd cousin. It was true they had Mr. Marten's opinion, but it was by stating a false pedigree which precisely gave them our title. You have not been in the great city long enough to tell whether you can endure a 6 months residence. The honey-moon has hardly expired. I am told you are to

adjourn the 2nd of Mar: this will be fortunate as you will be pretty well prepared by that time for the pleasures of home.

Your's

J. A. B.

WILMINGTON Dec 10th 1803.

MY DEAR SIR

Tis now one week since upon my return from Dover I received your last favor. I find the air of Washington extremely favorable to metaphors, there was scarcely a line of plain prose in your last letter. The climate here does not enable me to answer you in the same practical stile. But perhaps there is not so much in atmosphere as in occupation. I have been employed in the homely drudgery of making money, and you in the refined and elegant pursuit of attaining honour and reputation. I perceive plainly by the papers that you have not failed (as I knew you could not) in acquiring your object, and I have been as little disappointed as to mine. We are strange beings my friend, we contend for objects without knowing their value or insignificancy. The course of things forced us into a competition in which the successful Party was to be the loser. Tho' I do not like your politics, yet I should be much gratified that by some extraordinary event your interest was really promoted. I fear that the Virginia pride will never truly appreciate a Delaware Character. If they will do anything for you I will forgive your folly for going into public life. I know not that you would have expressed to

me the same wholesome admonition. But I fear you are disposed to do much more for certain men, than you will find them disposed to do for you. Believe me in the present times, (our Country is not in danger) it is better to be doing for ourselves, such is the object of all about you, tho' I am sure it does not present itself to you. In spite of your politicks I can't help liking you, and I am therefore but half gratified by the passing occurrences, as you are not here to partake, of them. You are not perfect, but you have so many pleasant qualities that I shall be quite glad when you return to our society.

Your's
J. A. B——

WILMINGTON Feby 24 1804.

DEAR SIR,

I derived much satisfaction from your last letter. I gave full credit to the assurances you were so kind as to give me of the continued friendship you have always borne me And I shall have great pleasure in cherishing that confidence in your honour and sincerity which first attached me to you. Political opinion need not have an influence on personal sentiment. That we are of different political Parties, and so likely to remain is very certain, but I do not know in what the difference exists as to our opinions upon the material principles of politicks, I believe you are a little more *peopleick* than myself, but that will wear off after carrying your share of the government for awhile.

I think you are likely to have a complete surfeit of Washington this Session. Four months almost killed me, and how will you contrive to survive 6 or 7 I do not know. There is little prospect of your being liberated before the month of May, & I suspect you will have to clip the session if you are present at the pleas in Kent. It appears from the papers that the harmony of social intercourse has been a little disturbed in your mess. Let us know something of the details, the public prints are so much in the habit, of giving their own colours to transactions, that I seldom trust them as to facts of a Party or Personal nature. Has the thing ended or how is it likely to terminate. If you were here at present we should be able to feast you. A most plentiful cargo of terrapins arrived the other day the largest & finest I ever saw. I got two dozen to my share, but as their weight is a little above the frank priveledge it is not in my power to send you one by mail.

Your's
J. A. B.

WILMINGTON 24 July 1807.

DEAR SIR

I had the pleasure to receive yesterday your favor of the 22nd Inst. It was a long time coming & I had begun to reproach you with forgetting or neglecting the promise you made me before we parted to inform me of things of consequence passing at the Seat of Government. I do view with you the present crisis of public affairs as very impor-

tant. Without substantial reparation for the crying offence
committed against our honour rights and independance
whatever the sacrifice, we must go to war. The nation
will not be & I trust the administration will not be satisfied
with empty apologies or with the mockery of a trial which
ends in a promotion or ends with anything short of the
signal punishment of the offender. I regretted being ab-
sent·from Wilmington on the occasion of the public meeting, which deprived me of an opportunity of joining in
the expression of that just sentiment of indignation which
the atrocious act of the British Commander seems to have
inspired in the breasts of all our Countrymen. To be an
American and not to feel upon the occasion would be impossible.

Your's.

J. A. B——

WASHINGTON Jan.y 11ᵗʰ. 1811.

DEAR SIR

I should have made a pretty business of it if I had connected my movement to Congress with yours to the Cabinet. Looking at the weather and roads I have little expectation of seeing you here during the month of Jany. We
have news here to day that Baton Rouge and the fort of
Mobile have been surrendered to our troops. The Bank
bill is before the House of R. and it is supposed will not
pass that body—intelligence from Europe is renewed &
contradicted every day, one knows not when to believe.

Your's

J. A. B.

Washington 10 Dec. 1811.

My dear R.

The conjectures you made as to a successor have been verified today by the nomination of Pinckney. There could have been no difficulty in the selection for no time has been lost in making it. We have still a chance for two representatives. A Committee of Conference of each house met on the subject of the apportionment and separated without coming to an agreement. As Chairman of the Comm^{ee} of the Senate I reported accordingly with a recommendation of the Com^{ee} to adhere to the ratio of 35,000. We shall take the question in the senate to-morrow on the report, which I have no doubt will be agreed to, and if the House do not recede the bill will be lost. I am still alone at Davis' and find solitude more agreeable than I expected.

Yours &c

J. A. B ——

Washington Dec 18th 1811.

Dear Sir,——.

The House have this moment voted to recede from their disagreement to the amendments of the Senate to the apportionment Bill· The vote of course establishes the ratio of 35,000, and gives for the first time to our little state two members.

Your's

J. A. B.

WASHINGTON, Dec 22nd 1811

MY DEAR SIR.

I am going to narrate to you an occurrence of the day which will surprise you. It is nevertheless true, and shall be narrated with exact fidelity. Your friend Paul Hamilton called to make me a visit and after other indifferent conversation I remarked to him that I had had a letter from our friend Rodney since I had seen him last, and that upon the fullest consideration since he had returned home he was wholly satisfied with the step he had taken, and what was that he asked with surprise. I refer said I to his resignation of the office of Atty: General. What he exclaimed with great surprise has he resigned? I understood from him I replied that he had communicated to you his intention before he left Washington. What has he left Washington? I never heard a word about the affair or otherwise it has entirely escaped my recollection. It is nearly three weeks Sir since he left us, and have you not known of Mr Pinckney's being appointed to his place? Not a word of it. It has been in the newspapers for a considerable time; I have never seen it; I never knew a word about it. I am really very sorry—Rodney was a very amiable man and I had a great regard for him. How do you account for this that one member of the Cabinet, should not know so long after that another was absent or had resigned? To me it is passing strange. We are going on here in a strange temper,—all talking about war which no one seems to expect. The Senate has passed a Bill for an additional regular force of 25,000 men. We expect the

house will send it back to us with a reduction & I very much doubt whether they will agree in the end to anything which is efficient. We have here Governier Morris and Dewitt Clinton. Their ostensible object is a canal from the lakes to the Hudson, which is to cost seven millions of dollars. A fine time for such an expenditure when we have not money eno' in the Treasury to pay the bounties to the troops we propose to raise. The characters of the two men are pretty well known, and it is rather supposed that they mean to open a road to the presidency than a Canal from the lakes. Tho' a young republic we are already old in intrigue. And the goodnatured people are transferred from one man to another with all the zeal which belongs to a work of their own doing. Being only a Looker-on I amuse myself with the scene as it passes by. You see we have got two representatives. In this I have had some hand, and I did not hesitate upon such a subject to make engagements which had a view singly to the Interest of our own State. The result however I believe a just one as it regards the States generally. Let me know how you passed the Court, what business was done and what became of the causes in which I [was] concerned.

Yours'

J. A. B.——

SENATE CHAMBER 6 Jany 1812

DEAR SIR,

I had the pleasure to receive yesterday your favour of the 1st inst and can readily conceive that the comfort &

happiness you experience in private leave you nothing to regret in having renounced the parade and distinction of public life. I should like much to be with you and am sure I should gain a great deal by making the same exchange you have done. I was concerned to hear of the accident which befel you, but as it rendered you more studious, & its only permanent effect will be to increase your stock of. knowledge, your friends will find a consolation for the pain you have suffered. The army of 25.000 is still before the House, but the number will remain tho' varied in composition from the nature of the force proposed by the Senate The navy will be augmented, but whether any or what use will be made of these new forces is too difficult at this moment to forsee, to allow me to express any opinion on the subject. Bauduy I understand is not disposed to render my offer of the house in Town of any service to you. The French are always polite but seldom accommodating. Pray let me know when Witherspoon is to be tried? If it be not before the Supreme Court, I shall probably come in for a share of the prey.

Your's

J. A. B. ——

WASHINGTON Jany. 26th 1812.

My Dear. R.

Affairs go on here with their usual snail pace as J. A.

anxious for war, but they don't know how to get at it. They find it almost as difficult to get men and money as to get the Orders in Council taken off. Gallitin's budget has made many wry faces They expected he would raise all the money which was wanted without any new taxes. Bradley says he has no objection to go to war, but he does not mean that it shall cost anything. That he does not intend to vote any more money than just what is in the Treasury. He is against taxes, or loans, and he wished to God it was a part of the constitution that the Government should neither tax nor borrow, for the purpose of making war! It looks very much as if we should be brought up by the war-taxes. There was no sensation while the question was about raising men, but the taxes are the rub with your popularity-men. I postpone all opinion now as to what is likely to happen, till I see how the ways and means are treated.———I have seen nothing done yet which has not pointed to popularity, when I see the needle vary, I may indulge myself in new speculations. I have some anxiety to know if you have wasted your money, and what progress you have made in the way of retrenchment. These enquiries could not be made if I cared nothing about you; But I know you are too much disposed to let tomorrow provide for itself and the motive must therefore excuse the enquiries. It is impossible for you to be too prudent the ensueing year. It will be one of experiment you will afterwards be able to calculate.

Your's

J. A. B

MY DEAR R.

Your letter of the 6th I had the pleasure to receive two days ago. Maugre my solitude I have upon the whole spent the winter more pleasantly than any former one in Washington, when entirely separated from my family. And for my location I am certainly indebted to you. Very little has been done in Congress for several days past. It is not intended to take any decisive step before the arrival of the Hornet. But it is difficult to divine what is expected by the Hornet. Barlow may have a treaty with France, but no change can be looked for in our relations with England. We are informed that the Comᵉᵉ of Ways & Means will report to-morrow, and in substance will adopt Mr Gallitin's report with some modifications and *additions*. I understand however that the taxes are not to be imposed till war is finally determined on. Your successor Mr Pinckney has greatly disappointed public expectations as to his oratorical powers. The first cause he was concerned in he refused to argue because the Court would not adjourn at 2 o'clock and allow him till next morning to prepare himself In the 2nd cause he left the Court about the same hour when it came to his turn to speak, apologizing that he had been summoned as a Cabinet Minister, The following morning we heard him. His manner is extremely violent and ranting & better suited to any purpose of public speaking than a law argument. Disappointment was universal. Our friend Horsey is certainly about to suffer a great metamorphosis. What kind of a being

the change will make of him the Lord only knows. He
has his own manner of courting. Tho' he might more
conveniently lodge in Georgetown he prefers making love
three miles off and takes great care that too frequent visits
shall not render the Lady too familiar with. One thing
is fixed tho' the time is not known when the old Bachelor
is to be merged. It can't well happen in Lent as the Lady
is a Catholic, and not allowed to *taste flesh* during the
quadragesimal fast. They still keep up a buz about ad-
journing, but I don't know what they mean by it. At all
events I expect to be with you in April.

God bless you.

J. A. B—

WASHINGTON 27 Feby. 1812

MY DEAR R.

We have at length got the Constitution but she brings
us nothing of any consequence. She left Cherbourg the
4th of Jany: at which time the Hornet had landed a Messenger in France, & sailed for England she is to return to
France, and to take in a full cargo of dispatches for the
U. States. The House of .R. yesterday had the report
of the Com^ee of Ways & Means before them and in a
Com^ee of the whole adopted the whole string of taxes
recommended by the Secretary. The Majority upon the
excise was the smallest and on the land tax the greatest.
I think there will be some flinching and skulking when they
come to the yeas & nays. It does not appear to me that

CÆSAR A. RODNEY.

Congress have more respect for the people's money now than they had in the time of John Adams. You know what may be the consequence.

Your's

J. A. B. ——

N. B. Secretary Hamilton told me the other day to remind you of the terrapins. If you don't send them I am sure I shall not see the inside of the Secretary's house, and if you do, I don't know that I shall—unless you put an invitation in the mouth of one of them.

———

SENATE CHAMBER. 6 Mar 1812

MY DEAR R.

I have just received your letter of the 29th Feby but postmarked the 4th March, your dates and those of the Postmaster have generally disagreed. Your time I presume passes very pleasantly as you seem to take no note of it, not so here. I have counted the days too regularly not to know the exact day of the month. The Terrapins may be on the road or possibly arrived, but I have heard nothing of them. If they were mailed on the 1st inst they certainly ought to be in Washington by this time. I fear our Secretaries are so much engaged in war affairs, as to have no time to think of eating even *terrapins*. We have been employed several days upon the nominations for the new army. They have all been sent in except from New-York & Delaware. There is a rumour afloat that war will be declared within two weeks. It is not discredited nor be-

2

heved. I cannot discover the source of it. It would not surprise me if the effort were made, but it is not likely that it will be attempted before the arrival of the Hornet. That may be however within two weeks

Your's

J. A. B ——

WASHINGTON 9 Mar. 1812

MY DEAR .R.

The Pearl river bill has passed both houses & your father's estate is two thousand dollars the better of it. I have great pleasure in congratulating you on the prosperous events and therefore I give you joy of the windfall. The Terrapins have arrived, and the good Secretary has been so civil as to send me 4 of them. They are really stout fellows and may rank with the grenadiers of their species. Mr Secraty [*sic*] also hints that when his appetite gets the better of a small fever which has laid hold of him, he will be glad to receive from me a lesson in the sublime art of cooking these strange animals who can fatten in air or water and live without either. I was out shooting on Saturday with Mr Attorney your successor. We found but 3 or 4 snipe and I killed only one, and as he did not kill as many, you may think what was his luck. The taxes caused at one time some wry faces, but they have all gone down pretty smoothly. The resolutions have been sent to a select comee to prepare Bills. No war, no taxes, not in bad combination. How results the specific gravity? w the war float the taxes, or the taxes sink the war? We are

waiting here with great impatience for a little insect called a Hornet. It is supposed it will arrive winged with peace or war. Of whatever magnitude impending events may be, people here seem to think very little about them. Winder of Baltimore has agreed to accept the rank of Colonel in the new army. He has a large family and is in good business, he pays very dear I think for a pair of epualettes.

Your's
J. A. B.

WASHINGTON Mar 16, 1812.

MY DEAR R.

I never was more surprised & shocked than at the account given in your last letter of the abominable & dastardly attack made upon you by Bradun. I had at the same time however a sentiment of pity for the man, because I am persuaded he had lost his senses at the moment he committed the violence. I always found him very decent and well behaved in his conduct, and must suppose that the transport of feeling at what he considered a cruel decision blindly hurried him to an act of which he must soon have repented. You have received I presume & hope no permanent injury & the affair must be considered as one of those unpleasant occurrences to which life is exposed, & which are disposed of the best when the least thought of. We will leave so ungrateful a subject to think of one that will revive recollections of a more gay and pleasant nature. While fortune treated you so hardly at New-Castle, think with how much beneficence she is treat-

ing our Friend Horsey at Washington. He has drunk the
poison of her eyes—Behold him tasting the nectar of her
lips, enjoying the thrilling sensations of an embrace,—
transported with the extacies of hope & desire and then
say if there be not moments of pleasure in the world, which
console us for the evils to which we are subject. Horsey
is now completely—The Lady has engaged her hand,
having given her heart, the father has approved and he
only waits for the fine· days of *May* to consummate his
happiness. He has removed to Georgetown, and the war
may commence and the battle rage loud & long before
he will know anything about them. This same war is much
talked of here but nobody seems to know when it is to
take place. Clay & Cheves spent part of last evening with
me & they both assured me that war was inevitable &
would be declared in a short time. Clay is certainly in
confidence, & I believe both are & they spoke in entire
sincerity. You will know how to appreciate the information. The Supreme Court adjourned· on Saturday having
done much business, & left much undone. Johnston called
last evening to take leave, and spoke of you with friendship Our friend Hamilton I told you sent me four of the
terrapins you sent to him & promised me a supper on those
he retained. But I have had no farther notice on the subject and I presume the terrapins have expiated all the
crimes they ever committed on the chaffing-dish before
this time. You have seen the President's Message
with Henry's documents. Were they worth think you
50,000 dollars? That sum was certainly paid for

them & Henry is off with the money. The Com^ee refused to send for him & the Executive has officially assured us they have no names. If there were traitors they ought to have been known The public should have been informed that its indignation might have marked the guilty. I will not complain of the times, for I know not that we are likely to have better; but with regard to men, I do not believe the Court at Washington is much behind any Court in Europe in intrigue & duplicity. In speaking thus of *your friends,* you perceive what a proof of confidence I give you. Adieu, and let me assure you you will want little when you possess all the good things I wish you.

Your's

J. A. B.

WASHINGTON March 22. 1812

MY DEAR SIR.

I thank you for your letter of the 15th inst. The plot does not take as was expected, even Wright says that it was a wicked thing to attempt to divide the people at the moment when every means of conciliation ought to have been employed. The payment of the 50,000 dollars is a fact of indubitable verity and is not denied by any friend of the Administration It was paid on the 11th of Feby & the President knowing that fact, sends a letter of Henry dated the 20th of Feby. at Philad^a importing to be a voluntary offer of the communication. It was known that the date was false & the offer not gratuitous. Is not this a

fearful prostitution of the first office in our country. A party never ought nor can be benefitted by such a transaction. I hope to be with you at the Supreme Court, but I dread the Hornet. I cannot be absent when the matter of war is to be decided on. But that in any event is not expected in a month.

Yours'

J. A. B.

WASHINGTON 6 May 1812

MY DEAR SIR.

I cannot tell you when or where the war is to begin, but I continue to think that it will have a beginning and that before long. It is not unlikely that it will be made before it is declared. We have four frigates out, and I understand with such orders, that if they meet with any British ships of war on the coast an engagement is highly probable. When the President has made the war I presume Congress will not be too modest to declare it, It is with great difficulty we can get or preserve a quorum in the Senate. On Monday no business was done for want of one, & we have not had since more than 2 or three beyond the majority.

Yours.

J. A. B.

SENATE CHAMBER 11 June 1812

M\ :sup R Dear R.

I received your letter of the 9th yesterday. You are very kind in saving the woodcock till my return. You

generally have mercy upon them, but it is a great concession not even to disturb them till we can enjoy the
amusement in common of beating up their quarters. Especially let no ———— ———— ———— ———— of any species violate
the sanctity of their retreat in the neighbourhood of the
Spring; that is a spot of our exclusive sport and upon
the occasion of one of our old delightful Parties at Cool
Spring will be the ground we will appropriate to ourselves,
while we send the boys back into the woods to search for
more distant & uncertain game. I have never met with
anything at Washington half so agreeable as one of our
Parties at Cool Spring. You want me (not that you have
asked it) to tell you something about our proceeding in
Congress. This I should be very happy to do, but the
vile padlock which they have hung to my lips prevents
me from opening them. But you have more than common
means of guessing & cannot therefore be much in the dark
as to the work we are employed in. The fable of the
mountain I fear will not apply. If the birth should be
equally harmless, I should be satisfied that it should be
equally ridiculous. If you have kept as good a lookout
with your spy-glass as you promised to do, I think you
must have discovered something ahead. At this moment
she is behind a point, but if the wind holds & she is able to
weather it, you will probably throw down your glass &
call all hands to quarters. You have thought the thing all
along a jest, & I have no doubt in the commencement it
was so, but jests sometimes become serious and end in
earnest. The denouement must be unfolded in a few days,

but the features of the result will I fear be better discovered
in the fable of Cadmus, than that of the mountain. You
have had a flourishing time of it at Wilmington while we
have been drooping here, you have actually lived in clover
during the spring while we have been starving.

Your's

J. A. B. — — — —

WASHINGTON June 20th 1812

My dear R.

You are now in possession of all our secrets & you find
I have been the better prophet of the two. I wish your
inspiration had prevailed, and I assure you that I would
rather have forfeited all pretensions to prophecy than to
have had my predictions fulfilled. However as we are now
at war we must defend ourselves; & I think you ought to
bestir yourself in organizing a military force. I am in
hopes we shall adjourn in 10 or 12 days, at all events I
think I shall return by that time, & see how the war comes
on in Delaware. I am very sensibly obliged by your ap-
propriation of the woodcock at Cool Spring to our common
sport & equally sensible of the obliging manner in which
you set aside the Taunton till my return. We will toss it
off to the success of Decatur Bainbridge & our other brave
naval commanders who I fear will have very unequal
battles to fight. I do not believe all our secrets are over.
I have heard that the President means to ask for authority

to take military possession of East Florida. If such should be the case no doubt our doors will be again shut.

Yours'

J A B.

My Dear R.

I had the pleasure to receive your letter a day or two ago to receive yours of the 9th inst. It was written as you rightly calculated the day we arrived at Washington. We are now quartered comfortably at the six buildings. The Bill raising an additional army of 20,000 men for 1 year has passed the house & been twice read in the Senate & committed. The ways & means are to be derived from loans. The Secretary proposes borrowing 20,000,000 not at 6 per cent you may be assured but at any per cent necessary to produce the money. No taxes are to be laid this winter—the Virginia & N. Carolina elections are still to come. A majority for the 2 ensuing years is no small matter. They pretend to have adopted this principle the war is to be carried on by loans & provision made only for the interest on them. While therefore the ordinary revenue is sufficient to meet the ordinary expences of the government & the interest on the debt which may exist no taxes are to be laid. The double duties on the importations will be equal to the object the present year. I saw a few evenings ago Col. Winder & Capt. Gibson, their account of the operations on the frontier beggars all description. Gib-

son states that the number of men which crossed at Queenstown was sufficient to have beaten any force the British
could have brought against them. But to [*sic*] thirds of
them skulked & altho' 900 were taken not more than 300
hundred could be brought into the field. The regular
troops behaved no better than the militia, for in fact they
had no more experience or discipline And yet we are
going to raise an army of 20,000 men for one year in
order to add to our defeats and disgrace, & to the triumphs
of the enemy. Jones passed the Senate as Secretary of the
Navy without a division, but Armstrong rubbed thro' as
Secretary at War with 18 to 15, & if S. Smith & Leib had
voted as they took pains to make others vote he would have
been rejected It is the common opinion that he will soon
set the Cabinet by the ears.

Yours'.

J. A. B.

WASHINGTON 31 Jany. 1813.

MY DEAR R.

I received yesterday your favor of the 24th. You will
not expect in me a very punctual correspondent this winter,
as the attentions belonging to a wife, in accompanying her
to Parties consume no inconsiderable part of one's time. I
saw a few evenings ago your quondam friend the late Secretary of the Navy. He forgot that I was an acquaintance
of yours as he did not enquire after you. He has lost all
character for the tameness with which he has crouched to

Madison since he has been turned out of office. The statements he made to several of his friends as to the harsh conduct of the President towards him, he has endeavoured to explain away in a publication in the Intelligencer. And so kindly has M^{rs}. H. met the humiliation of her husband that she has sent a present of a glass ship which belonged to the navy office to M^{rs}. M. since the gentleman has been dismissed from his office. But it is understood that if Mr. H. is not fit to be secretary of the navy a birth may be found which will suit him. It is therefore important that he should keep himself in some favor. It is said that he is to be Commissary of Prisoners at N. York. So that all men are not so quite proud & high-spirited as yourself. A State paper made its appearance yesterday, which has excited considerable sensation. It is a manifesto of the Com^{ee}. of Foreign relations which bring the war to the single point of controversy respecting impressment & proposes a law which is to remove the ground even of that. So that your prophecies as to the result of a winters intrigue may yet be verified.

Yours'

J. A. B.

SENATE CHAMBER 13 Feby. 1813

MY DEAR R.

I have heard nothing lately said about the repeal of the non-importation act & I think it will not take place during the present session. A summer session is in contemplation to commence about the 1st of June. This I had from the

President who said it would be recommended by the Com^ee of ways & means in the other house. This extraordinary session proposed it is said is designed to be employed only in digesting & imposing a system of internal taxation. The Virginia election will then be-over, and the N. Carolina & Tenessee elections pretty well secured. I saw a letter from General Harrison yesterday which softens in some degree the aspect of the picture first given of Winchester's defeat. His conjectures limit the loss to about 340 men. Few however escaped—600 must have been taken. This battle like that of Queenstown furnishes evidence of American courage exposing itself to extreme danger, & disaster, thro' the want of a proper head to control and direct it. I feel great pleasure in looking forward to the speedy termination of the session. In spite of all the routs & parties with which Washington abounds, I cannot like the place, and always rejoice when I find myself on the road to Wilmington. I hope to be shooting snipe with you before long.

Adieu
Yours' J. A. B.

WASHINGTON, 21 Feby. 1813.

MY DEAR, R.

I received yesterday your letter of the 18th covering the handbill containing the account of the splendid victory of the Constitution over the Java. I rejoice most heartily in the event, and the more on account of the brave Commander, of the Constitution who heretofore has been the

sport of so much perverse accident. You remember our forebodings when we heard of Bainbridge's sailing, which I am very happy to find have not been realized. Horsey left us to-day & is on the road to Wilmington, Ridgely has been gone these ten days past & the State now rests upon my shoulders. I shall try & support it till the end of the session. Treasury notes are likely to become very plenty, a law will be passed to-morrow authorizing the secretary of the Treasury to issue ten millions Dollars in addition to the five already issued. They will soon be as abundant as old paper money-bills. The expences of the Western Campaign are enormous. Flour at the Rapids has cost the Government 60 dollars a barrel. The Sec-y will find great difficulty in getting money this summer, but as he must have it I suppose he will pay a handsome price. If you can trust you may have reserved your money for a good market. Horsey's wife was in bad sailing trim and if she had remained here much longer, would have required heaving-down before she could have commenced her voyage.

Your's
J. A. B.

COPENHAGEN 27 June 1813.

MY DEAR R

We have stopt at this place which is directly in our route in order to obtain information as to what has lately passed & what exists on the continent & may concern us. Military details you will have received before this reaches

you, and the most important fact which relates to ourselves
is that the Emperor of Russia is with his army & that G.
B. has no minister at present at St. Petersberg   We intend
to proceed to that city to-morrow where we expect to arrive
in 10 or 12 days.   The first part of our voyage was bois-
terous rough & cold and consequently very uncomfortable.
Mr Tod & myself were the only part of our Company who
were not seasick.   Mr Gallitin suffered a good deal & was
not entirely well before we·entered the narrow seas.   Tho
the British represent the ocean as covered with their vessels of war, upon the whole passage we spoke nothing but
a Yankey Letter of Marque, till we entered the North-sea.
We had a strong wind in crossing the N Sea & passed it
in little more than 24 hours.   We found it very rough.
We stopt one day at Gottenburg which is situated among
frightful rocks but enjoys a fine harbour, and subsists by
commerce.   It is much affected by the interruption of trade
with America.   We were obliged to come to at Elsineur on
account of the sound duties, & availed ourselves of the occasion, not only to look at the town, but also to visit the
castle & the celebrated garden of Hamlet   It is impossible
to describe to you at this time these places or the impression they made upon me.   But you may well conclude that
I was highly gratified.   I abstain from any remarks of a
political nature as it is scarcely possible that this letter can
reach you without being opened & in such case you would
be little benefitted by the attempt to communicate political
information.   It is impossible to offer any kind of conjecture as to the time of our return.   If the Russian mediation

should not be accepted, it will be speedily, otherwise we may be detained God knows how long. Whatever I find of novelty abroad to gratify me for a moment it cannot quench my desire to be at home. I do assure you I shall hail the moment with great joy when the good ship the Neptune turns her head towards the shores of America.

Yours,

J. A. B.

St. Petersberg 30 August 1813–

My dear R.

The present is the first opportunity which has presented itself of writing to the U States since our arrival here. The American trade is at an end, and even foreign vessels are deterred from attempting the American by the blockade established by the British fleet. We arrived here on the 21st July & a few days afterwards were presented to the Count Romanzoff Chancellor of the Empire, but we found to our great grief, that the Emperor was in Silesia 1200 miles from his capital We cannot be received at Court till his Majesty's orders are received on the subject. A copy of our letters of credence was sent to the Imperial Head-quarters, immediately after it was delivered. But no answer has yet been received in return. This is a matter of no political importance because, as G. Britain has appointed no one to meet & treat with us, our having been presented at Court would have varied our situation very little. The mediation of the Emperor has not been accepted, nor yet formally refused by the B. Cabinet. How

long the course of events may induce us to remain, can only
be at present an affair of conjecture, but I am certain that
neither Mr G. or myself are disposed to protract a fruitless
residence abroad. I have been to visit most of the palaces
& churches so celebrated in the tales of Travellers. The
Winter Palace & the Hermitage which communicate with
each other are the most splendid & magnifecent. We.were
conducted thro' a suite of rooms which appeared endless.
The walls are covered with paintings of the most celebrated masters. Nothing can exceed the splendor & ex-
pence of their churches. I have been thro' the palace of St
Michael in which Paul lost his life. We passed thro' the
room in which he was strangled. And I fancied that I
saw the spot on which his struggles ended with the agony
of death. A new floor has been laid in the room, in order
that that should not remain which had been stained with
the blood of an Emperor. The Palace is stript at present
of all its ornaments & furniture & inhabited only by a few
domestics. I was highly gratified in viewing the Taurida
palace & especially the grand Hall in which Potemkin gave
the magic entertainment to his Mistress. It contains a vast
number of very fine statues. Sir John Carr gives you a
good description of it. The Empress Regent at present
resides at Zarsho-Zelo but comes into town occasionally
to hold her Court. We had an intimation given us when
the Empress would be absent & that we could use the occasion to view the palace. It is 22 versts from the city, which
is a ride of about two hours. We went out & were shew
[*sic*] the apartments & conducted thro' the grounds. All

I can say at present is that the whole is an Imperial establishment. But after all my dear R. I would rather be in Wilmington than in St Petersburg, and no one can be more anxious than I am to return to my family & country. This I hope will be at no distant period, and in the meantime believe me

Yours'

J. A. B.

St Petersburg 15 Oct 1813.

My dear R.

This place affords no news. Even the operations of the Russian armies are made known to us thro' the medium of the English papers. I have of course nothing to say to you which may not be communicated in very few words. After our arrival here this government renewed the offer of mediation to G. B. The answer of the B. Government has not yet been received. The R. Government does not consider the mediation as refused & that we look upon as a point for them to decide. We were yesterday presented to the reigning Empress. It is impossible to say how long we shall remain here, but we intend to send our ship immediately to Gottenburg. From that place we can sail at any season, but from Cronstadt there is no moving from the 1st of Nov: to the middle of May. We shall of course have to travel thro' Sweden & shall pass round the head of the Gulf of Bothnia, or cross from Abo to Stockholm. If we pursue the first route we shall approach near to the Polar circle, & that probably in the coldest month in the year.

The passage by Abo is the shortest but it is frequently impracticable. There is but little prospect of success attending our Mission. I have not thought since I have been here that the B. Government would admit the mediation of Russia. The Count Romanzoff seems to think differently, & it is from him we are to receive our final answer on the subject. I do assure you I wish myself home with all my heart. The novelty of this place is exhausted and nothing remains to compensate for the separation from my family & friends. I wish you all kind of happiness

Adieu,
Yours
J. A. B.

LONDON 1ˢᵗ May. 1814.

My dear. R.

I little expected when I left the United States to have had it in my power to address a letter to you from this great Metropolis. It is of no importance to you to detail the motives which brought me here, tho' I am well satisfied in their having justified me in coming. I arrived at the moment the wonderful & unexpected events occurred of the Abdication of Buonaparte of the Crown of France & Italy & the restoration of the Bourbons. This revolution may be considered as established, Louis 18th makes his solemn entry this day into Paris & Buonaparte is in custody on his route to Elba. All the authorities of France civil & military have sent in their adhesion to the new government. You will readily believe that these events have no

[*sic*] softened the temper of John Bull towards America. If the people are allowed to have their way there will be no chance of peace. The cry is for Lord Wellington's army to be sent over to inflict exemplary chastisement. There is no doubt that a great part of that army will be sent over if the negociation fail at Gottenburg. As yet no commissioners are appointed to conduct the negociation on the part of this government. Probably as soon as Lord Castlereagh returns from the Continent an appointment will be made. Till that event happens I shall probably remain here. I can offer you no conjecture as to the probable result of the negociation. I can only say I do not despair of peace. I have had an opportunity of seeing the Lords and Commons in Session. The Lords were sitting as a court of Appeal, and there were two Lords present beside the Lord Chancellor. Counsel were argueing at the bar. In the Commons there were a few more than a quorum, but the subject before them occasioned an animated debate, in which Messrs Stevens, Whitbread, McIntosh, Romilly, Marryatt, &ct took part. I will tell you what I think of them when I have the pleasure of seeing you. I have seen also the Courts of Chancery Kings-Bench & Common-Pleas in session. The halls in which they sit are miserable boxes. The whole of them put together would not contain half the number of the court-room at New-Castle. Their appearance was not wonderfully impressive and I think their long wigs excite rather a ludicrous than a solemn feeling. I do not expect to remain here very long, & I am quite satisfied to be off

whenever it is proper that I should go. I have seen everything which I was desirous of seeing; and it is really not pleasant to inhabit a country where there is no sympathy, & where you are to rejoice when they are sad, and to mourn when they are joyful. I have written to you several letters but have not received a line from you. Clay & Russell are at Gottenburg, but we have received nothing which they brought for us.

Yours'

J. A. B.

GHENT. 5th August, 1814.

My DEAR. R.

The conveyance of letters to the distance of 4000 miles is subject to much delay & many accidents. Your favor of the 28th of July 1813- addressed to me at St Petersburg, I received in this place July 11th 1814. & at the same time I received your letters of 14th August 15 Sept^r '13. & Feby. 14. If they had lost anything of their novelty, they were not the less historical & furnished much matter of interest & information. I wrote to you from Amsterdam, at the close of my journey from St Petersburg. You have a faint idea of the difficulty of reaching the Atlantic from the Russian Capital in the winter season. The gulf of Finland & the Baltic are not navigable, and the ordinary course is to cross the Gulf of Bothnia at Abo, or to go round the head of it by Torneo. The Gulf of B. during part of the season is not passable on account of broken & floating ice & then you must go

by Torneo. This was the route I expected to have taken & which I was relieved from taking by the revolution in Holland which opened a new road. When the winter approached we sent our ship from Cronstadt to Gottenburg, from which place we were informed, we could sail at any season of the year. It was from there we expected to embark. But when we learned that Holland was open, we sent orders to our captain to sail for some port in that country, and we commenced our journey by land to Amsterdam. We set out in Jany. & were upon the road all the month of Feby. the coldest in the year. We generally travelled during the whole night, which in the high latitudes you know in the month of Feby. is the greater part of the 24 hours. We passed thro' Riga, Revel, Konigsberg, & Berlin. In B. we stopt nearly a week to rest & refresh ourselves which I assure you I found very necessary. We arrived at Amsterdam the 4th of March. It was here I received advices from our government of the negociation proposed to be held at Gottenburg. This intelligence was mixed with pain & pleasure. It disappointed the fond hope I had entertained of speedily returning to my country, but opened at the same time a prospect of carrying home with me when I did return the Olive Branch for which I had been sent abroad. The messenger who delivered to me dispatches at Amsterdam was to proceed to St Petersburg with similar instructions to Mr Adams to repair to Gottenburg knowing that more than two months must intervene before [we] could assemble at Gottenburg. I determined to avail myself of the interval in paying a visit to

London. I did not venture upon this step without knowing that I should tread upon safe ground, tho' in an enemy's country. And indeed I had reason to think that the visit might be attended with a good political effect I proceeded thro' the Hague & Rotterdam to Helvoetsluys from whence I embarked for Harwich. We carried over with us several English officers who had been wounded, & the widows of others who had been killed in the attempt to storm Bergen op Zoom. This part of the company were not very cheerful. We made the passage in about 45 hours; the distance is said to be 100 miles from land to land. The shores on either side are dangerous in foul weather from the sands. Our captain would not go out in the night, and they never approach the coasts but when they can see the buoys. We had a dull passage, but a very quiet one considering the number we had on board a small vessel. Orders had been sent to Harwich for our civil treatment. The distance from Harwich to London is a little more than 70 miles, & having a very fine day in the beginning of April & seeing after a long & dreary winter the first appearance of vegetation, I had a delightful ride to the far-famed city. We arrived in the evening just in time to be able to see the parts of the Town thro' which we drove to our lodgings. We had about four miles to drive after we got into the Town, & it was nearly dark when we were set down at the Blenheim hotel. The limits of a letter will not allow me to detail the employment of my time while I remained in this Metropolis. The Houses of Parliament & the Courts of justice were of course objects of curiosity. St

Stephen's chapel is quite shabby, the Chamber of the house of Lords is better, but quite common. I attended the Lords when an appeal was argued from Scotland, & altho the House was in Session there were present only one Lord beside the Lord Chancellor. I heard part of the debate on what was called the Norway question & listened I assure you for 3 hours with great pleasure to a speech of Earl Grey. He is a very eloquent sensible & manly speaker. In the house of Commons I heard no good speaking but I was not present upon any very important occasion. The Hall of the King's Bench is scarcely large eno' to contain the Barristers. I attended sittings of the Court but observed nothing very remarkable but the wigs & robes of the Judges & Lawyers. I heard some motions argued in the common pleas where Sir Vicary Gibbs had lately taken his seat at the head of the Court, & I thought there were few of our legal Gentlemen who had been 14 years at the Bar who would not make very passable Seargeants. I was successively in all the Courts & found they had no great occasion for large chambers, for not a soul scarcely but the Counsel attended them. You will remember however they had nothing before them but matters of law. My stay in London was about 6 weeks and notwithstanding the politeness of a few people I most sensibly felt that I was in an enemy's country. The mass of the people are extremely hostile to us, & I verily believe hate us worse than they ever did the French. America has not a friend in any Englishman, & there is not an Englishman who would be satisfied to see the war terminated, till he thought we

were severely punished for our audacity in commencing it. It had been proposed by the British Government to Mr G. & myself to transfer the seat of negociation from Gottenburgh to Ghent, to which we readily assented, (the low countries being neutral at the time), considering this as a place more convenient to both Parties. Having time eno' before me I determined to visit Paris upon my route to Ghent. It was going to be sure something out of the way, but it was as well to be upon the road as waiting here for my Colleagues who I knew could not arrive for some weeks.

I crossed the channel at Dover in a vessel smaller than our common packets & crowded with upwards of a hundred passengers. We had a strong wind & heavy sea & such a scene of distress I never saw on board of a vessel. It was difficult to keep out of the way of the cascades & such an atmosphere I never breathed before. Fortunately we had a short passage & were landed in about 3 hours, & my stomach maintained the reputation it had acquired in crossing the Atlantic. We travelled at a delightful season of the year & thro' a rich & beautiful country from Calais to Paris. One ought to be in Paris at least six months to know anything about it & to acquire a proper taste for it,   had time only to indulge the eye, & that was quite satisfied before I left the city. The gardens of the Thuilleries & the Luxembourg are enchanting. The gallery of paintings in the Louvre is magnificent & the finest Statues that exist are found in the Halls of the same building. It was no small gratification to have a

sight of the celebrated Statues of Apollo & Venus which
had been brought from Rome. The King of Prussia took
back the sword of Frederic & some bronze horses which
the French had carried off from Berlin, but all the fine
paintings and Statues of which all Europe had been robbed
were suffered to remain. Certainly in this conduct there
was much moderation & forbearance on the part of the
Allies. Before I left Paris I took a walk of two miles
under it. You descend about 20 feet to the level of the
excavation; the passage at first was very narrow, but
soon opened into very wide spaces. You pass immense
walls of human bones, which are brought here from the
common cemeteries. The number was stated at 2,400,000
skeletons. We were under the direction of a guide from
whom we were cautioned not to separate. The passages
are so numerous & intricate that strangers easily lose themselves, several persons were said to have done so, & perished in the caverns. We had a company of about 14
persons & each one carried a wax light in his hand. If
any accident were to extinguish the lights, the Guide himself could never find his way out. We ascended two miles
from where we had entered, & I found it much more pleasant to be upon than under the earth. After leaving Paris
I went a little out of my way to see Brussels & Antwerp,
towns you know of no small celebrity in history. When
I reached Ghent I found Mr Adams & Mr Russell had
arrived two days before me. Mr Clay came a day after
me, & Mr Gallitin made his appearance at the end of
about ten days. We have *all* been here nearly 5 weeks

& have not yet heard of the B. Commissioners having left London. The Post which comes by Calais & moves slowly brings us the newspapers from London in five days. The British Government knew of our being here within three days after we were assembled. It is impossible now that anything can be done to affect the present Campaign. I can say little as to the probability of peace. I have seen no signs of it except in the Speech of the Prince Regent upon closing the Session of Parliament. But a speech from the throne is too hollow a thing to be much relied upon. Let the event be what it will, I hope to see the U. States before the winter. I have enough of Europe & sigh most dolefully to revisit my native shore

Your's

J. A. B.

August 7th

P. S.   The B. Commissioners Lord Gambier, Mr Goldbourne & Dr Adams arrived last evening, & this morning I had a visit from Mr Baker the Secretary to notify the fact—. 20th August. There can be no peace the British pretensions render the continuance of war inevitable.

GHENT 28th Oct. 1814.

MY DEAR R.

Here am I still at Ghent. When I wrote you by the John Adams which left us the latter end of August, I expected by this time to be near the Coast of America. The British Government have ordered it otherwise. The are not yet

prepared to tell us whether the war shall continue or peace
be made. They are looking to events on both continents.
They will be influenced greatly by the State of affairs in
America at the end of the Campaign, & also by the state of
affairs which may result from the proceedings of the Congress at Vienna. If the campaign terminates badly with
you, & if things should settle down peaceably on this continent we shall have no peace. Nothing exists here, which
would [lead] one to form a decided opinion. The negociation is evidently protracted to take the chance of what may
happen. Knowing this to be the fact we have done & mean
to do all that is in our power to defeat their project. But
discretion confines us within certain bounds, & they will
be enabled to take their own course. I think you ought to
count upon & be prepared for another campaign & a campaign in which the Government will exert its whole power
against us. If we can weather the storm another year,
they will give up the contest & we shall be safe & quiet for
a generation to come. This continent is generally in our
favour, but it is exhausted by long wars, & will reluctantly
embark in new conflicts. We must depend upon ourselves,
& if the contest be maintained as I am sure it can be if we
are united, America will establish a proud character
throughout Europe & the World. You may rely upon it
we shall not cede any point of National honor. We may
have much to suffer, but to an honorable mind no suffering
is so great as that of disgrace. It is better far to die than
to exist in a state of ignominy. Such I hope is the sentiment of every American, & if such be the sentiment of our

citizens the U States cannot be subdued or disgraced. I will not flatter you with vain prospects. Peace is not in our power, it depends upon our enemy. You are not to expect it unless events should render it the interest of the enemy to make it. You will not see me before the spring. Whether peace or war be designed, the negociation will be ·protracted for some months to come. I have long sighed to return to my family & friends. Europe may have its attractions for others, but everything which is dear & in-.teresting to me is in America.

Adieu sincerely yours,

J. A. B.

GHENT, Dec. 25th. 1814.

MY DEAR. R.

I am afraid we have put an end to your Military Career & deprived history of some brilliant pages which you were preparing to furnish. A treaty of Peace & Amity was signed yesterday by your Plenepotentiaries & those of the B. Government. The general basis is the Status ante Bellum. The British retain only the possession of some disputed Islands in the bay of Passamaquoddy, till a decision on the right takes place according to a provision in the treaty. Hostilities continue till the treaty be ratified by our Government. We shall not attempt to voyage in the winter, but you may expect us in the spring.

Sincerely, Yours '.

J. A. BAYARD.

PAPERS OF THE HISTORICAL SOCIETY OF DELAWARE.

XXXII.

BIOGRAPHICAL SKETCHES

OF

Prominent Delawareans.

BY

REV. SAMUEL W. THOMAS, D.D.

Read before the Historical Society of Delaware, April 15, 1901.

THE HISTORICAL SOCIETY OF DELAWARE,

WILMINGTON.

·1901·

BIOGRAPHICAL SKETCHES

OF

PROMINENT DELAWAREANS.

DELAWARE is a diamond whose lustre and value are seen in her sons, a peninsula all radiant with rich treasures of historic value, the brightest and best of her colonial sisters. She has produced men who have filled the annals of history with resplendent deeds, and who served their country with distinguished honor.

We shall speak of some of her illustrious sons, not as Plutarch wrote his "Lives," in parallels (an illustrious Greek by the side of an illustrious Roman), but rather take our subjects singly,—men we knew, except the elder Bayard. God lent them to their country; they left a legacy of which we are proud to be the trustees. Nor are we unmindful of the sacredness of the trust, for the names of these noble men were not born to die,—men imbued with transcendent virtues, monarchs of mankind, men whose lives and labors we share. May we ever keep fresh their memory, emulating their example, practising their virtues, while we bury their faults and forget their failings. "Great men are not their own; they are the

3

property of mankind." He is great whose goodness is not eclipsed by his greatness. Some of whom we treat walked on the high places of the earth, others in the valley of comparative obscurity, yet in all we find some jewel worthy of our notice, some characteristic that challenges our admiration.

In early childhood it was our lot to be associated with the Rodneys, which brought us in close touch with the ancestral line, but a short remove from Cæsar, who signed the Declaration of Independence, and among the heirlooms we possess, those we most prize, are the knee-buckles he wore upon that momentous occasion. No prouder name is found upon the Roll of Honor of this, our native State, nor has that name been sullied by those who bear it.

JAMES A. BAYARD, the elder (though not to the manor born, but who adopted Delaware as his home), stood a giant in forensic debate. Astute, cogent, and clear, he left an imperishable name His descendants were among the foremost men in the time we have lived.

JAMES A. BAYARD, his son, had few superiors in his chosen profession, was the equal of Clay and Calhoun, and conserved the interests of his country with marked ability. True, he represented a small State, but he filled the land with admiration for his rare genius. When he arose in legislative halls, his stately presence, commanding tones, and charming manners commanded the attention of his hearers in those supreme moments of his life when fully put upon his metal. He was a courtly gentleman, a well-mannered man. Some thought him haughty, but

he was never arrogant. Reserve was chosen lest he might suggest familiarity, and prudence in speech he prized more than a flippant tongue. He honored and never betrayed the State that honored him.

THOMAS F. BAYARD was the honored son of an honored sire. He was born in 1828, in the city of Wilmington, State of Delaware, and practised law in New Castle County from 1851 until he was elected United States Senator in 1868. He was re-elected in 1875 and 1881. He served as Secretary of State under Cleveland from 1885-1889, and March 30, 1893, was appointed Ambassador to Great Britain.

His stay at the Court of St. James was marked with ability, and did much to cultivate the spirit of fraternal regard for us which, more recently, has manifested itself among our English cousins.

He was prudent and persuasive. Still, he was chided for remarks he was said to have made upon public occasions, on the breaking out of the Civil War, and while representing this country abroad, but, taking him all in all, we may well be proud of his record.

Had he represented a large State, there is no doubt that he would have been a nominee of the Democratic party for the Presidency, nor could they have found a better.

He was tinctured with Methodist blood, for he was related to one of her proudest sons, Governor Richard Bassett.

Seventy years bore no mark of misused opportunity.

He leaves an untarnished name, and died comparatively poor as the world in these days counts riches. Yet there is enough left to make his family fairly comfortable.

JOHN M. CLAYTON, a man of massive brain and a body of goodly proportions, of fair estate and many friendships, social in disposition, but of a retiring nature, found in his elegant home, shaded by trees of his own planting, with ample fields dotted here and there with herds of choice cattle which were his pride, and well-bred horses that bore him on journeys about the neighborhood, a source of great delight. He was a master in political science, broad-gauged and catholic, as well as courteous in spirit. The horizon of his vision was not bounded by partisan lines or personal preferences, but reached over the map of this mundane sphere. He studied great international questions with the assiduity of a Premier and the accuracy of a mathematician, making himself conversant with the needs of humanity. He was every inch a man, and had he represented a State whose numerical power would have weighed heavily in settling political preferment, he would have been nominated as President of the United States by the old Whig party.

His warmest personal friend in Philadelphia was that genial and cultured gentleman, Morton McMichael, with whom he frequently consulted upon public and personal affairs. Mr. McMichael's respect is best evinced by the fact that he named one of his sons after John M. Clayton. I imagine it has never occurred to you that the former efficient City Treasurer of Philadelphia, Colonel Clayton

McMichael, was named after Delaware's distinguished son, but such is the fact.

The trio of SAULSBURYS were dissimilar in taste and disposition except in their ambition for office.

GOVE was an autocrat, and an aristocrat as well, who, like the Iron Duke, would never brook the slightest offence. His will was law, his plans must be respected, and his purpose served. Yet he would scorn to do a mean act, or use unfair means to accomplish a purpose. In State politics he ruled with an ungloved hand, and, usually, was allied with the Bayards, for they shared honors between them. His inflexibility and indomitability perplexed his adversaries, but held his friends as with hooks of steel. There was that about the man which impressed his associates that he was born to rule. He was true to his friends, but implacable to his enemies. He never held out the olive branch; he never apologized, compromised, or surrendered, unless it proved a forlorn hope, then, to gain his point, would make concessions.

WILLARD was a generous soul, full of the milk of human kindness. His face would radiate beams of pleasure such as gladdened all who caught the warmth of his social nature. He was attractive in person, had lustrous eyes and winning ways, which captivated his willing worshippers. He fascinated by his mirth and humor, and drew about him congenial and often convivial companions, who would accept from him what they would resist from others. The tones of his voice were mellifluous and his oratory matchless. Had he followed the dictates of his conscience,

and what he believed the voice of God, he would have been a minister of Christ, and not a Congressman. He yielded (to his great regret) to the promptings of ambition, which led him to the forum rather than to the pulpit. His love of society and unwisely chosen associates created a want of carefulness which brought him many hours of sorrow and bitter repentance. This is no fancy sketch, for we heard his lamentations over murdered hours and privileges. He was a man of deep religious instincts, and called to mind those hours of sweet serenity he enjoyed while living a life of devotion to God and His cause. How our heart yearned for this lovable, affectionate, and true man, and we have good reason to believe he found rest in Christ ere he passed that bourne from which no traveller returns.

ELI was the happy medium between the brothers. His quiet demeanor, his keen mind, his careful, calculating methods, his unquestioned integrity, his ability to win and keep friends, the pureness of his life, his candor, high conscientiousness, his retiring nature, modest almost to a fault, but correct as a chronometer, all conspired to beget confidence. He squared his life by the rule of right. No man could bribe him by money or flattery; he kept the even tenor of his way despite all the storms that may have raged about him. His word was his bond, for, when once given, it was not recalled. " He swore to his own hurt and changed not!" A sincere Christian, a true patriot, a zealous politician, and a rigid party man, peerless in purpose, positive in action, uncompromising in devotion

what his judgment approved and his conscience con-
ned,—all honor to these noble sons of Delaware! They
ved their country well and left a good name.

MEN IN AND ABOUT MILFORD.

Peter F. Causey was a man of honest purpose, plain,
pretentious, amiable, generous, and kind, cautious and
iservative, but diplomatic, and avoided all contests that
uld expose him to censure. He was affable and con-
erate, and was greatly beloved by the people of Kent
l Sussex, where he was best known. Governor Tharp
l his brother, the Harringtons, Ralstons, Voseys, Mar-
s, Flemings, John and James Sharp, Benny Lofland,
tailor, who had seven sons, each of whom in his
ler was told to bring the goose that ironed the new-
de clothes, but each in his turn bade the other bring
and at last the old man had to get down from the
le and get it himself (a sad example of parental au-
rity); the Smiths (and they were many); the Pretty-
is, the Dills, the Nealls, and hosts of others of whom
cannot make other mention.

)r. Burton, a sturdy character, always kept himself
in hand. He was not only the servant of the people
vhom he ministered as a physician, but a slave to his
ession. He did more work for little money than any
in his line we ever knew, and was a good friend to
poor, and ought to have acquired a fortune. If his
endants are alive, they should claim a pension, and

those who failed to honor his fees should be compelled to pay.

Trusten P. McColley was not a great man, but good. and kept open house for the itinerant preacher, and his home was graced by a kindly wife. No man was more sought after on funeral occasions, for it mattered not what kind of a character the person had, he treated all alike. Every one of whom he spoke was given a free passport to heaven, so that all bereaved people knew that their feelings would not be wounded and the virtues of their friends extolled and their vices forgiven.

Curtis Watson hewed to the line, asked no favors, and gave to the penny all those he owed, and demanded it from those who owed him. A just man of good business ability, a true friend and a good hater, a man of sterling worth, a first-class citizen, and an honor to any community.

Daniel Godwin, a man of generous impulses, of an affectionate disposition, easy-going, and full of charity for the weakness of his fellow-men.

George Atkins was a polished gentleman, an ardent friend, and a fair financier. His home was honored by an excellent wife and lovable as well as beautiful daughters. His brother John was capable and painstaking. Captain George Primrose, John Sherwood, Clement Clark, Isaac Taylor, Captain Bailey, Squire Porter, were men we liked, and who deserve extended remarks, but we must pass on.

John Darby was the father of one of the most devout

and intelligent daughters. Fannie Darby and Sallie Atkins (afterwards Mrs. Marlatt) were like twin sisters,
and they were the pride of Milford. Everybody, rich and
poor, did them reverence. Both were early crowned; they
seemed too good for this evil world. Their memory is
like ointment poured forth,—not any young person of
either sex but who was better for having known them.

Mrs. ANN E. GRIER, a noble type of womanhood; her
superior would have been difficult to find. She was an
oracle at whose shrine all were willing to bow. Her approval was desired by all, for she was the embodiment
of wisdom, purity, and love. Her queenly bearing, her
gentle manners, her mild reproofs, her sweet lessons of
helpfulness, her tender regard for all young people, and
willingness to assist them in well-doing, gave her a place
in the hearts of all who knew her and enjoyed the privilege
of sharing in the wealth of her mature mind. She was
worthy to be classed with Lady Jane Grey, Susannah Wesley, and Lady Huntingdon. How proud we were to count
her our friend, and, though she long since joined the great
majority, her memory lingers about us, and the spell of
her charming manners and loving ways never cease to
impress us while life shall last. I pay this tribute because
I owe her a debt of gratitude I can never repay. Mr. James
Hall is proud to call her aunt, and her spirit of mother-
hood broods over all those who were blessed by her counsel and inspired by her words of cheer.

Delaware may well be proud of the women who grew
up upon her soil. Indeed, so far as we are concerned, if

circumstances would permit and the occasion required, we would avail ourselves of the privilege of recording the virtues, the intelligence, the piety of the women who were foremost in the places where we dwelt, or even made temporary sojourn, rather than pay tribute to the men we knew. Still, we cannot dismiss the Milford contingent without making mention of the Drapers and Dorseys, the Collinses, Loflands, Currys, Captain Clark, Captain Binly, Hudsons, and Captain Elias Smithers, who sailed the " Packet Wave," a quaint, steady-going man, whose relict still survives him.

Comparisons are sometimes odious, but extremes abound, yet there were many about Milford who were worthy of a high place on the scroll of fame. But we must forbear.

FREDERICA was honored by men of no mean calibre such as JAMES S. BUCKMASTER, whose heart was big enough to take in the world, and made numerous friends, who courted his society and shared his hospitality. He was a man of the people, ardent, earnest, and true, and never was more happy than in helping some forlorn brother out of distress.

WILLIAM TOWNSEND, the sharp, shrewd, business man, quick-witted, but never sordid, staunch in his adherence to justice, truth, sobriety, candor, and conscience, was neat in appearance, cultivated in taste, polite and modest, rigid in his demand for good, and sufficient reasons why he should serve another, but when convinced, did it royally.

His wife, Elizabeth Barrett, was a daughter of John Barrett, a grandson of the founder of Barrett's Chapel.

EDWARD ANDERSON, the gentle gentleman, loath to offend, was quick to apprehend a well-meant kindness, and always ready to return the compliment. His widow died in the Methodist Episcopal Home for the Aged, Philadelphia, October 29, 1900, in her eighty-second year.

One of the men who impressed us most was a farmer (Caleb Burchinal by name) who lived near by, full of quaint sayings, rich in native genius, ready in repartee, always well-poised and sharp as a needle. He was full of goodness, but despised cant, of rare judgment, a sage who never learned at school, a savant in the science of agriculture, a model farmer, an astute politician, so far as weighty facts go, but had no fancy for office.

JOSEPH LEWIS, a man of mark, a local preacher who loved to preach, but seldom knew when to stop. It is said, after all the congregation had left, the sexton stayed awhile, but he grew sleepy and laid the key on the pulpit, saying, "Brother Lewis, when you are through, please lock the door and put the key under the steps."

Samuel Grace, Captain Waitman Sipple, the Wests, and the Boones, were goodly men of no mean order; John Hall, who built up a fortune by diligent attention to business,—each of these left a good record.

What a galaxy of graces gather around Camden.

The restraining power of the Quakers lingers about this quiet town, but who can think of Hugh Jenks without feeling a disposition to lift the hat and do honor to

the name? "None knew him but to love him, nor named him but to praise." The broad acres, cultivated by his skilful direction, have proved an object lesson to every passing farmer, who, on his return home, tried to improve his estate and brighten his home.—. Many a whitewash- and paint-brush have been put to use by the example of this tidy farmer. But time would fail us to speak of Mr. Coursey; Mr. Creadick, who lived near by, his noble son the doctor, who lately died in Philadelphia; of Edward Lord, the merchant; of Mr. Land, the retired landholder; of the Coopers, Temples, Simpsons, and other honored names associated therewith.

And what shall we say of Dover's distinguished inhabitants—of Daniel M. Bates, of the Harringtons, of the Days, the Comegys, the Jumps, the Whartons, of Elijah Crouch and his famous brother, of that noble family of Ridgleys, of the Wallcotts, the Pennewills,—sons of noble sires,—of the Cowgills and Stevensons, of John Cullen, and Nathaniel Barratt Smithers and his kinsfolk, but particularly of him?

What a noble man he was, the noblest Roman of them all,—foremost in defence of the oppressed, of the downtrodden, the leader of reform, the conscientious advocate, who never stooped to dishonest acts, or smirched the character of his bitterest foe, the jurist, the gentleman! He stood like a brazen law in the maintenance of righteousness, and never faltered in the defence of truth. He was a grandson of Dr. Elijah Barratt, and thought to possess

in a marked degree many of the characteristics of that distinguished physician.

CHANCELLOR BATES, the protégé of Daniel, whose meek-
ness was next to that of Moses, whose mind was keen,
whose sunlight soul flashed with intelligence, probity, pureness, and holiness. Saintly in appearance, almost ghost-
like, he never seemed to live but in the shadow of death,
and only dwelt in the affairs of earth because necessity required the sacrifice. His saintly spirit seemed like a caged
eagle trying to escape to its native heaven. Thanks be
to God that such men as he ever graced this earth, for
without such God might repent that He ever created it;
they are the salt of the earth. If Delaware bore no other
name than his, it would be enough to glory in; not because he was so great, for his attenuated body never gave
him any chance to spread his wings, to test his metal, or
unload his full-freighted soul.

We recall DR. BONWELL, who measured the miles he
travelled by a cyclometer of his own construction, and
was a genius in his way, a many-sided man.

SMYRNA, once the depot of trade, a mart to which was
brought the growths of various kinds from distant parts,
was, in our time of association with it, most distinguished
for its storekeepers and its traders. Its industries were
few and its merchants many.

Two characters impressed us strongly. Mr. Mansfield
and Dr. Perkins were men of mark; but we cannot dare
to give an outline of their character, except to say that
these two men were types of a former generation, men of

sound mind, of sober habits, fine discrimination, and tender sensibilities; but, taking the community as a whole, they were fair representatives. We recall others whom we can only name,—Judge and George Davis, the Cumminses, Clements, Edward Beck, James Clements, the Bewleys, Carrows, Goulds, Raymonds, Stockleys, Hurlocks, M. Hoffecker, Reynoldses, Bells, Goutys, Fox, McDowell, Mumford, and others equally worthy of mention.

MIDDLETOWN and vicinity gave to the State men of energy, of solid worth,—the Biggses, Coxes, Townsends, But these were but little known to us, for our work seldom brought us in touch with them.

WILMINGTON, the place of our birth, the emporium of trade, produced some of the best specimens of active business men and educators. Teachers such as Sheward Johnson, Caleb Kimber, Edward Smith, President Prettyman, the Bullocks, the Hilleses; manufacturers, such as Harlan & Hollingsworth, the Prices and Canbys, the Puseys, Lobdell, Jarrett Megaw, and Stotsenburg; merchants, Kennard, Dunott, and Pennington; ship-builders, such as the Thatchers and Thomas Young, the Moores (Edward and Charles), John, William, Edward, and Robert Robinson, Ed. Merrick, the Flinns, the Talleys, Jesse Lane, John Turner, and Colonel Davis (the father of three sons, called New Castle, Kent, and Sussex). We remember the old gentleman when he carried an immense staff, and how he could catch the boys on the street with its crook; the Careys, Captain Kelley, the Clarks, the Jacksons, Delaplain McDaniel, who was an apprentice to my father;

Harry McComb, who was his helper at the bellows and anvil; Sammy Wollaston, the sturdy Quaker; neighbor Moore, the motherly teacher; Friend Williams, who took the boys to Brandywine and taught them how to swim; and James Riddle, the cotton spinner and cloth weaver, —simple as a child, artless and good, but one of the truest that ever came from the Emerald Isle; the Bringhursts (Edward's wife had one of the sweetest faces on which we ever gazed. She was full of good works) ; the Milligans, the Morrows, Haganys, Boddys, Birds, Sparkses, McCauleys, Merrihews, Turners, Simmonses, Grubbs, Betts, Noblitts, Hardys, Taggarts, Johnsons, Billamys, McCleeses, McCorkles, McClarys, Booths, Williamses, Hedges, Plunkets and Williamsons, Garasches, Duponts, Dr. Askew, Dr. Porter, Dr. Higgins, Dr. Lewis P. Bush, and Bishop Lee.

One name more particularly merits mention—WILLARD HALL. Who can tell the matchless worth of this beautiful character, so spotless, so free from every vice, selfpoised, even-tempered, chaste, noble, generous, hospitable, and kind, a man whom the gods would honor, his face a benediction, his society a charm, his words full of wisdom! In life's young morn, we almost looked upon him as a prophet. We thought of Elijah, and often wondered why he was not caught up.

Another person breaks upon our view, stately in carriage, nimble of step, neat as a pin, gentle as a child, true as steel, learned in his profession, able in service, conscientious in its discharge. A lovely Christian char-

acter was Dr. Gibbons. We have often said we shall never see his like again.

And what more shall we say, for the time would fail us to speak of Abner Bailey, of the Bushes, of the Townsends, of the Wales and Lore families, Adams, McInall, of Benny Bracken who professed great courage, but was a mortal coward. And who shall tell of Jack Gardner and George Robinson, Caleb Rudolph, George Topham, the Schofields, and the many lesser lights too numerous to mention?

These are the reminiscences of one who loved many of the persons he has named. But those he loved the most were too nearly related to himself to make such reference as he would gladly have made as to their character and conduct. The grave-yards and cemeteries in Delaware retain as bonny dust as ever mingled with its mother earth, and memories as dear as ever come to mortals gather about names cherished in many thousand hearts. Their offspring have gone into every part of the world to bless mankind, and no sweeter spot is known to them than that of Delaware.

He that is not proud of being a Blue Hen's chicken should never listen to her cackle nor catch the clarion notes of her lawful mate, the chanticleer, who ever pipes her praise, nor see the flapping of his wings which fan the world with refreshing reminders of the gallant band who have made the world better for their living in it.

COLONEL SAMUEL B. DAVIS.

THE

BOMBARDMENT OF LEWES

BY

THE BRITISH, APRIL 6 AND 7, 1813.

HISTORICAL completeness is short-lived; detail, in actual fulness, dies with the era in which it is born. Eighty-seven years after an engagement, attempt to recall its specific occurrences, and insurmountable difficulties will present themselves. Legend survives in companionship with crisp official facts, dry and dwarfed. In an out-of-the-way recess, research may bring to view imperfect data; the common-place talk, the shades of the transaction, the little things, which aggregated make the big things, are wanting. Go to the locality vibrating with the hero's name, once the scene of his engagement,—town oracles are dead; the graveyard seals with silence mute lips. What is desirable has been lost. Sometimes there is no difficulty encountered in successfully grouping the more prominent facts, such as the trite details of the engagement at Lewes. Certain facts are ascertainable. The place where the fort stood is easy of location; the force behind the guns can be approximated; the once deep pond, now shallow, on whose uprise of surrounding land

3

the volunteers encamped, can be designated. These are incidents with which we are familiar. We know about the guns and men behind them, of the twenty-two hours' bombardment, because bullocks, hay, vegetables, and water were not forthcoming. These statements are narrated briefly in Commodore Beresford's, Colonel Davis's, and Governor Haslet's interchange of despatches, and, with a few meagre accounts from the papers of that day, now inaccessible to the masses, complete the recorded history of the British assault and the American defence of Lewes, occurring on the 6th and 7th of April, 1813.

Irreverent time, the intermeddler with men's affairs, permits to remain the grandeur of the unalterable ocean, the magnificent stretch of bay, and the creek where pilots quenched their thirst during those memorable days when they stood beside the guns, twelve in number, four of which at this distant time look sullenly seaward, searching for disappearing ships, with armament gone and without possibility of return.

In Pilot Town is standing the former residence of Colonel Davis; it was built by Dr. Fisher, father of the late Henry; a simple, old-fashioned, two-story house, with attic and peaked roof. It has no occupant, and is closed against all would-be tenants. To a pilgrim it has the appearance of having sheltered greatness. In its isolation it has become the scene of homage and patriotic worship. All around it is hallowed ground, and if the past has a voice, it certainly speaks thereabout.

Would that my granary were filled with such imper-

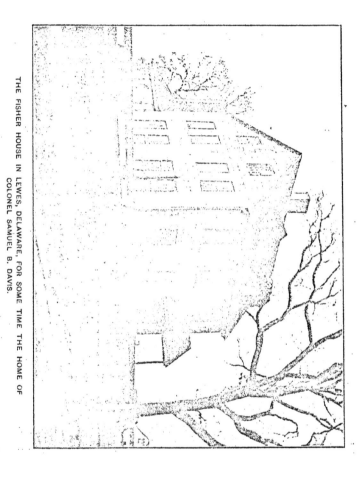

THE FISHER HOUSE IN LEWES, DELAWARE, FOR SOME TIME THE HOME OF COLONEL SAMUEL B. DAVIS.

ishable wheat! I have gathered the little I have been able to find from a field left by the late reapers at sunset hour. Their lips have on them the seals of silence, and much of truth is interred with their bones.

Beresford's bombardment of twenty-two hours was bloodless to Americans and exasperating to the English. The king should have recalled him. We have to regret that the explicit despatches of that day were so brief. It was before the age of news enterprise and exaggeration. The officers who forwarded the incomplete account of the engagement, and those who furnished the papers with what they printed about it at the time, boiled their statements down to occupy a narrow space.

In historical adornment, the purest diamond in the tiara of Delaware, worn by her during the war of 1812, is the assault of the British on Lewes and the defence made by the garrison of that town. The story has a feverish interest. Where the Delaware Bay and the Atlantic Ocean unite and sing in chorus, Lewes uplifts her head and looks forth over that magnificent stretch of water. In the inland distance spread the fertile plains of Sussex, suggesting their origin in the British island, whence they came associated with ancestral memories of the past. Cape Henlopen has had since 1813 more than a light-house to flash its rays abroad, whose future influence cannot become the less significant, since it will ever prove a beacon burning steady and luminous.

Lewes and Pilot Town, one and a quarter miles apart, were hamlets in 1813, inhabited by a hardy, fearless peo-

ple, engaged principally in fishing; some of whom were
professional pilots. Lewes is distant from the sea three
miles. It stands on the main-land, slightly elevated, above
a strip of marsh and sand lying between the Delaware
Bay and Lewes Creek, which runs along between it and
the main-land to the bay. The strip varies in width, being
about a quarter of a mile across from the main-land, where
the fort was located, to the bay. The Lewes Creek is a
dark, narrow, unprepossessing stream of no great depth.
It is sometimes asserted that a growth of wood stretched
from the creek to the bay. Trees grew only in distant
places; there was no continuous growth. An unob-
structed view was had from the fort to the bay, and of
the sails on its broad bosom.

Interest centres in Lewes in consequence of its earlier
history. In the dawn of American shipping its harbor
was a refuge in storm for craft compelled to seek security
from ocean perils. It was settled as early as 1631, on
a site where stood the renowned and romantic wigwam
of the untutored and uncivilized red man, that race of
defiers of your civilization, which perishes rather than accept your boasted blessings as heritages.

In the first era of Delaware, at Pilot Town, a fort
was constructed. During the war of the Revolution one
stood there. In 1813 it was replaced by that at Lewes.

Lewes enjoys the honor of being the original county-
seat of Sussex. A court-house was erected in 1730, but
was abandoned in 1792, Georgetown stripping it of its
laurels.

· Count D'Estaing, in the war of independence, arrived from France with his fleet on the Virginia coast, and sailed for and anchored in the Delaware, and was saluted by the fort at Pilot Town when he reached there on the eighth day of July, 1778.

During the Revolution English naval ships under Admiral Howe were familiar with the locality. The crews of the enemy's boats foraged along the shores of the bay. They were of the original hungerers after juicy bullocks, with decided thirst for water, possibly to dilute something stronger. Their most notable achievement was the burning of the interior of the light-house, the friendly guide of the mariner.

The defence works at Lewes were simple intrenchments. An account of their construction I have taken from the *Republican,* of Fredericktown, Maryland, March 31, 1813, as follows: " On Saturday last the Fort for the protection of this borough was commenced; it is, we understand, to be finished by the citizens, who have voluntarily undertaken the task without regard to rank or distinction."

Dr. H. R. Burton, answering my inquiries, states: " Mrs. Marshall, of Lewes, remembers the appearance of the two forts, one of which stood on a prominent point commanding the entrance to the then deep and navigable creek known as ' Horn Kill.' Mrs. Marshall says the forts were constructed of rough logs and brush, filled in with earth, sand, and gravel, each having what she terms a log watch-house."

Samuel B. Davis, commandant of the forces assembled

for the defence of Lewes, was of imposing stature; decidedly fine in appearance, prominent features, large cheek-bones, heavy jaw, large nose and mouth, expressive of great firmness. He was six feet in height, courageous, possessing qualities of discipline and intellect for the management of men.

During his residence in Lewes he adopted in his family a young girl, whom he regarded affectionately as one of his children. She was in after-years celebrated and well known as Myra Gaines, the New Orleans litigant. It has been said that in her prosperity she did not forget her foster-father. He often spent weeks with her as her guest in New Orleans.

Colonel Davis was born in Lewes, December 25, 1765, and died in Wilmington, where he was buried, September 6, 1854. In youth he was a midshipman in the French fleet, beaten by the English naval force June 1, 1794. During his absence abroad he was united in wedlock to a French lady. On returning to America he resided temporarily in New Orleans. When the war of 1812 was declared, he offered his services to the United States, and was commissioned lieutenant-colonel of the Thirty-second Regulars, March 17, 1813. Subsequently he was transferred to the command of the forty-fourth regiment, which he resigned, and located in Wilmington, whence he moved to Philadelphia. While residing in that city he was elected a member of the Legislature of Pennsylvania. He returned subsequently to Wilmington, where his last days were spent.

· He was fond of Lewes and made frequent visits to the place. At such times he was welcomed by a military salute fired by a company. He occupied a suite of rooms in the hotel by the site where the battery stood.

During the last years of his life an iron rod was run from the first floor to the second, on which his rooms were located, to assist him in going up and down stairs, which rod remains.

Prior to the engagement at Lewes, a British fleet had blockaded the Delaware Bay. March, 9, 1813, there were at the capes the Belvidere, Poitiers, La Paz, and Ulysses. It was their purpose to replenish their exhausted supplies from the farmers on the coast, a correct list of the names of all of them, from New Castle to Lewes, being in their possession.

From a large naval force assembled by the enemy near Norfolk, the frigates Poitiers and Belvidere were detached and ordered to the Delaware, and by March 13 that bay was rigidly blockaded by three frigates of seventy-four guns each and smaller vessels. The Belvidere had a narrow escape from capture. Commodore Rodgers, in the President, gave chase to her; she escaped by throwing overboard movable articles, outsailing the President. A well-directed fire from the latter vessel seriously injured her, but a favorable wind enabled her to escape.

The arrival of the blockading fleet in the Delaware was thus mentioned in one of the papers: " Our inhabitants are in a great state of alarm. On Saturday a British

·seventy-four came into the Delaware, and is now about ten miles within the capes. On Monday a frigate anchored alongside. Last night, at twelve o'clock, two of the Cape May pilot-boats were driven in Maurice River and captured by the enemy's tenders."

The blockading fleet conducted no movement which was not watched. They made soundings and placed buoys in the bay. The coast was under strict surveillance by the militia. The use of spy-glasses was availed of by them to detect the manœuvres of the enemy's ships. Those people of Lewes who gained their livelihood on the deep found their occupations gone, so they turned soldiers; men of their hardiness and endurance were good ones, as the sequel proved. They were the nucleus, holding the body of those who poured in for defence firm and steady to that purpose.

Niles' Register furnishes the following account of the uprising of the people: "At Dover, on Sunday last, in consequence of the movement of the enemy, the drum beat to arms. The whole population of all the various sects and persuasions, religious and political, capable of shouldering a musket, assembled; arms were liberally distributed, and from four hundred to five hundred men were ready for service. It was pleasant to remark that all the soldiers of the Revolution in the neighborhood were present. One old gentleman, who deserves to be named, Mr. Jonathan McNatt, tottering on his staff, received his musket, and with a hearty will went through the manœuvres. Sunday as it was, the venerable man (a worthy member

and a strict observer of the rules of the Methodist Church),
returning home, set himself to work making ball cartridges, affording the youth the fruits of his experience,
and presenting an example irresistibly leading to patriotism. The force musters frequently for drill, and have
made great progress in essentials. At Smyrna the people
are all alive, munitions of war are prepared, and all possible means are taken for the defence of that place and
vicinity. At New Castle the chief control of the defensive measures has been confided to the veteran Captain Bennett, of the much-extolled Delaware Blues, who,
with General Greene, earned unfading laurels in the
Southern States. This brave man is in his element, and,
as a colonel, has the command of some well-disciplined
militia, artillery, and infantry. At Wilmington the general measures of defence appear submitted by common consent to Colonel Allen McLane, a seventy-sixer, and as true
as steel. To aid him in his operations, all the men of
other years, a veteran band of gallant hearts, are on the
alert assisting. Batteries are erected below New Castle
on the Delaware, and on the Christiana River that leads
by Wilmington. The former is much exposed to the
enemy; but the latter may be defended, if the people are
true to themselves, as they appear to be."

The foregoing perfect picture of a people's preparation
for deadly conflict could have been taken out of its old
frame in which it has been held so long, reframed, re-
colored, and encased in a new frame, but such alteration
would dissipate its charm. I shall leave such old pic-

tures as I have found them. This one is refreshing in the distinctness of its outlines; terse, explicit; and graphic amplification would ruin its appearance.

The story is fluently told how, along the line of the Delaware River, the bay, and in the interiors of States bordering thereon, defensive preparations were prosecuted. Lewes was in a similar condition of fermentation, and finally was the rock hurling back the gory wave to the sea.

The volunteers were prompt and their presence assuring. They varied in length of time of service. Of those at Lewes, five, eight, and thirty days were among the periods of their detention. Some of these, called out when Beresford made his demand on Lewes, were discharged before the bombardment under the impression that danger was over. They were emergency men, returned to their homes when their services seemed to be no longer required. Those of them who made application subsequently received one hundred and sixty acres of land for their services.

The presence of the blockading fleet in the Delaware assembled the militia on the coast. Governor Haslet was alive to his obligations. On the 17th of March the British burned a sloop, and would have set fire to another but for the appearance of the volunteers, who prevented the conflagration. Annoyances to shipping were numerous. A schooner from Charleston, voyaging to Philadelphia, was chased ashore at the mouth of Town Creek; four barges of armed men were sent from the fleet to take possession of it, and would have done so, but that

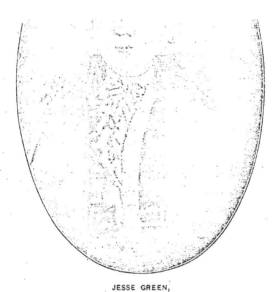

JESSE GREEN,

BRIGADIER-GENERAL OF THE DELAWARE STATE MILITIA IN THE WAR OF 1812.

the people, aided by the efforts of the militia, boarded the vessel and took from it two cannon and a large amount of ammunition, which were conveyed to land. It was a warfare of useless destruction on the part of the British, which roused the indignation of the country.

Under date of the 20th of March, General Green, of Delaware, wrote the following letter to a friend in Baltimore:

"We have a British fleet at the capes of Delaware. They have burned several vessels and taken others. We have had an engagement with them from the shore. Our ammunition gave out, or we would have prevented them from burning the Charleston packet. They had four large boats full of men, and came within two hundred yards of the shore. I am now on my way to Lewistown, where there are one thousand men under arms. . . . We have men sufficient to prevent them from landing, but we are in want of ammunition, which we shall be supplied with in a few days."

Captain Warner, with his Wilmington troop of horse, forty members, accompanied by fifty volunteers, rode to Lewes. Along were Captain Hunter, of Philadelphia, and Major Robert Carr, of the United States army. A company of troops from Laurel and its vicinity, under Captain Thomas Rider, besides a company commanded by Captain Samuel Laws, also presented themselves at the threatened town. The companies named, with other rallying ones, were incorporated into the Ninth Delaware Regiment, whose colonel was Mitchell Harshaw. Captain

Hunter was probably assigned to a post in the battery, and Major Carr doubtless to an important place. The entire force was subject to orders from Colonel Davis.

The national government sent gunboats down the Delaware to check the depredations of the British. They took no part in the engagement which followed; that on the enemy's side was participated in by four launches of twenty-four- and eighteen-pounders, two sloops carrying thirty-two-pounders and a mortar, a pilot-boat having six-pounders, and the schooner Paz mounting twelve-pounders of twelve caliber each, covered by the frigates Belvidere and Poitiers, belonging to that formidable class of naval warsmen known as "seventy-fours." Altogether two hundred and forty-one guns thundered and exploded at the defiant town.

Less than a week elapsed after the arrival of the blockading squadron before the men on shipboard were in need of vegetables and beef. The silly commodore believed he was sufficiently formidable to enforce his demand; he haughtily addressed "to the first magistrate of Lewistown," the following letter sent from "His Britannic Majesty's ship Poitiers, in the mouth of the Delaware, March 16," not forgetting to politely append "Sir."

The text of the letter ran in this wise:

"As soon as you receive this, I must request you will send twenty live bullocks, with a proportionate quantity of vegetables and hay, to the Poitiers, for the use of his Britannic Majesty's squadron, now at this anchorage, which shall be immediately paid for at the Philadelphia

prices. If you refuse to comply with this request, I shall be under the necessity of destroying your town." Which comforting message had this ironical conclusion: "I have the honor to be, sir, your obedient servant, J. Beresford, commodore commanding the British squadron in the mouth of the Delaware."

Such a precious document inviting the "first magistrate of Lewistown" to act as commissary officer on shore to the British fleet, and thereby place a halter round his neck, got into the hands of Colonel Davis, who transmitted it to Governor Haslet. Neither the governor nor those acting under him were ignorant of "Article 56 of Articles of War," which read, "Whosoever shall relieve the enemy with money, victuals, or ammunition, or shall knowingly harbor or protect an enemy, shall suffer death, or such punishment as shall be ordered by the sentence of a court-martial." The governor left Dover and repaired to Lewes, and from the latter place, under date of March 23, he answered Beresford, saying, "As governor of the State of Delaware, and as commander of its military force, I improve the earliest time afforded me, since my arrival at this place, of acknowledging the receipt of your letter of the 16th inst., directed to the chief magistrate of Lewes. The respect which generous and magnanimous nations, even when they are enemies, take pride in cherishing towards each other, enjoins it upon me as a duty I owe to the State over which I have the honor at this time to preside, to the government of which this State is a member, and to the civilized world, to inquire of you whether

upon further and more mature reflection, you continue resolved to attempt the destruction of this town. I shall probably this evening receive your reply to the present communication, and your determination of executing or relinquishing the demand mentioned in your letter of the 16th inst. If that demand is still insisted upon, I have only to observe to you that a compliance would be an immediate violation of the laws of my country and an eternal stigma on the nation of which I am a citizen; a compliance therefore cannot be acceded to."

Beresford probably smiled when he read that sentence in the governor's letter which inquired "whether upon further and more mature reflection" he "continued resolved to attempt the destruction of the town?" Beresford must have rubbed his eyes and wondered what he and his fleet were there for, if not for such purpose. The governor evidently was playing for time, which was permissible war strategy.

The commodore sent the governor, the day of the receipt of his letter, this response: "In reply to your letter received to-day, by a flag of truce, in answer to mine of the 16th inst., I have to observe, that the demand I have made upon Lewistown is, in my opinion, neither ungenerous nor wanting in that magnanimity which one nation ought to observe with another with which it is at war. It is in my power to destroy your town, and the request I have made upon it, as the price of its security, is neither distressing nor unusual. I must therefore persist, and whatever sufferings may fall upon the inhabi-

tants of Lewes must be attributed to yourselves by not complying with a request so easily acquiesced in."

Captain Byron, prior to March 27, had sent ashore a flag of truce at Cape Island, to procure supplies and water, without success. The obstinate people would not hold communication with the enemy. Beresford subsequently, when too late to retract, was informed of his error. He permitted Captain Page, in charge of ship Robert Wallen, whose health was desperate, to pass to Philadelphia. He told Page "he was ignorant that it was high treason in the magistrate in Lewistown to supply him with provisions, as he had required, or he would not have made the requisition in the manner he did."

Correspondence was at an end. Beresford's first demand was of the 16th of March, his last letter of the 23d; he had procrastinated in making his attack, which did not take place until the 6th of April. This paragraph relating to his tardiness is taken from the *National Intelligencer:*

"Commodore Beresford would seem to have suddenly altered his mind with respect to burning down Lewistown, to make fire to roast the Delaware oxen by. It would be too offensive to suppose a British officer would threaten without meaning to be as good as his word. But certain it is that the commodore has fallen into a dilemma, which 'his friends' at the coffee house have not explained. Delaware beef is highly seasoned, and if served up with forced meat balls, might not prove as palatable to this nautical hero as the roast beef of old England."

Beresford felt the necessity of acting, so he ordered the attack. Colonel Davis despatched the governor, "This evening the Belvidere and two small vessels came close into Lewes and commenced an attack by firing several thirty-two-pound shot into the town, which have been picked up; after which a flag was sent, to which the following reply was returned:

"Sir,—In reply to the renewal of your demand, with the addition for 'a supply of water,' I have to inform you, that neither can be complied with. This, too, you must be sensible of; therefore I must insist the attack on the inhabitants of this town is both wanton and cruel. I have the honor to be your most obedient servant, S. B. Davis, Colonel Commandant."

From the foregoing it appears that Beresford concluded to try shot on the nerves of his disobliging shoresmen. He did so, and to ascertain the effect he sent a flag of truce, which was met outside of the fort, when he made a last effort to have his demand complied with. After the flag had returned unsuccessful, the reluctant commodore parleyed still further. About five o'clock the same day Captain R. Byron continued the correspondence dropped by Beresford, and sent the following letter to one whom he addressed as "S. B. Davis, Esquire, Colonel Commandant." He thus pleaded his hungry and thirsty cause:

"No dishonor can be attached in complying with the demand of Sir John Beresford to Lewes in consideration of his superior force. I must, therefore, consider your refusal to supply the squadron with water, and the cattle that the

neighborhood affords, most cruel, upon your part, to its inhabitants. I grieve for the distress the women and children are reduced to by your conduct, and earnestly desire they may be instantly removed." Incongruously enough, he appended a postscript to his letter, which read, "The cattle will be honorably paid for." To which Colonel Davis verbally replied that he was a gallant man, and had already taken care of the ladies. Colonel Davis sent the letter of the British officer by a man on horseback to the governor. Before the courier started, Davis added, "The attack immediately commenced, and continued till near ten o'clock. The fire from our battery silenced one of their most dangerous gunboats, against which I directed the fire from an eighteen-pounder, for which I request you will immediately send me a supply of shot and powder, as it is uncertain how long the bombardment will continue. They have not succeeded with their bombs in reaching the town, and the damages from their thirty-two-pounders and canister cannot be ascertained until daylight." Colonel Davis closed his note saying, "In this affair you will find the honor of the State has not been tarnished." An N.B. of course was usual and to be expected, which read, "The enemy" (have) "recommenced firing."

The condition of Lewes as to its defence is gleaned from a letter of date April 7, sent from Dover to the Baltimore *Federal Gazette,* appearing on the 9th. According to the writer, when the bombardment began, two eighteen-pounders were serviceable, but without ball; two nine-

pounders, ball too large; there were but fifteen casks of powder. One of the eighteen-pounders mounted on the 6th played on a sloop and silenced its guns. Our men behaved well; the women and children left the garrison; the Belvidere came within two miles of the town, too close for her shot to fall in it; the smaller vessels sent balls flying over the town. On the 5th of April there were 286 men, 418 muskets complete; 8000 cartridges; 25 bags of grape-shot; 15 kegs of powder; 2270 flints; 41 twelve-pound ball; 88 nine-pound ball; 167 six-pound ball; 216 four-pound ball; 434 kegs of lead; 2 eighteen-pounders, one mounted; 2 nine-pounders, badly mounted; 4 six-pounders, badly mounted; 3 four-pounders, mounted.

The Executive of the State convened the Legislature in special session, and while the British fire circled the town the Legislature appropriated the sum of two thousand dollars for its defence.

The eyes of the country were at this juncture on Delaware. A despatch from Cape Island to the Baltimore *Patriot,* April 7, read: " This morning a very steady smoke was seen in the direction of Lewistown, supposed to be occasioned by throwing rockets into that place." The same paper contained this further despatch: " Our brave citizens being short of cannon-balls, the enemy was so accommodating as to fire eight hundred on shore, which on picking up and finding they suited the caliber of our cannon remarkably well, the loan was immediately returned with *interest.*"

A spectator of the closing scene thus described it: He

THOMAS STOCKTON,

MAJOR IN THE UNITED STATES ARMY IN THE WAR OF 1812, AND AFTERWARDS GOVERNOR OF DELAWARE.

said he gained a situation above the town, commanding
an open view; the British ships were ranged in line of
battle; the fire ceased about two o'clock, when he visited
the earth-works; the weather was threatening, wind easterly. Captain Byron drew off his squadron at four o'clock,
a few miles, where he remained until sailing for the capes.
About five hundred shots were fired. A collection was
made of one hundred and fifty of small sizes and a few
bombs. Houses were injured, chimneys cut almost in two,
the corner-posts, plates, and studs cut off in several houses.
The foremast of a schooner was cut away, and another
received a shot in her hull. Of two particular rockets
thrown, one fell on a lot, another in a marsh. A fire
was directed at the breastwork, where more than thirty
men were stationed. Shot struck the battery and broke
the pine logs. Two shots entered by the guns. A further
account mentions that one bomb-shell fell in the town, but
failed to explode; the rockets passed over the town, likewise the shots of the Belvidere, and fell some distance
beyond. The damage suffered by the destruction of property was estimated to be two thousand dollars.

A letter from Dover to the editor of the *Aurora* contained this passage: " We tried some schemes to get them"
(the British) " ashore and trap them, but they seemed
to have anticipated our purpose, and kept close to their
boats. . . . I am told by good authority that a major of
militia and a physician of Cape May have been presented
on board to the British commodore. Some inquiry into
this appears necessary, and a little expenditure of hemp

would perhaps save a ton of gunpowder. They water at Newbold's pond; and the tavern of ———, at Cape May is like a tavern at Wapping, with English officers and every species of debauchery."

It was stated, after the English ships reached Bermuda, some vessels from the coast did a paying business by furnishing them with supplies. The charge was boldly made in the papers of the day, and proves how strong is greed for money when it can suppress the inspiring strains of the heart prompting to patriotism.

Governor Haslet was in Dover in the discharge of his executive functions, actively engaged in calling out and forwarding troops to the scene of action, and performing other official acts necessary in such a crisis. After the foregoing despatch from the colonel commanding to the governor, a subsequent despatch was received from his Excellency, stating that he had "left Dover for headquarters," evidently Lewes, "to superintend the movements of the militia, all of whom are determined to sacrifice everything, rather than treasonably submit to the demands of the enemy." Mention was made in this despatch that the Belvidere was "within" (less) "than two miles of the town."

On the 10th of April, in the evening, a letter reached Philadelphia from Dover, dated 8th inst., and written at a quarter-past eight o'clock, saying, "Lewes is yet safe. Mr. White left there at eleven o'clock yesterday, and says the enemy cannot, in his opinion, destroy the place unless they land, which he thinks they would probably do in

the course of the day. The barges, to the number of
five, were full of men. The house of Peter Hall (a tavern
on the bank) was demolished, and several others damaged; the bombs and rockets fell short of the town."

The paper containing the foregoing account had this
concluding paragraph: "By yesterday's Southern mail
we learn that the British withdrew from Lewistown on
the 8th inst., after bombarding and cannonading it inces-
santly for twenty-two hours, without doing any material
injury to the place, most of their shot and shell falling
short of their object."

Another newspaper had the following account: "The
armament of the British, four launches, twenty-four- and
eighteen-pounders; two sloops, thirty-two-pounders; mortar and pilot-boat, with six-pounders; schooner Paz,
twelve-pounders, covered by the frigate Belvidere, on the
6th and 7th inst. fired six hundred shots, wounded two
or three horses, killed a chicken, and have made fine
sport for the boys in digging the shot out of the sand,
of which they have found and safely lodged in our battery, ready to be returned should occasion offer, ten
thirty-two-pounders, ninety-six eighteen-pounders, one
hundred and fifty-six of twelve and nine [-pounders], with
a large quantity of sixes and grape, with shells and remains of rockets. The militia fired but few shots, as they
had only one eighteen- and one nine-pounder and but few
shots for them, and of which they endeavored to make the
best possible use, and have reason to suppose they gave one
of the sloops the contents of the eighteen-pounder, as she

was obliged to haul out of the line soon after it was seen to strike her.

"We are assured the inhabitants of Lewis and Pilot towns, the volunteers and militia under the command of Colonel Samuel Davis, behaved in a cool and determined manner. The pilots who were stationed in the fort deserve the highest praise, and the whole was so judiciously stationed by the commanding officers that had the British landed they would have been able to give a good account of themselves."

Powder from Dupont's mills in Wilmington was rapidly sent forward to Lewes, and ball was hurried there. The general government had furnished Delaware one hundred and fifty stands of arms, part of its war quota; these were distributed among the volunteers at Lewes. The British made an attempt to land on the 8th; a number of small vessels with armed men approached the shore; the militia and volunteers hastening to the beach to receive them. The British were called back by a signal from their squadron. Colonel Davis resorted to a ruse eminently successful. He marched the militia and volunteers along the water front up to where, unseen by the enemy, they could enter a back street of the town, countermarch to the water front and along it, go and return; thus deceiving the British into believing that an advancing army was flooding Lewes with troops.

On the 8th, the fleet was at its anchorage at the capes, foiled and dispirited, without bullocks, vegetables, hay, or so much as a cup of cold water, and having ignomin-

iously failed to vindicate the boast made by its commodore that it was " within his power to destroy the town."

April 28 the Belvidere put to sea, sailing for the Chesapeake with a few prisoners who were unlucky enough to have been captured.

Mr. Congressman Ingersoll, of Philadelphia, in his history of the war of 1812, devotes about one dozen lines to this important engagement which saved the upper country from visitation, his chief statement being, " Colonel Samuel B. Davis and Major Hunter stood a bombardment of some severity from the Poitiers and Belvidere." May we not whisper to Ingersoll and say, " Friend, had it not been for thy neighbors of Delaware ' standing a bombardment of some severity,' thee would have gotten thyself up and had to git in great haste, as thee once did before under somewhat similar and constrained circumstances?"

In several histories no mention of this gallant action is made, although usually recording the fact " that the British fleet in the Delaware captured or burnt every vessel within its reach," as Hinton remarks, who omits any reference whatever to the engagement. This may be partially due to yourselves; let us believe not so any longer.

Strange, indeed, that this engagement at the gateway of the Delaware, saving the inland from invasion, should be so little understood and so under-estimated.

A complete roster of the officers and men present at the bombardment of Lewes is not to be had. The entire force was, as already stated, about one thousand, some

of whom were without arms, and were required to march with sticks.

The late Dr. Mustard, of Lewes, possessed the diary of William Marshall, a pilot by profession and pursuit, and lieutenant-commander during the bombardment, which diary is in the possession of the doctor's heirs, and was willingly placed by them at my disposal for use. That diary records the names of the following persons who were in the battery,—viz.:

John Ganns, Second Lieutenant-Commander.

Job Cornell, Sr., private.		Charles Baker,	private.
Job Cornell, Jr.,	"	William Edwards,	"
John Rowland,	"	Thomas Norman,	"
Richard Poynter,	"	John Saunders,	"
Samuel Rowland,	"	Moses Nichols,	"
Asshur Pointer,	"	Jacob Art,	"
S. P. Davis,	"	William Masten,	"
Samuel Thompson,	"	James Nicholsen,	"
Simon Edwards,	"	B. Atkins,	"
George Orton,	"	David Hall,	"
Joseph Ort,	"	Nathaniel Neumon,	"
Jerry Shillenger	"	John Davis,	"
John Clampitt,	"	Simon Edwards, Jr.,	"
Samuel West,	"	John Norman,	"
William Jeffries,	"	William Lewis,	
J. W. Batson,	"	Cook Clampitt,	"
William Johnson,	"	Gilbert McCracken,	"
J. W. Norwood,	"	William West,	"
Thomas Virden,	"	William Art,	"

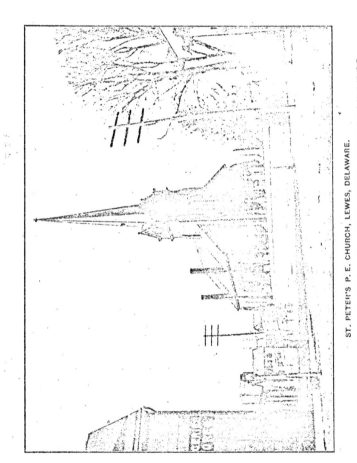

ST. PETER'S P. E. CHURCH, LEWES, DELAWARE.

THE BUILDING AT THE LEFT WAS OCCUPIED AS A STORE BY CALEB RODNEY AT THE TIME OF THE BOMBARDMENT, AND A CANNON-BALL SHATTERED THE DOOR SHOWN IN THE PICTURE.

On authority of Commander Marshall the guns were worked by thirty-eight men, exclusive of their officers.

The same responsible authority numbered the troops encamped at Block House Pond at five hundred. He says that when the fleet appeared, an effort was made to land a force to make incursions in the country; there were two forts, one opposite the spot where the United States Hotel now stands, which suffered bombardment, and the other one located at Pilot Town. The guns were taken from the latter fort to the former, mounted on carriages, and used during the engagement. An arsenal was located on the corner of Second and Shipcarpenters Streets. His account of the several vessels comprising the fleet employed in the bombardment agrees with the names and number already given. He says the Belvidere fired upon the town from the roads; that the store-door of Caleb Rodney was struck by a ball and defaced, which mark it continues to bear; that a house standing on the site of the United States Hotel, the property of a Mr. McIlvaine, was damaged. No lives were lost by the Americans, and no one was wounded. The damage done by the enemy, who thought he had the town at his mercy, was rhymingly described by a soldier:

> "The commander and all his men
> Shot a dog and killed a hen."

Poets will have their say. In this instance the versifier was brief. He might have continued,—

Beresford, Beresford, 'tis rough,
  You drink not our blood or water;
The bullocks are hardy, not tough,
  Nor will they lead to your slaughter.

Your wrath like our wells keeps boiling;
  Your manners grow sensibly worse;
For water your liquor is spoiling;
  Hold! send us your shot, but don't curse.

Your flagship might come up nearer,
  A little closer in to the town;
Before our guns please to steer her;
  Are you afraid of running aground?

Go away, Sir Trumpeter, go;
  You have become the laugh of us all;
To some other place speed and blow,
  But mind ye, a gunpowder squall. ·

Until the closing of the war the battery was garrisoned
by troops. A company was organized by Lieutenant-
Commander Marshall, September 27, 1814, John Ganns,
Second Lieutenant-Commander. The names of the pri-
vates enrolled were at one time fully stated on the roster
in possession of the heirs of the late Dr. Mustard, which
roll suffered mutilation before the doctor received it, supposedly by heirs of those soldiers whose names were upon
it, and were clipped out by their descendants, wishing
the names as evidence to prove army service in pension
applications. A copy of so valuable a paper should at
least be had by this Society.

The names recorded by Commander Marshall, as those in the battery during the bombardment, almost reach the complement in full of the braves who served the guns. I do not know whether the diary was kept during the fight or was written afterwards; no doubt it is measurably correct. Gilbert McCracken, who served on that occasion, had next to him a companion in arms, Greenbury Brown, whose name does not appear upon the roster.' It is likely with this addition all are mentioned who were present. McCracken had an interesting history. He was a soldier during the Revolution; captured by the British and placed in the Jersey prison-ship in New York, at which time he was twelve years of age. Afterwards he served on board a privateersman as armorer, it being his duty to clean and oil the guns. The ship on which he served burned twenty vessels in the British Channel.

In quest of new facts to give additional interest to what must ever remain an incompleted chapter of a glorious event, I made a visit to Lewes to ascertain if such material could be obtained. It was then that I realized fully what I have stated in my introduction,—the town oracles were dead; the graveyard had sealed with silence their mute lips. Two years previously I was there, and met Dr. Mustard, who was thoroughly posted on the history of the engagement at Lewes. He accompanied me to the various historical locations; afterwards, when in his library, he placed before me his wealth of modern newspaper clippings and memoranda. When I left him, it was with the promise to return and avail myself of

his material. When I did so, he was gone from among us. With him perished a great amount of history of which his mind was the only tablet containing it. Seeking others to serve my present purpose, I learned through Samuel McCracken, son of a man of similar surname behind the guns, of two worthy, intelligent ladies, Mrs. Edmund Simmons, four years of age when the drum beat at Lewes, and her sister, Miss Emily T. McIlvaine, a few years her junior. From those excellent people I obtained certain facts which through long years they had treasured, which I have woven in a narrative.

The appearance of the British ships of war and the announcement of their hostile intent, at first created a panic among numerous non-combatants. At the beginning of the engagement, the affected ones manifested a feverish anxiety to leave the town and flee into the interior. Mr. Thomas Rowland told his wife, "Put your trust in God; bury the tool-chest in the garden, and set your face for Cope's,"—a place seven miles distant, the home of a worthy minister, who with his parishioners were shortly visited by more friends than they could house and feed. Cope's was a veritable haven of refuge for the timid, who remained there until the thunder-storm was over.

A lady in Lewes, whose nerves caused her constant uneasiness, visited Colonel Davis, and warmly exhorted him to save the town, the homes, and lives of the people by letting the British have the bullocks. The colonel was kind and considerate; he showed no impatience, blandly

telling her that "the enemy could have plenty of bullets, but no bullocks."

The majority of the population declined to leave. The town had its large and small sized people in it, who after the initiatory cannonading were unmindful of danger. The men behind the guns laughed, chatted, smoked, and fired as though it was the fourth day of July, and they were merely giving a national salutation to the day and the flag. The road leading to the town soon rolled up its cloud of dust; the militia and volunteers flocked in rapidly; then everybody who did not bear arms had all they could do to minister to the gastronomical wants of the soldiers. The mother of my informants, Mrs. Jane McIlvaine, was kept busy throughout the day cooking for them; when one pot was taken off the fire, another one replaced it. Her neighbors were similarly employed. The presence of the soldiers added to the gayety of the occasion. Joshua Hall, when the ships appeared, made certain suggestions, which were accepted, for the strengthening of the fort. Being located on the brow of the main-land, which is slightly elevated above the creek and the waste of sand and marsh, it was not thought to be within the range of possibility for the enemy to reach it in a shore attack.

An attempt towards landing at Cotton Duck Shoals was prevented by the ever-ready and irrepressible pilots, the militia, and volunteers. The British barges, filled with selected armed sailors and marines, at one stage in the game were inclined to such a venture; their movements

in the direction of the land called forth showers of shot, which were discharged upon them with such telling effect that they were unable to endure it, being compelled to withdraw. Several sailors and marines in the barges were seen to fall; the number killed and wounded was unknown to our people.

Those citizens of the town who enrolled for service were designated " Sea Fencibles." They had charge of the guns. They were in the heat of the engagement. The volunteers were kept drilling and marching. The gunners in the battery had to be sparing of ammunition; at one time it gave out. The United States government forwarded torpedoes to blow up the hostile ships, but no good resulted from their use. Many of the balls which the British fired fitted our cannon and were returned to their owners, especial care being taken to secure accuracy of aim when used. The firing was distinct, at regular intervals; the frigates fired at long range; the gunboats and smaller vessels approached closer to the shore, keeping up a severe cannonading. The fire of our men was at longer intervals, and was said to have been well directed. The British were prodigal in the use of flying shot, filling the air with their balls, which passed over the fort. Richard Howard, who resided at the " Cedars," is said to have kept an account of the number of times the British fired their guns, which was upward of four hundred.

The guns fired in the battery were effective, damaging the ships and wounding many on board. Whenever exe-

cution was done, bands of music played lively airs, heard on shore, supposedly to drown the screams of the wounded. It cannot be stated what numbers of the enemy were killed on shipboard. His Majesty's officers suppressed such facts. Mrs. Moore's house was struck by a ball. The interesting feature of which was, she had been entreating her neighbor, Mrs. Rowe, not to be afraid of the British; they were such bad marksmen; that no one was in danger from their guns, when her chimney was hit, and fell, the bricks flying about in various directions. The dwelling of Benjamin McIlvaine, back of the fort, and a storehouse owned by a Mr. Parker, were both injured. During the engagement Mrs. McIlvaine heard a whistling sound over her head. She asked her husband, "What is that noise?" He answered, coolly enough, "Bullets, my dear."

Salt was a scarce commodity during the blockade. The supply became exhausted, when a plant was contrived for its manufacture; it was located on the flats on the Rehoboth side at a place called Salt Springs. The demand for the article was such that it readily sold for three dollars a bushel.

A sloop called Black Duck, loaded with cotton, was captured by the British previous to the bombardment, and retaken by the Americans. The British made a final effort for the sloop's recapture. During the fight Colonel Davis was in the midst of his men, urging them on; beside him was Henry F. McCracken. A musket-ball fired by some one in a barge grazed Colonel Davis, who turned to

McCracken and remarked, " Henry, an inch more and that
ball would have fixed me." The cannon fired at the time
of the engagement were of sufficient force of propulsion
to send a ball six miles. The shore was so slightly elevated above the sea, that British-guns seemed unable to
focus an accurate range.

The confidence of the commander of the British fleet
in his ability to reduce the town was shared by many of
the townspeople. His inability to do so was a surprise
to himself and a gratification to the townsmen universally.
Niles, in his *Register* of the 24th of April, published the
following:

" The people of Lewistown are making themselves quite
merry for the late bombardment of that place. They
enumerate their killed and wounded as follows: one
chicken killed, one pig wounded,—leg broken. It was a
ridiculous affair on the part of the enemy. We have nothing new from this quarter except that Sir John Beresford
has captured five oyster-boats, and, after a severe engagement, caused these whole cargoes to be devoured."

Of course, ludicrous stories emanated in consequence of
the bombardment. Two negroes crept into a cellar for
refuge. A ball passed through the house and expended
itself on a milk-chest in the rear. The negroes, although
demoralized by fright, their eyeballs glaring like those
of maniacs, could not suppress their curiosity, so they
cautiously poked their heads through an aperture, and
observing a generous flow of milk streaming in richness
from broken vessels, one of the couplet, forgetful of his

surroundings, exuberantly exclaimed, "For the Lord's sake, brudder, if they ain't throwing milk at us."

At the first fall of shot in the town, a colored woman, who had a large bundle of clothes on her head, which she was taking home to wash, was felled to the earth from the effect of a passing ball, her bundle first falling; she was not hurt, and, supposing mischievous boys had knocked the bundle off her head, she jumped up and, loosening her adjectives, began to swear what she would do to the boys if they perpetrated that trick again. Turning to strike them dead with an indignant look, she was filled with consternation, for she observed no one near her. A hissing sound demonstrated the passing of another ball; she flung herself behind the bundle of clothes, where she remained for hours.

No official report of the bombardment was made to the national government. I have communicated with the War Department, and have received an answer to that effect. I have written to the State authorities of Delaware to ascertain whether Colonel Davis submitted to Governor Haslet a report of his final operations, which communication remains unanswered. It is probable none was made, otherwise its presence would have become known in the channels of my search.

A memoranda of Dr. Mustard's states, two barges were converted into torpedo-boats, connected by long and strong chains; the barges were set adrift at ebb of tide, above the British fleet, with the expectation that they would eventually come in contact with the vessels of the fleet

and explode. No such result was obtained. They produced a bad effect on British nerves, however, alarming them seriously, so that a watch was set and constantly on the lookout for such contrivances.

The defeat of the British assailing fleet did not quench their thirst for water or appetite for beef. There were other places along the Delaware coast where such articles abounded. Beresford concluded they could be had and he would have them, so he dropped down to Newbold's Pond, seven miles from Lewes, and sent armed men in boats for the shore with water-casks and halters for bullocks. Colonel Davis, anticipating such a movement, ordered Major George H. Hunter, with one hundred and fifty men, to the scene, who drove the British detachment back to their ships. They were obliged to sail to Bermuda for supplies, and thus the gallant little State of Delaware was victorious in every phase of the conflict.

Of the twelve cannon mounted in the fort, four have recently been placed in position where they formerly stood, having been taken from the creek for that purpose. They sullenly point seaward and watch and wait. A few others of those guns have been degraded to the menial office of sidewalk sentinels at street corners; one or more fell into the unhallowed clutches of mercenary junk dealers, sons of greed, among whom sentiment is without vestige of relationship, who broke them in pieces, perhaps to be moulded into cart-tires, wheel-boxes for ox-carts, or manacles for the use of a certain class of our nobility who now and then are bound at that haven of serenest joy

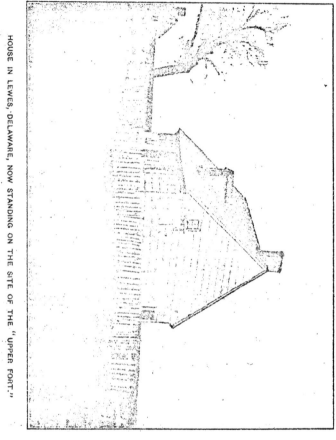

HOUSE IN LEWES, DELAWARE, NOW STANDING ON THE SITE OF THE "UPPER FORT."

and acutest sensations,—the thrilling and not to be forgotten whipping-post.

One other of those guns had a mournful and tragic history: being fired on a civic occasion, it burst and killed one man and wounded others; it now stands at one of the street corners of Lewes in dejected loneliness.

Apart from the cannon mentioned, I have been told. that eight brass pieces were supplied for the emergency, some of which possibly were used by the militia, and all of them on hand to give an account of themselves. You will recall, in the course of the narrative, that mention has been made of the use of such guns in the soldiers' hands, independent of those worked by the men in the fort. After the war, those eight cannon were placed on board a small schooner to be taken to Philadelphia. In going out of Lewes Creek, the boat grounded on a bar; in order to float it, three of those guns were removed from the vessel to the beach; before they were put back, a northeast storm of exceptional severity prevailed, and during it the landed guns disappeared. They are supposed to have sunk beneath the sand.

The weary trail of war finally dragged to an end. The hour arrived when Lewes heard no longer the cry of the sentinel, "All is well." The man behind the guns ceased to watch the movements of the ships at the capes; they spread their white wings and hastened away. A discharge of the garrison followed on March 15, 1815. How solemn sound the closing words of Commander Marshall's diary! they are pæanic: " This day discharged all the

men; took the keys of the magazine; nailed up the guard-house, and stopped the touch-holes of the cannon."

"Took the keys of the magazine." The door need not in the future be unlocked; no powder would be wanted, no more firing of guns whose brazen voices should answer similar dogs of war over the deep. He had that day discharged all the men; they had severed comrade-ship in arms, henceforth their vocations would be peace-ful. They could venture over the ocean as of yore, 'mid storm, darkness, prevailing winds, day and night, bring-ing ships with rich cargoes over the bars into havens of safety, until the stars of their destinies should set in the earthly vortex of dissolution; but aided by the life-boats of heaven, mounting every heaving billow, finally reach the calm and unvexed waters, where pilots are not needed at helm or gun, where ships sail in only and never out of the final port of rest.

"Nailed up the guard-house." How suggestive. The men who could be trusted at the guns to watch over the sleep of babes of innocence, mothers and daughters, prop-erty and country, could not always defend them against themselves. No more the door of the guard-house was to swing open on its hinges for the unlucky inmate; it was nailed up; the room would henceforth be vacant, chilly, and damp, without a soldier occupant, thus to re-main until the sure processes of decay should obliterate it from the sight of things once existent.

"And stopped the touch-holes of the cannon." The last act of war on returning peace conferred. The hour

for Old Hundred's lofty breaking sounds of gladness.
The cannon henceforth were to be voiceless; no more were
they to speak of danger to the town, invoked by the presence of frigates and sloops of war. Their ears stopped
and their flaming tongues silent; they had become merely
memorials of stirring days and anxious nights, when they
were heard with the loudness of the convulsive shout of
the earthquake's shock, suppressing the roar of the waves
by thunders of severity which rose deafening over all com-
peting sounds in assertive supremacy.

Will you permit the suggestion that your Society will
enrich its lore in recovering additional incidents belonging to the chapter read this evening?

There is needful work for you to do in securely guarding its remaining relics and landmarks. The drama
enacted at the fisherman's town of Lewes is imperishable;
the more its facts are examined into, the greater will
become their importance. What you have learned of it
is in the highest degree creditable to all who were engaged in it; neither weakness nor incapacity detracts or
disfigures the perfect portraiture.

> No white feathers shone in the air,
> The days those British ships were there.

Patriotism was luminous; the people and their rulers
gave neither aid nor comfort to the invader; exhibiting
of greater value their honor as citizens and bravery as
soldiers; preferring the trench, with twenty-two hours'
bombardment, to a stain upon the flag or dishonor upon

themselves. They wreathed "old glory" with the smoke of their guns, and taught anew the lesson that the plain American can easiest of all things be a soldier.

You and I,* who are fortunate sons and grandsons of the sires of 1813 present at the call of the roll at Lewes, when evening blushed a deeper red, when was written in the streaming sky, "We have bullets for them, but no bullocks," hail our fathers' memories with proud acclaim; let them be spread on the everlasting parchment of the ages; guarded by flaming swords, swift and burnished, as when they were seen at the gate of Paradise, the day Adam and Eve left it to roam the thorny path of the world.

Gentlemen of the Delaware Historical Society, you will go forth to ennoble the dead. The grateful work of collecting facts will prove to you a sublime inspiration. Among the records you shall read, do not forget those of the Bureau of Pensions, Department of the Interior. It is a rich depository where the curious eye has seldom gazed; where are papers aged with stains of years, rich and real, fragments whose unities shall become the verities of history. Where are filed applications for land bounties on the part of participants in the war of 1812, whence can be obtained other names than those you have to swell the number known as having served this State;

---

* William Knowles, the speaker's grandfather, was a member of Captain Thomas Rider's Laurel Company. Rider was related to the wife of William. John, William's brother, was a member of Captain Law's company.

evincing fidelity and patriotism of Roman firmness and Grecian sublimity. You will find in those overlooked files facts of value for whose discovery the muse of history waits.

An English poet of exquisite sweetness, whose song of matchless verse will live as long as a churchyard shall be found to exist, the most sacred of all places, wrote, " The pathway to glory leads but to the grave." An English general on his way to glory and the grave, as he sat in his boat and was rowed by that city soon to fall before his victorious troops, quoted the line, and shortly afterwards illustrated its truth. Bloodless, Lewes teaches of a fame without a grave on the part of its defenders, a circumstance unparalleled in an engagement of its consequence in the warfare of the world.

Lightning Source UK Ltd.
Milton Keynes UK
UKHW031334031218
333390UK00012B/733/P